THE
CHEATING
CLASSES

THE
CHEATING
CLASSES

*How Britain's Elite
Abuse their Power*

Sue Cameron

SIMON & SCHUSTER

London · New York · Sydney · Tokyo · Singapore · Toronto · Dublin

A VIACOM COMPANY

First published in Great Britain by
Simon & Schuster UK Ltd, 2002
A Viacom Company

1 3 5 7 9 10 8 6 4 2

Simon & Schuster UK Ltd
Africa House
64–78 Kingsway
London WC2B 6AH

www.simonsays.co.uk

Simon & Schuster Australia
Sydney

A CIP catalogue record for this book is available from the British Library

ISBN 0-684-85130-X

Typeset by M Rules
Printed and bound in Great Britain by
The Bath Press, Bath

For my mother, Dorothy, and for Keith. With love.

ACKNOWLEDGEMENTS

I would like tho thank all those who have helped me during the long gestation of this book including Luigi Bonomi, staff at NACAB and at the Campaign for Freedom of Information, my longsuffering family and friends and above all my husband without whom this book would most certainly never have been finished. I am particularly grateful for the forbearance of Cassandra Campbell, Helen Gummer, Catherine Hurley and Katharine Young at Simon & Schuster.

My special thanks to Maurice and Audrey Balchin, Frank Cunningham, Godfrey and Sissel Fowler, Hugh and Liz Lowther, the Wood family, Keith and Gill Dray, Ian and Richard Wise, Neil and Emma Palmer and the friends and family of The Handyman. I wish that one day all your stories my have happy endings. If the telling of them helps even a little to prevent others suffering as you have done, then it will be worthwhile.

Perhaps I should give a mention also to my acquaintances among the cheating classes whose antics, I fear, will continue to provide a rich seam for writers of unjust tales.

CONTENTS

CONTENTS

INTRODUCTION

The cheating classes are among the most privileged members of our society. They are people with clout. Often they are wealthy – lawyers, bankers, politicians, bureaucrats. Few think of themselves as cheats. Yet rarely a day goes by without some of these influential individuals inflicting injustices, great and small, on ordinary men and women. The kind of men and women whose stories are told in this book: those who find there is little they can do if they are victimised by the authorities, those who are starting to recognise that their right to a fair deal is being hijacked by an unaccountable and mainly unelected elite.

In Britain today there is an ever widening gap not just between rich and poor – though the gulf there is growing – but between those who have influence and those who do not. More and more people feel excluded from decisions that affect their lives, decisions that are often arbitrary and against which there is no appeal. This book is about them. The voiceless ones. Those whose freedoms are being curtailed, whose demands for decent treatment are being ignored and who find it almost impossible to get redress when they are steamrollered by the big battalions, by Whitehall, by greedy or incompetent professionals or by officialdom in all its forms.

There are mechanisms for ordinary people to achieve justice. There is the law, there is Parliament, there is the Ombudsman and there is a legion of regulators. Yet those who challenge the System can find it takes years of fighting through the courts or battling with the bureaucracy to have their wrongs righted. As the stories in this book show, our old institutions are no longer up to the job of protecting the public. Despite piecemeal reform, all too often they fail those who are outside the small, select circle of influence.

The Victorians used to talk of the Upper Ten Thousand – the ruling elite that controlled much of the country's wealth and nearly all of the power. That concept of an Upper Ten Thousand is alive and thriving in the twenty-first century. The centres of influence may have shifted over the years: the landowning set no longer holds sway while those in the media have become more prominent. Yet as in the Victorian era, a close-knit and largely self-appointed group of people still dominates. They are found among the key personnel of the Government, the Opposition, the civil service, business, the universities, the law, broadcasting, the press and the City.

Despite the glitz and the bonhomie, today's elite is becoming progressively more authoritarian, more impatient of democratic controls, more determined to dictate what others may say and more ruthless about strengthening its own grip on public life, often by stealth.

Some of its members are talented enough. Some are highly principled. But increasingly they are not answerable to the public for the influence they wield. For all their gifts and good intentions, they cannot help a tendency to arrange things to suit themselves. They are the leaders of a new breed – the cheating classes.

They operate in different spheres and at different levels. Not all belong to the elite. Some are comparatively humble. But it is those at the top who make possible the abuses lower down.

They rig the rules to suit themselves. They charge excessive prices. They ride roughshod over others in the name of cost-saving and efficiency. They cover up mistakes to avoid embarrassment or blame.

Some are lawyers whose fat fees help to make justice the preserve of the rich. Some are town hall officials who waste thousands of pounds of public money prosecuting sick, elderly people over a few hundred pounds of unpaid debt. Some are bankers who try to boost profits by squeezing vulnerable families.

Some are bureaucrats – like those in the Child Support Agency – who have been ready to hound parents to the point of suicide in the interests of Government cost saving. Some are company directors who preside over redundancies and profit slides yet still collect bonuses worth millions when they are sacked.

Some are politicians who hand out jobs and peerages to their friends, friends who have often made big donations to party funds. Some are local councillors who refuse to pay compensation when their plans for a new road destroy the value of a family's property.

Of course it would be wrong to suggest that all those who have influence at national or local level abuse their positions or even that most of them do so. Clearly that is not the case. Many figures in the political, financial and legal worlds are people of integrity who are striving to do their best by the public often in the face of difficulties beyond their control. Some are acutely aware of inadequacies within the System and they would dearly like to see changes.

It is also true that failure to ensure a fair deal for ordinary people can be – and often is – the result of muddle and confusion rather than conspiracy. And if those in influential positions then try to put the best possible construction on honest mistakes that is no more than most of us do when we are in a corner.

Yet, increasingly, a seemingly out-of-touch elite is presiding over failing institutions that no longer safeguard the interests of ordinary people. Examples abound in our political system. What is perhaps less recognised is that it is not just at Westminster and Downing Street that the rottenness has taken hold. It can also be found in our spawning bureaucracies, both nationally and locally. It can be seen in the legal and financial sectors that underpin our democratic traditions. Everywhere, members of the public are finding that the System no longer responds to their wishes or their needs. Small wonder if people feel cheated by those at the top.

Several factors have helped destroy trust between the elite and the public. One is the way political power has been progressively centralised over the last two decades. At the same time there has been an erosion of democratic checks and balances on both political leaders and officials. The power and scope of British bureaucracy has expanded apace.

Meanwhile the great self-governing institutions that once guarded high standards in the law, in the City, in medicine and the other professions have started to atrophy.

The old public service ethic is waning. Once almost everyone in responsible positions whether they were civil servants, City men, lawyers, bankers or even politicians felt that they owed something to the public good and should conduct themselves accordingly – even if practice did not always live up to principle. Some still follow that code. But as the stories here show there is evidence that a narrow, more self-centred ethos is gaining ground.

Perhaps the change was triggered by the discrediting of long-held ideologies and the emergence in the 1980s and 1990s of the competition culture with its single-minded emphasis on cutting costs and boosting profits. The new drive to economic efficiency in both the public and private sectors brought very real benefits. Yet it seemed to leave less room for compassion or fair dealing or accountability to the wider community. It is a trend that continues today.

There are too many cases where those in key positions fail to protect or promote the public interest or to listen to ordinary men and women. The rich and powerful have always tended to look after their own but in the past, in Britain at least, they also had some sense of obligation to those lower down the scale. It is that which is changing.

For at least two decades influence in Britain has been draining away from the elected to the unelected, from those who are accountable to those who are not, from those who can be pressured into action to those who are largely immune to public opinion. After years of neglect old safeguards in our unwritten constitution are being undermined and – crucially – they are not being replaced by fresh guarantees.

A long tradition of ensuring that there are limits on the power of any one individual or group is being eroded – often deliberately. Old notions of openness, tolerance and fair play are giving way to values that are harsher, brasher and altogether less susceptible to popular influence.

What we are seeing is the disempowerment of large sections of the British people who find it ever harder to make their voices heard, their needs and wishes felt.

Foremost among the cheating classes are those who inhabit the upper circles of Government. Yet the rot did not start with New Labour or even with the Thatcherites though both have played their part. It began long before.

The pillars of the British system – Parliament, the civil service, the great newspapers, the legal system and the professions – were created largely by the Victorians. Their beginnings were often much older but it was the self-confident men of the nineteenth century who took the institutional relics of medieval times and gave them a shape that is still recognisable today.

They reformed Parliament, extended the franchise and embraced Gladstone's great dictum that the job of the House of Commons was not to rule the country but to hold to account those who did. They gave the court system a radical overhaul. They ended jobbery in the civil service and replaced it with a system based on merit.

They founded national newspapers like the *Telegraph* and the *Daily Mail.* They laid the foundations for a golden age of local government. The Victorians built to last and the institutions they created served the nation well for more than 100 years.

Of course the System they created had flaws: the description of the law courts in Charles Dickens' novel *Bleak House* shows that justice in the nineteenth century was even slower and costlier than today; and latter day cash-for-favours deals are as nothing compared to the blatant way that Liberal Prime Minister David Lloyd George sold peerages to boost party funds.

Yet for all its weaknesses, the Victorian system was robust enough to last until the latter part of the twentieth century. By then an overhaul was needed. A few senior figures recognised this. In 1976 the Tory Lord Hailsham, later Lord Chancellor, said in a lecture entitled 'Elective Dictatorship':

> I have reached the conclusion that our constitution is wearing out. Its central defects are gradually coming to outweigh its merits and its central defects consist in the absolute powers we confer on our sovereign body and the concentration of those powers in an executive government formed out of one party which may not fairly represent the popular will.

His analysis may have been sound but it had little practical impact. Perhaps it was complacency, that very British vice, or perhaps it was the Cold War which laid down that everything to do with Western democracy was good while everything to do with the communism of the Eastern bloc was bad. For whatever reason, reform never came. People took refuge in comforting assurances that the British way was best and superior to that of other nations.

Slowly British democracy and the institutional mechanisms

that supported it began to stultify. By the 1980s the cracks had begun to show. As Lord Hailsham had foreseen they were most apparent in the political system.

Twenty years before Tony Blair, Margaret Thatcher was riding roughshod over Cabinet Ministers, centralising Whitehall and largely ignoring backbench MPs who were ruthlessly bullied into following the party line on an ever wider range of issues. Crucially, the role of MPs as conduits for public opinion helping to keep senior Ministers in touch with the electorate, started to diminish and it showed. It showed, for example, in the fiasco over Margaret Thatcher's plans to introduce a poll tax. Power had become so concentrated in the Prime Minister that her own Tory MPs, who realised how unpopular the tax would be and who privately opposed it almost to a man, did not dare warn her.

The Labour Government under Tony Blair has gone further in dismantling the checks and balances of our democracy. It has sidelined Parliament to an even greater extent. It has bypassed impartial civil servants and downgraded the Cabinet. It has replaced unelected hereditary peers in the House of Lords with unelected Labour cronies.

It has tried to rig elections in Wales and London. It has demanded the right to appoint MPs to the very House of Commons committees that are meant to call Ministers and civil servants to account. It has packed Downing Street and Whitehall with political advisers – powerful, unelected, unaccountable placemen.

These placemen, whose first loyalty is to Labour not to the public interest, increasingly call the shots. Some are allowed to give orders to politically neutral officials. They are allowed to circumvent Cabinet Ministers as well as civil servants so as to impose Downing Street's line on the rest of the Government. They do it in the name of an increasingly presidential Prime Minister. As Professor Peter Hennessey of London University has pointed out, the words 'Tony wants' have become the most important in Whitehall.

Yet the Number Ten courtiers are not in touch with the public except through focus groups and polls. These may offer a snapshot of public opinion but they do not allow for ideas to be tested in open, democratic debate. The result is that often propaganda takes precedence over policy, a favourable headline is valued more than hard thinking and the constraints of democracy are regarded as tiresome.

New Labour has talked much of 'modernising' the political system. Yet as Peter Riddell of *The Times* points out in his book *Parliament Under Blair*, reforms in the Commons have all been on the executive's terms and none really inconvenience Ministers.

'The illusion must be fostered that the Commons reigns supreme and that a few improvements here or there will sort everything out,' he argues. 'Making sonorous claims about the sovereignty of parliament and how it is being abused and must be defended is a substitute for thought, for seeing how real accountability can be achieved.'

New Labour gave fair warning. When he was a Cabinet Office Minister, Peter Mandelson, one of Tony Blair's closest confidants, said publicly that 'the era of representative democracy might be coming to an end'.

As the great Labour parliamentarian Tony Benn has said, the British people are no longer represented – they are merely managed.

The waning of democracy has had a knock-on effect way beyond Westminster because it is the political system that is the driver for reform elsewhere.

With the public exercising less influence over political decision-making, the opportunity for ordinary people to insist on a fair deal from the bureaucracy, from big financial institutions or from self-regulating professionals has also dwindled. And when the public protests, all too often redress is denied.

Admittedly, Conservative and Labour governments have

talked about reform and have made some shift to bring it about. They have set up regulators like the Financial Services Agency. They have tried to streamline the legal system and make it more responsive to customers. They are attempting to change the culture of the medical profession so that it is easier to weed out incompetent doctors. Labour even ordered the Office of Fair Trading to investigate the professions though little came of the resulting recommendations.

Undoubtedly there has been progress, sometimes in the teeth of opposition from vested interests. Yet politicians of all parties have proved timid and inadequate in delivering reform. The thoroughgoing changes needed to guarantee the public a fair deal have not happened. The injustices continue.

So how do the cheating classes get away with it? Their main tools are secrecy, delay and self-regulation. Procrastination is a particularly valued technique. Some lawyers find that delay can be made to pay handsomely while there are bureaucrats who take years to investigate injustice.

But most effective of all, usually the cheating classes can rely on being able to police themselves. This is particularly true of the professions. As Simon Jenkins put it in *The Times* (11 April 2001): 'Britain's professions are the last great scam. They never rock their own boat.'

Just as the integrity and competence of politicians have been brought into question by the voters, so the last few years have also brought a rising tide of complaints from the public about negligent doctors who cause suffering or death to their patients, civil servants who refuse to take responsibility for the kind of bungling that ruins people's lives and incompetent lawyers who rip off their clients. Yet nearly all these groups are allowed to regulate themselves.

Take the lawyers. The body that deals with complaints against solicitors is the Law Society – the solicitors' own trade union. Its slowness and ineptitude has become notorious. It has managed to bring the number of *outstanding* complaints against its members down but they are still running at 6,000 a year. It has admitted

that when it writes to members about complaints four out of five
solicitors ignore the letter.

The public therefore has nowhere to go when lawyers behave
ineptly or overcharge – and even wealthy individuals can find the
costs of going to law crippling. One couple found themselves
paying £830,000 in legal costs when their divorce case went all
the way to the House of Lords. Lord Nicholls, one of the Law
Lords who heard the case, described the costs as appalling.

True, there has been a real attempt to cut the law's costs and
delays, notably the implementation of the civil justice reforms of
Lord Woolf, now the Lord Chief Justice. The Woolf reforms,
brought in three years ago, were designed to make the legal system
simpler, more open and less adversarial. Most people believe that
they have succeeded in speeding up cases and making it easier for
people to reach settlements. But they have failed to make any
impact in other crucial areas – most notably in cutting legal costs.
In January 2002 Lord Phillips, Master of the Rolls and head of the
civil justice system, said the 'very serious problem of costs' in non-
criminal cases was the 'Achilles' heel' of the reforms. He warned
that it was a problem that would be 'very difficult to sort out'.

There have been a number of other changes on the legal front.
The Government is allowing customers to sue barristers for negligence for example. And the courts have been ordered to
conduct business in English rather than legal gobbledegook.
Lord Irvine, the Lord Chancellor, has even publicly criticised a
number of leading lawyers for overcharging the legal aid fund.

Welcome though these and other measures are, they have not
been enough to make justice affordable and accessible to the
majority, as Lord Phillips' comments show. And if the public
complains . . . well, that's when they find themselves up against
self-regulation.

It is a similar story in medicine where the last few years have
brought worrying evidence about the incompetence of some
doctors and the lengths to which they and hospital administrators will go to cover up medical negligence. One of the most

prominent cases was that in Bristol where the low standards of some hospital doctors put the lives of hundreds of babies at risk.

The Government has talked of taking a tougher line over negligent doctors and has promised a White Paper on medical negligence but progress is slow. The doctors still police themselves via the General Medical Council. Admittedly, the GMC is introducing reform including more representation for laymen although the latter will still not be in the majority. Meanwhile the public's lack of confidence in the System can be gauged by the latest figures on medical negligence claims; the National Audit Office says the number of claims almost doubled in 2001 and the likely cost to the health service rose by £500 million.

Yet though the public can sue doctors for negligence it brings them up against the lawyers. Just as bad doctors can endanger your health, so the legal profession can seriously damage your wealth. And it may take years.

Perhaps the worst example of professional self-regulation is the civil service where it can be hard indeed for the public to appeal against officialdom's foul-ups. Pensions provided a classic case. For ten years Social Security officials failed to warn people about plans to halve the value of the State Earnings Related Pension Scheme (SERPS) as it applied to widows.

Worse, the Government initially decided that only those who could prove they had been misinformed by the civil service would receive compensation – not the thousands who had simply been kept in the dark.

Eventually there was a change of heart and the introduction of the new rules was delayed but there was no attempt to apportion blame or to demand an apology or a penalty from the civil servants and Ministers concerned.

The most spectacular Whitehall scandal of recent years was the arms-to-Iraq debacle when the Government prosecuted British businessmen for doing something that Ministers and civil servants knew about and connived at – breaking a ban on the export of arms to Iraq. Senior officials were ruthless in trying to cover up the facts and spare the Government embarrassment. In one case, later described by the Lord Chief Justice as 'disgraceful', Foreign Office civil servants interfered with defence witnesses at a trial, putting pressure on them not to turn up. When they duly failed to do so, the accused businessmen were found guilty.

Ancient history? Irrelevant to the twenty-first century? Sadly it is not. The businessmen wrongly convicted after their witnesses were nobbled had their convictions quashed. Each received £125,000 in punitive damages from the State, the first such payment in 300 years. One, Reginald Dunk, was eventually paid £2m for miscarriage of justice. But it took until 1999 – nearly seventeen years – for that to happen. Meanwhile the officials who abused the justice system by interfering with the trial witnesses were promoted. Others in the arms-to-Iraq scandal had to wait until 2001 before they were given compensation. Labour did little in Government to ensure fair settlements.

The mores of the cheating classes are not confined to politicians, civil servants and members of the professions. Dubious standards can be found among the upper echelons of the business community. Some top executives give themselves huge payouts when they fail yet show little compassion or consideration to those lower down the ladder.

The head of British Airways, sacked when losses led to a fall in the share price, was rewarded with a £2m payoff. It was a similar story for the bosses of BT and Railtrack and – most outrageous of all – for Lord Simpson, who presided over Marconi at the time of a £30bn fall but was still in line to receive over £1m when he was finally forced out.

Who decides to give fabulous deals to these failed top people? Other top people. It is fellow Board members or friendly 'outsiders' of equal wealth and standing who decide on pay. Small-scale shareholders have little influence – let alone customers, other employees or members of the public.

As the *Financial Times* observed in a leader column headed 'Time to Stop the Gravy Train' (22 August 2001):

> The pay explosion in Britain's Boardrooms is running out of control . . . Executives sitting on each other's remuneration committees continually bid up the going rate – for the benefit of all.
>
> Since 1992 the total earnings of large company bosses in the UK (excluding share options) has nearly doubled in real terms. That is more than four and a half times the real rise in average earnings.

Predictably, the politicians have done a good deal of hand wringing but have failed to address the cash-for-failures issue. They bluster about it being up to shareholders to act yet this is exactly the kind of issue that requires a strong lead from the State – difficult though it may be to find a practical solution. Small wonder if the public suspects that the Labour Government is more concerned about looking after its wealthy City friends – who contribute to party funds – than about forcing them to share the pain with ordinary people when things go wrong.

As John Edmonds of the GMB union has said: 'It is one thing to reward success but too many of these directors are being rewarded for failure with the most disgraceful amounts. And their failure can mean job losses for thousands of workers.'

Perhaps the biggest cheat is indeed the very different treatment meted out by the business world to more humble workers, particularly those who lose jobs through no fault of their own. That is when they can find themselves being hounded by the cheating classes for what little savings they have managed to salvage. One of the stories here shows how the law allows wealthy banks and building societies to wait for years before pouncing on the little people and pursuing them for ancient debts they did not even know they had – plus interest.

One rule for the cheating classes, one rule for the rest.

Not that the elite avoids all criticism. The press inveighs regularly against big payoffs for failed executives, against the high charges and slow service of some professionals, against cases of sharp practice by the banks and against the muddle, waste and callousness of which bureaucrats can be capable.

It is becoming hard to open a newspaper without finding reports of some new piece of spite or stupidity inflicted on the public: bailiffs charging over £800 for *trying* to tow away a car that they were not entitled to take in the first place; traffic wardens fining a near-blind lady for putting the disability sticker in her car the wrong way round; Whitehall officials forcing farmers to sign the Official Secrets Act during the foot and mouth epidemic. And these are the petty irritants not the big injustices.

Some of the stories in this book have featured in the media and they have been given sympathetic treatment. Yet despite the much-vaunted power of the press and the broadcasters, often publicity does little to help the victims or to bring about change.

Perhaps one reason why some bureaucrats, lawyers, bankers, planners and the rest behave unfairly to the public is because they themselves are struggling to cope with what is, for many of them, a new phenomenon: the pressures of competition. Often they find that they are being urged constantly to cut costs, improve efficiency and meet new, ever more demanding targets.

The competitive pressures on many sectors of society are becoming fiercer. Maybe we have been slow to recognise fully the effect that this is having on the conduct of people who work in the public service, in the professions and even in private sector commerce or finance. This is not to excuse the conduct of some of them but it may explain it.

Solicitors, for example, were for years free from any real competition. They had a monopoly on conveyancing, which guaranteed reasonable incomes for many of them. At the same time the fees they could charge were laid down by the Law Society, which also imposed a blanket ban on advertising. It was all highly restrictive but there was less incentive for them to shortchange their clients or inveigle them into paying higher fees than necessary. Most would have been outraged at the thought of touting for business among people suffering personal crises such as a marriage breakdown.

Today, in a much more competitive climate and with their old restrictive practices being steadily whittled away, they are under greater pressure to maximise income for their firms and there is more incentive to spin out cases so as to bump up the bill or to turn in slipshod work. Some even seem to prey on human misery, encouraging people to get divorced with adverts that urge 'Ditch the Bitch'.

It is a similar story with bankers. Banks have always had to face competition yet time was when a bank manager was a prominent member of the local community who knew many of his customers personally.

Usually he would have been reluctant to pull the rug from under a long-standing customer because of short-term or cyclical difficulties. If he treated someone badly then word would get round and his own standing and reputation might suffer. In the case of house repossessions and mortgage debt shortfall – much rarer in the past – banks nearly always wrote off the outstanding sum.

Today banking has become more impersonal. Orders come from distant head offices to squeeze more profit from customers and if that means harsher treatment for the very poor then, as one of the stories here shows, so be it.

This is not to suggest that bankers, lawyers or other professionals should or could return to the cosy, complacent and often anti-competitive world of thirty years ago. It is a question of striking a better balance between profit and decent standards of conduct.

Paradoxically, it is in the public sector where there is usually no question of personal profit that the new culture of hard-driving, cost-saving competitiveness is often most apparent. It can be seen, for example, in local government. There are planners who are prepared to ruin innocent householders for the sake of saving the local council money. In the health service some administrators will go to inordinate lengths to cover up medical mistakes so as to avoid paying compensation to the victims of negligence.

The cost-saving imperative is all too evident in the Child Support Agency. The agency has financial targets set by the Treasury and designed to save the State having to pay for the upkeep of children. This may sound reasonable enough but, as one of the tales here illustrates, in practice it encourages some CSA bureaucrats to bully and harass parents.

Nobody doubts that it is in the public interest for the State sector to be prudent about spending and about saving taxpayers' money. But again, it is vital to get the balance right between financial discipline and the old public service ideal of fair treatment for individual citizens. The evidence suggests that the two are seriously out of kilter. There are all too many examples of Treasury cost-saving taking precedence over fair dealing. For example, that bungled effort by Whitehall to cuts SERPS payments to widows without proper warning happened because officials wanted to cut the bill to the Government from £13bn to £8bn.

Sir Christopher France, former top civil servant at the Department of Health, summed up the dangers of substituting financial management for government.

Government, he said, is about more than economics, it is about 'creating and sustaining a society'.

He is right. What we need is a society that is prosperous and well run, certainly, but a society that is also caring and compassionate, a society that values justice, a society that has greater, nobler goals than mere efficiency.

One of the most notable aspects of today's cost-conscious, autocratic style of government is that it places a high premium on conformity, on discipline and on so-called political correctness. It is a culture that makes it easier for the few to dictate to the many. We may mock those who stay slavishly on message but the concept of 'right' and 'wrong' thinking has gained acceptance in our society with frightening rapidity. The new orthodoxies seem to be less about ideas than about control. Today the thought police are on permanent patrol when it comes to race, gender, religion and almost anything that can be put under the heading of 'modernisation' – including most Government policies.

There is less tolerance for those who display independence of mind. Dissent is stamped upon sometimes with black propaganda designed to ridicule or ruin reputations, sometimes with more blatant tactics.

It can happen to journalists felt to be unsympathetic to the Blair Government such as those from the BBC's *Panorama* programme who were banned from Labour press conferences during the 2001 general election. The Labour machine later tried to stop the broadcast of a *Panorama* programme critical of the Government's record on health.

It can happen to ordinary people who dare to criticise the Government or its allies. Ministers used the police to harass peaceful, legitimate demonstrators who had gathered to protest against the leaders of China's repressive regime during a visit to Britain in 1999.

Meanwhile mechanisms designed to safeguard the citizen against overweening authority are being eroded. Rights once enjoyed by the majority, sometimes age-old rights, are being whittled away. For the first time in centuries there are moves to imprison people without trial and to curtail the right to trial by jury. The Government also wants to introduce identity cards and centralise control of the police.

The risk with this steady increase in the powers of bureaucrats and politicians is that there is a ratchet effect. We can see this happening on the agricultural front. As the Aristocrat's Tale shows, during the foot and mouth epidemic some farmers quite legitimately questioned Government moves to cull their flocks and herds. Now the Government is determined to give itself tough new powers to go on to farms and kill the animals against their owners' wishes. Ministry inspectors will not even have to have evidence that an animal is suffering from a dangerous disease. Anyone who opposes them will face up to two years' imprisonment.

The new rules are also intended to allow Ministry officials to seize animal owners' computers – during the foot and mouth outbreak many farmers went on line to help each other resist illegal Government culls. Other officials are demanding power to pry into our computers with few safeguards for ordinary citizens. Officially this is to help fight terrorism and big-time crime while making the UK fit for the electronic age – and no matter if an army of government cybersnoopers would be more suited to a Stalinist state than to a democracy.

Meanwhile long-promised reforms like a Freedom of Information Act are deliberately watered down so that politicians and bureaucrats can continue to keep their secrets secret.

The hand of unaccountable and often anonymous officials is being steadily strengthened. What we are witnessing is the bureaucratisation of Britain and there are few new safeguards being introduced to protect the citizen.

In the summer of 2001, at a public lecture in London, Geoff Mulgan, one of Tony Blair's bright young advisers who runs Downing Street's Forward Strategy Unit, spoke about the need to give the citizen redress against injustice.

'There has been a decline in public confidence in the monarchy, the judiciary, the civil service and other institutions over the last twenty-five years,' he said. He added that this was of 'particular concern' to the Labour Government and listed some of the areas that needed to be tackled, smiling ruefully when he reached the issue of redress. 'We're still weak on redress,' he confessed. 'I think it'll take at least eighteen months to get redress right.'

Do not hold your breath . . .

*

Do the public notice? Do the public care? Of course they do. There is growing popular concern over the direction of our society. It is reflected in the widespread disenchantment with politicians of all parties. It is reflected in the anecdotal evidence of ordinary people complaining that the only thing those in authority care about is money, that quality of life takes second place to boosting profits or cutting costs. There are signs too that sections of the public are becoming more willing to take to the streets in a bid to make the cheating classes listen.

At first sight there appears to be nothing new about that – people have been demonstrating on Britain's streets for years. But today we are seeing a tendency for a wider cross section of the public, many of them mainstreamers not fringe groups, to back protests born out of frustration at the authorities' refusal to listen. The well-supported protest against high fuel tax in the summer of 2000 was one example.

Another was the Countryside Alliance, a broad-based group of people protesting over a variety of causes but united by a sense of grievance at the way their interests were being ignored – a grievance that the mishandling of the foot-and-mouth epidemic will have done nothing to assuage.

We have seen people in places like Portsmouth taking to the streets over the authorities' failure to stop convicted paedophiles being released anonymously into the community after jail terms.

Often these grievances are not about great, abstract, national issues. They are about the kind of small-time injustices, the practical, day-to-day questions that can have a devastating impact on people's lives.

Our system is based on a nineteenth-century model that no longer works for us. It cannot keep up in the twenty-first century. Today, in a more complex society, where governments demand the right to interfere in more and more aspects of our lives, it looks like a sham.

What we need is a new democracy that is quicker on its feet, that is more accountable, that gives the public a real input and provides a much more rapid response to the day-to-day injustice that people suffer at the hands of the cheating classes. We need a fresh look not just at our political arrangements but at the other great bulwarks of our System: the law, Whitehall, local councils, the banks, the City and the ever more powerful bureaucrats of all sorts who are scattered throughout our society.

We need to stop the rot. We need to give ordinary people a better chance of standing up to the cheating classes when they are faced with the kind of unfairness that the people in this book encountered. These eight tales are not life and death tragedies nor are they the stuff of which legends are made. They are the every day stories of what can happen to ordinary people when they are let down by the System, when they discover that there is no adequate way of having their injustices redressed. What happened to them could happen to any of us. Their stories show some of the weaknesses in our social fabric, the agonising slowness with which we are moving towards reform and the need to start thinking afresh about ways of ending the kind of injustices related in these tales.

1

THE RICH MAN'S TALE

Wealth is no protection against the cheating classes. Nor is education, eloquence or friends in high places. You can be rich, able and articulate. You can win sympathy and support from some of the most influential people in the land – Ministers, judges, and Members of Parliament. Little good will it do you if the cheating classes put a black spot against your name.

The Balchins' tale is about the bureaucratisation of Britain. It tells how the public's traditional bulwarks – a vibrant local democracy and a strong Parliament – are on the wane, while cost-cutting, legalistic officialdom is on the up. As the old system fragments, there seems to be nobody willing or able to take charge and insist on fair treatment for people like the Balchins.

Politicians with the power to act, such as local council leaders or Government Ministers, abdicate their responsibility. Infected by the bureaucratic mindset, they are more interested in obeying regulations than in shaping them. Anyone who tries to break through the administrative monolith, such as a conscientious backbench MP, is run into the ground by hair-splitting arguments. Or ignored. Even the writ of a High Court judge can be frustrated by the new super-bureaucrats.

Ask Maurice Balchin. He was a man who had life's riches in abundance . . .

Maurice Balchin had it all. Well, if not all, most of it. He had a happy and enduring marriage. He had two children who were doing well at good schools. He had a highly successful building business. And he had Swan's Harbour.

Swan's Harbour was the most perfect place on earth in Maurice's eyes. It was set on the Norfolk Broads with grounds that swept down to the River Bure. Cutting back through the gardens from the river's edge was a dyke that carried a long, gleaming strip of water where swans cruised gracefully towards the house itself.

Occasionally they came inside. Maurice had once found one investigating the utility room. At the other end of the dyke was a private island, a haven for the wildlife of the Broads. Beyond was the mooring where Maurice kept his cruiser. He always said that he would never want to go on holiday as long as he had Swan's Harbour.

Swan's Harbour had been his dream throughout his adult life. Once when he and his wife Audrey were very young – barely out of their teens – he had borrowed an old banger and they had driven out beyond Wroxham to the Broads. They were not married then and he had little money. He had decided to train as a chartered surveyor but it would take time. She was working in a shipping office where she earned two pounds a week more than him – much to his chagrin.

As they walked beside the water that day, both of them were touched by the quiet beauty of the place. And Maurice promised Audrey that one day he would build her a house there. Even if it were only a two-up, two-down they would live at that spot beside the River Bure.

*

Time passed. Maurice Balchin qualified as a surveyor. He and Audrey married. He started a business building houses. It prospered. In the early sixties a son, Warren, was born to the Balchins and later a daughter, Lesley. The family started moving to ever larger homes. By the time the children were in secondary school they were living in an elegant, rather grand Georgian house at Swaffham. It had its own grounds and a heated swimming pool. But it was not the home of their dreams.

Then Maurice heard of a plot of land coming up for sale on the banks of the Bure. It was several acres and it had on it a covered squash court – an old, rather ramshackle, wooden structure. There was outline planning permission to build a house on the site. As soon as he saw it, Maurice knew that this was the place he wanted to live.

He took his bank manager to see it. The two men had become if not friends then more than mere acquaintances. Over the years Maurice had borrowed regularly from the NatWest bank to expand his business and he and his banker had built up a good relationship. Maurice and Audrey sometimes had dinner with him and his wife and occasionally the four went to dances together.

Maurice had no doubt the NatWest would lend him the money for the two and a half acre riverside site. The asking price was £80,000, which was a substantial sum in the early 1980s. But the Balchins only wanted to borrow £30,000 – enough to secure the maximum mortgage tax relief. All the same Maurice wanted a second opinion from the man who was going to lend him the cash.

His bank manager's view was more than favourable.

'Maurice,' he said, when they had strolled round the site, 'if you don't buy this land then I will.'

Above the hedgerows and beyond the dyke it was possible to see ships going past on the river. Sometimes it seemed as if they were gliding over the fields, as if they sailed on land instead of water. It was all part of the magic of Swan's Harbour.

Not that everything had gone smoothly with the building of the Balchins' new home. Maurice had secured his bank loan only to find that Audrey had reservations about leaving her beautiful Georgian house. She had no doubts about the site – she shared Maurice's passion for it. But a quick inspection of the dilapidated squash court that was the only building there left her refusing to move.

Maurice protested but Audrey remained unmoved – literally and metaphorically. He found a rented place for her and the family. Then he started work on Swan's Harbour. He kept the walls of the old squash court but everything else, inside and out, was planned and built anew to the Balchins' exact specifications. Not that the result seemed unfittingly modern. The finished house was half-timbered and looked as if it could have been part of the landscape for years.

It took more than twelve months for Maurice to design and build their new home. In the end it was not until 1985 that the family moved in but the wait seemed worth it. From the very first moment they all loved Swan's Harbour.

If they felt adventurous they could go down to the forty-foot boat shed Maurice had built on the river and take out their cruiser for a sail. But neither he nor Audrey wanted to go further afield.

'The only way they're going to take me out of here,' Maurice would say, 'is in a box.'

The first sign of a shadow falling on their paradise came early one morning in 1987 just as Maurice was setting off for work. It was eight a.m. and he was about to drive to Wroxham where he was building some retirement homes. Just as he was getting into the car he saw Liz Holt walking down his drive.

Liz and her husband David were the Balchins' new neighbours. Maurice and Audrey had been at Swan's Harbour for nearly two years when the Holts moved in next door. They had bought Heronly, a big, old house, which had once belonged to comedian George Formby.

Maurice wound down his window and waited until Liz reached the car. She was out of breath and she looked troubled.

'Maurice,' she said, 'have you heard about plans to build a Wroxham bypass? Apparently the council has been thinking about it for months – and there's talk of it going through here.'

Maurice smiled at her.

'No, Liz, I haven't heard about any such plans,' he said. 'But if I were you I wouldn't start worrying about rumours. I can assure you that this is the last place anyone is going to build a bypass. Well, they're not, are they? Not in a place that's a beauty spot and a wildlife sanctuary. And some of the most expensive homes in the area are here on Beech Road. Nobody in their right mind is going to allow all this to be destroyed to make way for some motorway.' He patted her arm. 'I promise you – it won't happen.'

'I hope you're right,' she replied and she seemed reassured by his confidence. She stood back and waved as he turned out of the drive.

Maurice wondered where Liz had picked up such a notion. Searches by the Holts' lawyers had not uncovered any proposals for a new road when they had been buying Heronly only a few months earlier. They would not have bought it if there had been any plan for a bypass. The whole idea was preposterous. He put it from his mind.

Neither Maurice nor Audrey saw the Holts for some time. When Liz did come to see them again several months had passed. Unbeknown to the Balchins events had moved on swiftly.

'You know we're leaving, don't you?' said Liz.

Maurice was stunned.

'Leaving?' he repeated. 'But you've barely been here for a year – and you've spent all that money on redecorating.'

The Holts had indeed spent over £30,000 refurbishing Heronly.

'So why are you going?' demanded Maurice.

Now it was Liz's turn to sound surprised.

'The bypass, of course,' she said. 'I mentioned it to you months ago. We checked with the council: it is going ahead and it's coming through here. It's going right across our land. And it's going to be big – the road will be up on stilts. Anyway David and I went to see them and they offered us compensation so we're off.

'I think Jerry over the road has been negotiating with them too because it's going to cross his land. I don't think it'll go through Swan's Harbour but you'll be affected by it. I'm amazed that you don't know about it. Hasn't the council been in touch?'

For a while Maurice just looked at her. He felt surprise, fear, bafflement and anger in quick succession. For several minutes he said nothing then he nodded at Liz.

'Well, I'm glad somebody's bothered to tell me,' he said quietly. 'I'd better get in touch with the council right away.'

And so it was that Maurice fell into the hands of his local bureaucrats. From the outset they showed all the hallmarks of underhand, uncaring officialdom. Had they been honest and open they would have contacted everyone living in the immediate vicinity of the proposed bypass at the earliest possible opportunity. They would have explained their plans, told everyone what the timetable was for final decisions and given outline details about compensation.

Even if they knew that their news would be unwelcome or that what they were offering would be unacceptable to some, it would still have been fairer and less painful if they had been up front. All too often secrecy is a precursor to cheating. The two go hand in hand. And Maurice Balchin was about to be cheated big time by Norfolk County Council.

When the council confirmed to the Balchins that there were plans to build a Wroxham bypass right beside Swan's Harbour, Maurice gave full vent to his feelings. He had a huge row with an assortment of officials but no one seemed to be in charge. Maurice demanded to see someone more senior.

In the end the council staff took a more conciliatory line. They agreed to send someone from the planning department, an inspector, to discuss the whole matter with the Balchins face to face.

An inspector came to see them just before Christmas in 1987. He sat in the living room at Swan's Harbour and Maurice placed a small tape recorder on the table.

'I don't want that thing on,' the inspector objected.

Maurice made no demur. 'I'll switch it off if you prefer,' he said and leant over to press one of the buttons.

Immediately the inspector seemed to relax a little. What he didn't know was that Maurice had actually pressed the 'on' button. It was his first tactical move in what was to prove a marathon war of attrition with the authorities.

Maurice realised almost immediately that he might not be able to stop the building of the bypass. He would try, of course, and if he could not halt the project altogether then he would try to have it re-routed away from Swan's Harbour.

But he was a realist. He decided that his first task was to ensure that he and his family would be properly compensated if the road did go ahead. Apart from anything else, Swan's Harbour had been pledged to the bank as security for the loans that Maurice had taken out to finance his property development business. The work that had been done on the house and grounds at Swan's Harbour meant it was now a substantial asset. Maurice reckoned it was now worth £400,000.

The Balchins had established that although the bypass would not cross their land, it would be horribly close. It was to rise up on its concrete pillars just thirty metres from their bedroom window.

The peace of Swan's Harbour would be shattered, its beauty scarred and the wildlife – the swans, the kingfishers, the Canada geese – would be driven away. And for the Balchins there would be serious financial loss. The council inspector agreed whole-heartedly when Maurice insisted that 'no-one in their right mind will want to buy Swan's Harbour now'.

The inspector seemed sympathetic. He appreciated the points Mr Balchin was making. He was sorry that the bypass would have such an impact on Swan's Harbour but he begged the Balchins not to worry too much. The council, he insisted, would look after them.

That Christmas of 1987 was a time of worry and uncertainty but Maurice had been somewhat reassured by what the inspector had said.

The Balchins discovered that the Holts had been given £500,000 to leave Heronly. Part of that money was the compul-sory purchase price of their land which the council needed to build the road. Part of it was compensation for the upheaval and distress of having a move forced upon them. The Balchins' neighbour on the other side of the road had apparently received even more – £600,000. Maurice knew that Jerry was a good negotiator but if he could get that much for a plot of land that had no moorings then maybe the Balchins would not do too badly financially.

They would still have to give up Swan's Harbour of course. They would never find anywhere quite as perfect.

Early in the New Year Maurice had a phone call from the bank. The bank wanted to know what 'Mr Balchin' knew about the Wroxham bypass. The bank wanted 'Mr Balchin' to come in and have a chat.

Maurice had been on first-name terms with most of the area's senior NatWest managers for years. He did not like this sudden formality. It irked him not least because there was no reason why the bank should be worried. However terrible the loss of Swan's Harbour, he would have full compensation. The bank's money was safe enough. He went to see them. He told them frostily that he had been to see the council, that he would be paid out, that there was no reason for the bank to worry.

They started calling him Maurice again.

That was at the beginning of the week. On Friday morning Audrey came and asked him if he had any cash. She had run out and she needed to go shopping. As it happened, Maurice had no money on him either but he offered to nip down to Wroxham and get £50 housekeeping. He drove into town, parked and went to the bank.

The clerks were courteous but firm. It would not be possible for him to draw out any money that day. Every single one of his accounts had been stopped. His business account, his personal account, Audrey's account, the account for his employees' wages – all had been blocked.

That day he had to draw cash for their food from his building society account.

When he reached home he rang the bank's main office. He was told they could not talk to him over the phone. And they started calling him 'Mr Balchin' again.

The nightmare had begun.

The bank wanted to recall all the money it had loaned Maurice. It wanted him to pay it back at once. The bank manager showed scant sympathy. He was sorry, of course, but he had a job to do.

The bank seemed unimpressed by Maurice's assurances that Norfolk County Council would give him compensation for Swan's Harbour. The manager and his colleagues at NatWest asked if Maurice had any proof, in writing, that Norfolk County Council would pay out. Maurice did not.

He rang the council. He was put through to a Mr MacLeod. Mr MacLeod was firm. The council had NOT said it would compensate Maurice for having the bypass so close to his home.

But what about the inspector? He had told the Balchins the council would look after them, hadn't he? He must have recommended a pay-out in his report.

Mr MacLeod was unmoved. The council had discussed the matter. The council had no plans to pay Maurice any compensation.

Had he but known it, Maurice's fate had been sealed before Christmas. Norfolk County Council had first started talking about building a Wroxham/Hoveton bypass in 1984 – soon after the Balchins had bought Swan's Harbour and started creating their dream. Neither the Balchins nor their neighbours the Holts had been alerted to the proposals when they bought their homes, as the plans had been put forward too late for the solicitors to uncover them when they carried out the usual local authority searches.

Slowly but surely the council had pushed ahead with the proposed bypass. An inspector reported back to the council on the impact the new road would have on Swan's Harbour. The council's planning and transportation committee had met on 17 December 1987 to discuss the Balchins' plight. The minutes of that meeting said:

> The value of the property is considerably reduced by the proposed bypass. And Mr Balchin uses the property as security for business loans. He claims that the decrease in value due to the bypass will reduce the amount he can borrow and he believes this will adversely affect his business as a property developer. The bypass, when built, would completely alter the character of the house. If the council does purchase, the price would be in the region of £325,000 to £375,000.

Another note in the planning committee minutes stated pertinently:

If the council does not purchase Swan's Harbour, the owner will only be entitled to claim for depreciation due to physical factors. It is difficult to assess the extent of these in advance but it is unlikely that more than £50,000 in current values will be payable.

The impact of the bypass on the Balchins' was spelt out quite clearly. But the planning inspector and his fellow officials were not going to allow themselves to be swayed by sentiment or by any sense of natural justice. Their advice to Council Members was unequivocal. Their report said: 'As the owner has no statutory rights to insist on the property being acquired, Members are recommended not to agree to this purchase.'

Seven years later Members of the House of Commons were asked by the Balchins' MP, Michael Lord, now Sir Michael, to remember that date of 17 December 1987 when the planning committee met. It was, said Mr Lord, the 'date on which Norfolk County Council set its face against doing what was right.'

The County Council was able to set its face against what was right because of an omission in the law.

English law lays down that authorities can make a compulsory purchase of land when this is deemed to be for the public good – so as to build a new road for example. If the authorities decide to make a compulsory purchase then they must pay a reasonable price. If there are questions as to whether they are offering a fair deal then they can be taken to an independent adjudicator.

In addition, authorities have discretion to pay out extra money on top of the purchase price to compensate for the upheaval and inconvenience suffered by people who are having to move from their land.

Maurice and his family had no right to a fair deal under any of these provisions. The catch is that the law does not force the authorities to pay up when someone's property will be blighted by a motorway that is going to run right beside their land but not on it.

The motorway would go within fifteen yards of Maurice and Audrey's bedroom window but it would not actually cross their grounds. The council therefore was not required to purchase their land.

As the report to the planning committee made clear, the Balchins would have a right to claim for depreciation because of physical factors such as noise. But they would be able to claim only after the bypass had been built and the sum involved would be nothing like the overall loss in the value of Swan's Harbour. Maurice had a letter from one local estate agent saying bluntly that 'at this particular moment in time the property is unsaleable on the open market'. The agent explained: 'The prospect of the construction work and ultimate usage of the bypass would, without doubt, dissuade any potential purchaser'.

In other words, the law allows local councils to slash the value of someone's main asset – their home and land – and to do so with impunity. Individuals just have to hope that the council concerned will have the decency to pay up voluntarily. Norfolk County Council did not.

All it could offer were excuses. Councillors claimed to be worried that they did not have the power to make a large, voluntary payment to the Balchins. They said they were concerned that this might set a precedent which could tie up scarce council funds in the future. Cost cutting not justice was Norfolk's goal.

The council's claim that it had no power to help the Balchins was dubious at best. But it was to be a key issue in the long legal battles that followed.

Maurice and Audrey found themselves living an increasingly hand-to-mouth existence. Not that they were thrown into penury on Day One – far from it. Maurice was a wealthy man. He had squirreled away various sums of money, he owned a number of other houses besides Swan's Harbour that he rented out to obtain an income and he still had his business. He had a couple of house-building projects in the area, which he hoped at first he would be able to keep going.

But as the weeks and months went by he found himself having to draw on his own savings and assets to pay his builders' wages, to meet household bills and to keep food on the table. One by one he sold off the houses he had bought. Audrey's little sports car was sold. Then the boat.

Maurice was determined to carry on fighting the bypass scheme but resistance came at a price. Lawyers would be needed to fight the battle and they did not come cheap. The Balchins were not entitled to legal aid. They were not poor enough – yet.

On the other hand, they were not entirely alone. There was to be a public inquiry into the council's proposals and a local group had been set up to fight the bypass. Aside from those who had been compensated because the bypass would cross their land, there was only one other family, the Evans family at the opposite end of the village, who were going to be as badly affected as the Balchins. Yet, there were plenty of others who were deeply dismayed at the prospect of a noisy road destroying the tranquillity of the area. The protest group set about raising cash for legal fees. Maurice found himself contributing a couple of thousand pounds.

The inquiry was held at Hoveton village hall and lasted three days. Maurice, like most of the objectors, felt that their barrister did a good job and that they were given a fair chance to put their case at the inquiry. It was to no avail. They lost.

By this time Maurice and Audrey were becoming desperate. Money was getting tighter all the time and the shortage of cash was starting to affect the business. Maurice was becoming increasingly worried about whether he could pay his men's wages at the end of each week. Eventually the day came when he knew he could not. Some of the men who had been with him a long time offered to help. They said they would be prepared to work for nothing if it would enable him to keep going and if it would not be for too long . . .

Maurice was touched. He thanked them but he knew he could not do it. All he would achieve would be to bring them to ruin as well as himself.

That year – 1990, the year in which the Balchins and the other objectors lost their fight at the public inquiry – Maurice's business folded.

Maurice and Audrey were penniless. Their debts were huge and growing. Interest charges of over 20 per cent had turned Maurice's original borrowings into a crippling £200,000 debt.

Audrey's health began to suffer. The doctor gave her medication but that did not stop her worrying constantly about being evicted.

In the end the doctor told Maurice that the best thing would be to have done with it and move his wife out of Swan's Harbour. Terrible as that would be, it might be better than having her brood about whether and when she was going to be put out of her home forcibly.

Swan's Harbour itself had become a sad place. There was no money even to do basic repairs on the house let alone to keep up over two acres of garden. Everything had taken on a derelict air. Perhaps that would make it easier to leave. That was what they told each other. In any event they had little choice.

In 1991 Maurice and Audrey left Swan's Harbour for the last time.

They moved to a little cottage in a village called Broome. They eventually sold Swan's Harbour for £220,000 – about half the price it would have fetched had there been no bypass. The money all went to pay off borrowings and even then they were still in debt.

Maurice found himself being pursued by Broadland District Council because he had refused to pay his poll tax. They chased him relentlessly. One day a couple of bailiffs even came to Broome. They knew all about Maurice. They had read about his case in the newspapers and they were sympathetic. They told him – unofficially of course – not to pay a penny.

Eventually Maurice told the council that he would not and could not pay his poll tax but that he would be happy to go to prison. They left him alone after that.

Despite everything, the Balchins had not given up all hope of justice.

Norfolk County Council had to have approval from the Transport Secretary before it could go ahead with the bypass. Maurice and Audrey thought they might have made a breakthrough when they received a copy of the report by the Department of Transport's inspector. The inspector expressed his concern at what had happened to the Balchins, and stressed that if approval for the bypass was granted then 'adequate compensation arrangements should be made urgently in respect of Swan's Harbour, particularly in view of the owner's financial situation'.

It was a view echoed by Transport Ministers themselves. The Transport Secretary at the time was the Conservative John MacGregor, now Lord MacGregor but then the MP for South Norfolk. For a while the Balchins had been his constituents and he was anxious to avoid any suggestions that he might be biased in their favour while taking a quasi-judicial decision on the future of the bypass. He therefore handed over the decision to one of his junior Ministers who could be totally objective.

The decision, reached so impartially and announced in June 1992, still went out in the Transport Secretary's name – and it favoured the Balchins. The bypass could go ahead but the Government expected Norfolk County Council to offer proper compensation to Maurice and Audrey. The letter telling Norfolk County Council that it could go ahead with the bypass noted that the Transport Department's inspector had called for 'sympathetic consideration by your council to the plight of the owners of Swan's Harbour'.

The letter said that the Secretary of State was 'confident that your council will give these matters early consideration'. Small wonder if the Balchins' hopes were raised. It looked as if the Government was going to force Norfolk Council to behave honourably and give them the compensation they should have had years earlier.

Maurice and Audrey should have read the small print. At the end of the letter from the Transport Department in Whitehall to Norfolk County Council came the catch:

'Details of the compensation arising in consequence of the confirmation of these Orders are for negotiation with the acquiring authority, not with the Secretary of State.'

What that meant was that Ministers, for all their avowed sympathy towards the Balchins, were not going to lift a finger to help them. They were going to leave it up to Norfolk councillors, the very people who had behaved so shabbily towards the Balchins in the first place, to decide whether or not to behave honourably and pay them compensation now.

Unsurprisingly, they decided not. Maurice and Audrey were back where they started. It is one of the oldest tricks in the book but it is no less effective for that: one group of bureaucrats and/or politicians sloughs off responsibility to another set of bureaucrats and/or politicians.

Each group protests that it cannot find a way to help, saying perhaps the unfortunate citizen should go and talk to the *other group* and/or its political masters. It is the *others* who really count.

The tragedy is that when the authorities start playing their game of pass the parcel with other people's lives there is nobody to make the music stop.

The Tory Government later explained its refusal to help the

Balchins by claiming that the Transport Secretary had no legal right to force Norfolk to pay compensation. Technically this may have been correct but politics is the art of the possible. Could more robust Ministers less concerned with sticking to the brief officials had written for them not have found a way? Having ensured that the bypass decision was taken by a colleague with no special constituency interest, could John MacGregor not have done more to ensure that his junior Minister's recommendations on the Balchins were followed?

Certainly that was the view of one of the Transport Secretary's own Tory colleagues, MP Michael Lord. Mr Lord, who became the Balchins' MP when they moved into his constituency at Broome, told the House of Commons that the Transport Secretary could have guaranteed a fair deal for Maurice and Audrey by refusing consent for the bypass until the council paid compensation. This Mr Macgregor had failed to do. Mr Lord tried to find extenuating circumstances for the Minister's behaviour.

'I suppose,' he told the Commons, 'that in some ways it was not unreasonable for the Secretary of State to think that Norfolk County Council might behave as he wished – with reason, fairness and a little compassion; but I am afraid that he was gravely mistaken. Norfolk County Council hid behind the letter of the law and refused to help.

'In the hope that I might persuade someone on Norfolk County Council to realise just how unfair the council had been,' Mr Lord said, 'I wrote to the leaders of the three main political groups – Mrs Cameron, Mrs King and Mr Revell – explaining Mr and Mrs Balchin's distress and urging them to look at the case again.

'I received a reply from Mr Barry Capon, Norfolk County Council's Chief Executive and Clerk. The final paragraph stated: "The decision not to purchase Mr Balchin's house was taken without dissent by agreement across all parties and they do not see any good and sufficient reason to raise the matter again."

'I hope,' said Mr Lord, 'that those ladies and gentlemen are able to sleep soundly in their beds at night – in their unblighted homes – and that they do not call to mind too often the way in which they have destroyed one family.'

Michael Lord visited Maurice and Audrey at their cottage in Broome and told them there might be another avenue they could pursue. It so happened that he was a member of the Commons Select Committee on the Parliamentary Commissioner for Administration – the Ombudsman. It is the Ombudsman's job to investigate cases of maladministration.

Mr Lord had been an MP for a dozen years and in that time he had come across many cases like that of Maurice and Audrey but as he said later: 'Mr and Mrs Balchin's case was the worst that I had ever seen. I was more than happy to refer it to the Ombudsman in January 1994.'

At the time the Ombudsman was a man called William Reid. The case Mr Lord put to him on behalf of the Balchins was that they had been victims of maladministration by the Department of Transport.

Norfolk County Council might be the real villains of the piece but as everyone kept pointing out they had not broken any rules. They had not even acted cackhandedly – indeed the reason they had been able to screw the Balchins so blatantly was because they believed that their shabby behaviour was protected by the letter of the law. The Department of Transport was a different matter.

Michael Lord pointed out that both the Transport Department's own inspector and Transport Secretary John MacGregor had agreed that unacceptable harm would be caused to the Balchins' property by the building of the bypass. That, argued Mr Lord, gave the Transport Secretary more than adequate grounds for withholding his consent to the bypass until Norfolk County Council offered a fair deal to Maurice and Audrey.

'These are administrative measures and they were mishandled,' Mr Lord later told the Commons. 'What can be more maladaministrative than that?

'What is the purpose of a public inquiry, an inspector's report and the Secretary of State's scrutiny if it is not to ensure that mistakes – and this is a huge mistake – do not happen?'

It took William Reid, the Ombudsman, almost a year to investigate the Balchins' case and deliver his findings. Why it should have taken him so long is not clear.

He did not question the facts that had been put before him. He accepted that Maurice and Audrey had suffered great harm.

But he found in favour of the Department of Transport and against the Balchins. In his view the Department had not been guilty of maladministration.

The Balchins were shattered by the decision. Michael Lord was outraged. He went to see William Reid and asked him to reconsider. The Ombudsman refused to change his findings. Dreadful case – yes. Maladministration – no.

He had accepted the argument put forward by the Transport Department that the Secretary of State had no legal right to tell Norfolk Council that he would not approve their bypass until they paid compensation to the Balchins.

Well might Michael Lord describe the Minister and his officials as talking in 'Pontius Pilate platitudes' while they washed their hands of the whole affair.

The Balchins were not through yet. Nor was Mr Lord. Maurice and Audrey went to court to see if they could challenge the Ombudsman's findings there. And they had found themselves an expert on planning law.

The Balchins were now living on social security but the upside of being so down in the world was that they were eligible for legal aid. Their planning law expert, working with another barrister,

Charles George QC, and with the Balchins' solicitor, would get it for them; they would not have to worry about legal fees.

Meanwhile Michael Lord was pursuing the Balchins' oppressors. He had in his sights the top civil servants at the Department of Transport.

In November 1994, just a month before the Ombudsman found against the Balchins, a Treasury Minister, Tony Nelson, had appeared before Mr Lord's Select Committee. The committee was trying to establish what did and what did not count as maladministration. Mr Nelson was most helpful.

'Failure to mitigate the effects of strict adherence to the letter of law, where this produces manifestly inequitable treatment, will now be an example of maladministration,' he said.

Three months later, *after* the Ombudsman had decided that the Balchins had *not* been the victims of maladministration, Sir Patrick Brown, then the top civil servant at the Department of Transport, appeared before Mr Lord's Committee.

Mr Lord seized the opportunity to ask him whether he accepted that failure to mitigate the unfairness of the letter of the law now counted as maladministration. Sir Patrick confirmed that this was the Government's position. Mr Lord pressed him for further clarification.

'What we are really saying,' said Mr Lord, 'is that even where everything has been done precisely by the law of the land and is defensible in that sense, where that clearly produces distress and problems, then maladministration may well be shown to have occurred.'

Sir Patrick replied: 'That is the current arrangement for dealing with cases of this sort.'

Had he been a stickler for accuracy, Sir Patrick might have said that this was meant to be the current arrangement for dealing with cases of this sort. It was not the way the Department or the Ombudsman had dealt with the Balchins' case. Ministers, officials and ombudsmen seemed only too happy to take refuge behind the letter of the law – regardless of whether it might amount to maladministration.

The exchanges in Michael Lord's Select committee suggest there is a black hole somewhere in the British System of Government. Ministers and top civil servants publicly spelt out Government policy which was that it was maladministration to allow someone to be treated unfairly even if the letter of the law had been observed. Yet Ministers, top civil servants – and the Ombudsman – had ignored the Government's own rule in the case of the Balchins.

There would seem to be little hope for ordinary people when those at the top ignore the rules with impunity.

In July 1995 Michael Lord gave a blow-by-blow account of the whole sorry saga on the floor of the House of Commons. The occasion was an adjournment debate. Technically MPs simply vote on whether or not they should go home for the night. In practice adjournment debates give backbench MPs the chance to raise constituency cases like that of the Balchins. The Government of the day puts up a Minister to reply to the points made.

When Michael Lord placed the tragedy of the Balchins before the House, the Minister who responded was Steve Norris. Mr Norris, later to achieve notoriety for his string of mistresses and fame as the Tories' unsuccessful candidate to be London's first mayor, was then a junior Transport Minister.

Mr Lord made it clear that he did not hold Mr Norris responsible for what had happened in the past but insisted he would hold him responsible – with others – for what happened to the Balchins in the future.

'In recent weeks I have had meetings with the Secretary of State to plead the Balchins' case yet again,' Mr Lord told MPs. 'He listened sympathetically but insisted that the Government was unable to help.

'This sort of inhuman treatment, dealt out to innocent citizens by the authorities, whoever they may be, might be understandable in some lawless banana republic but surely not in this country in 1995.

'What is absolutely clear in all the evidence – and it has never been denied by the Government – is that it was acknowledged that harm would be done to Mr and Mrs Balchin and their property. It was also acknowledged that someone had to look after them. The Department of Transport which had the power to ensure that that was done before allowing the bypass proposals to proceed, singularly failed to take the steps that could have turned the pious hope into a fair and reassuring reality.

'The Balchins' plight is desperate. They have no money and their health is suffering. A solution must be found and found quickly.'

Michael Lord's speech in the Commons was an eloquent and moving plea for justice. It was made in the highest place in the land. Yet it did not bring a solution to the Balchins' desperate plight.

Why was the Commons incapable of making things happen, of forcing Ministers, officials and the Ombudsman to act? After all, the constitutional experts insist that Parliament is sovereign. What is more, the Balchins' case was not a party political matter.

Yet in the last twenty years or so Ministers – and even more Prime Ministers – have done their best to neuter the Commons. Backbench MPs are treated by both main parties as cheerleaders who should accept the party line unquestioningly.

Democracy is the poorer. So too are ordinary members of the public who have in effect been robbed of one avenue for having their wrongs righted. For the undermining of Parliament means MPs find it harder to achieve much when they raise the grievances of individual constituents in the Commons – no matter how eloquent they are.

Yet Michael Lord's passionate plea on behalf of the Balchins did not go entirely unanswered. When Steve Norris rose to speak he said he might have something useful to offer to his honourable friend Mr Lord . . .

Steve Norris started his reply by rehearsing the usual arguments for not helping the Balchins . . . Compensation was a matter for the local council not central government . . . It would be improper for a Minister to attempt to put pressure on a local authority to make it do what he wanted . . . Ministers had no right to impose their views on local councils no matter how often Mr Lord said they did.

But, said Mr Norris, there might be another way forward for the Balchins. He explained that in 1991 – years after the Balchins began their battle for a fair deal – a new section was inserted into the 1980 Planning Act, stating that all highway authorities had the right to make discretionary payments to anyone who was going to be badly affected by a new road. The payments could be made in advance before building work started.

Norfolk had decided not to use these advance discretionary powers in the case of the Balchins. The council claimed that the fall in the value of Swan's Harbour had had more to do with a general drop in property prices than with the bypass proposal – an allegation that lacked credibility with just about everyone. Even Mr Norris seemed unconvinced. Norfolk's plea that tightness of funds had been a factor when it decided not to use its new discretionary powers was far more believable. Whether it was defensible was another matter.

'It is not for me to obtain legal advice in this case,' Mr Norris told the Commons, 'but there may be a question about whether the decision not to operate a discretionary scheme for which statutory provision had been made by Parliament can be justified.'

Mr Norris hoped that by raising the issue of discretionary powers, he had now given Mr Lord a realistic prospect of pursuing the Balchins' case further. He added: 'No Member of this

House – certainly not my right honourable friend the Secretary of State – would wish to stand by and see an injustice occur where it is within our power to correct it.'

This pious remark sums up much of what is wrong with the System. It *was* in the power of Ministers to correct the injustice suffered by the Balchins – if only they had had the political will. The power of backbench MPs may have waned but that of governments has not.

Ministers and civil servants could have leant on Norfolk Council or they could have changed the law and *forced* them to comply. After all, they had already changed it once to ease the impact of planning blight by spelling out councils' discretionary powers to buy up property in advance.

The pity of it is that John Macgregor, Patrick Brown, Steve Norris and William Reid are not monsters. All four are able men, well meaning and indeed likeable. The question is whether they could have tried harder.

Steve Norris clearly believed that he had given the Balchins fresh ammunition to attack Norfolk County Council. In the event Maurice and Audrey used it against Mr Norris's own Department of Transport.

The Balchins went to court to challenge the Ombudsman's finding that they had not suffered from maladministration. Their case was heard by Mr Justice Sedley. Norfolk County Council claimed that it would be 'setting a dangerous precedent' if it used its discretionary powers to help the Balchins. Mr Justice Sedley dismissed this argument saying that it made a nonsense of the word 'discretion'. The whole point of 'discretionary' powers was that they should *not* be governed by precedents or hard and fast rules. This was a 'textbook example' of what he called 'a fettered discretion'.

But it was not just Norfolk County Council's conduct that raised doubts in Mr Justice Sedley's mind. What Steve Norris had not perhaps foreseen was that the judge was not satisfied with the way officials in the Department of Transport had behaved. He was particularly unhappy that officials had given the Minister a background note on the Balchins' case that made no mention whatever of the new law specifically stating that councils, like Norfolk, had discretionary powers to buy properties suffering from planning blight.

Mr Justice Sedley described the Department's conduct as 'on the face of it, highly questionable'. Maurice and Audrey were over the moon.

'It gave us such a lift,' says Maurice.

Maurice and Audrey knew that Mr Justice Sedley's ruling was not final but it meant that the Ombudsman would have to think again. It was in 1996 that Mr Justice Sedley found in favour of the Balchins – almost ten years after they had started the battle over Swan's Harbour. So great had been the delays in the System and the procrastination by the authorities that the final surreal touch, when it came, should have been no surprise. In the middle of their High Court battle, Norfolk County Council decided that the Wroxham/Hoveton bypass would not, after all, be built. Nobody at the council wrote to Maurice to tell him. He was left to read it in the local paper.

Not that it made much difference to the Balchins. Unlike the Evans family who had held on to their home, they had long since lost Swan's Harbour and they would not benefit when the property rose in value as it would do now. They would still be ruined unless they could force the authorities to admit that they had been wrong and should pay compensation.

Yet after Mr Justice Sedley's decision, the Balchins had little doubt that this time the Ombudsman would change his mind. The Ombudsman was now Michael Buckley, who had replaced Sir William Reid on his retirement. Maurice and Audrey felt he would have to come down on their side.

They were wrong. The Ombudsman was unmoved by the findings of Mr Justice Sedley. He refused to change his mind. He did not explain why but he still believed there had been no mal-administration.

The incredible thing about ordinary men and women is that they sometimes display quite extraordinary determination. Maurice and Audrey had lost another battle but they did not give up. They went back to the High Court again citing the Ombudsman's failure to give adequate reason for his refusal to alter his decision.

One key factor this time was the Department of Transport claim that it had NOT overlooked the new law which spelt out Norfolk County Council's discretionary power to buy Swan's Harbour. The Balchins said the Department HAD overlooked it. Surely the Department should have pointed it out to Norfolk County Council and urged that the discretionary powers be used.

This time in the High Court the Balchins' case was heard by Mr Justice Dyson who took a tough line with the Department. He said that it would be 'plainly very damaging from the Department of Transport's point of view' if its officials were found to have overlooked the new law because they did not know about it. The judge said it did not matter that some officials somewhere in the Department might have known about it. What mattered was whether the ones dealing with the Balchins' case knew.

Sir Patrick Brown, the top civil servant at the Department, had, as the judge put it, chosen his words 'very carefully'. Sir Patrick had never expressly stated that officials handling the Balchins' case knew about the new power but he had implied that they did. The result, said Mr Justice Dyson, was that the Ombudsman had 'been led into error' by Sir Patrick Brown's evidence.

The judge also said that if the Ombudsman had thought about it more carefully, he would surely have pressed Sir Patrick about who knew what and when. After all, the documentary evidence 'pointed very strongly' to the conclusion that those involved had overlooked the new power. Mr Justice Dyson said that the court had not seen a shred of evidence to suggest that the officials dealing with the Balchins' case had taken the new power into account.

And he insisted that the conduct of Departmental civil servants had to be viewed against the fact that the Minister had told officials he wanted to know how they were going to ensure that Norfolk County Council helped the Balchins.

Mr Justice Dyson found for the Balchins. It was the second time Maurice and Audrey had been victorious in the High Court. Yet again their hopes were raised that this time the nightmare might be over. They believed that if they finally won they could demand substantial compensation, perhaps as much as £2m, from the Department of Transport. But they tried not to be too optimistic. Experience had taught them that the System might yet refuse them justice.

The Balchins were right to be cautious. Even if the Ombudsman could be persuaded to change his mind, their chances of winning compensation for their years of misery were – and are – slender. The Ombudsman system, loosely based on the longstanding and much tougher Swedish model, is designed to give ordinary people redress against the authorities. So the British authorities have rigged the system in their own favour and against the public. With one exception, our Ombudsmen have no teeth.

The exception is the Financial Services Ombudsman, who can order malefactors to pay for their wrongdoing if he finds against them. The other Ombudsmen, and there are a number of them looking after areas, such as local government, can merely make recommendations. Michael Buckley, who covers maladministration in central Government and also health complaints, could not force a Government Department or a local health authority to pay compensation even if he wanted to do so.

It is true that his recommendations are often followed voluntarily by Whitehall. It is also true that some of those who take their grievances to him are not looking for compensation but for an apology and for action to ensure that others do not suffer as they have done. Yet that is cold comfort for the Balchins and those like them. A system that cannot compel the authorities to right wrongs in a tangible way is one that is failing to serve the public.

Not that Michael Buckley seems keen to right the Balchins' wrongs.

So slowly does the machinery of English justice operate that it was only in May 1999 that Maurice and Audrey won their second court victory and Mr Justice Dyson ordered a further reconsideration of the Balchins' case by the Ombudsman. The couple were given a hint that they might perhaps expect another ruling from Ombudsman Buckley in the September of that year.

The autumn dragged on, the Millennium came and went, the new century began to get into its stride. Still the Balchins waited.

Eventually, the Ombudsman pronounced yet again on their case. And yet again he turned them down. This time he admitted that Transport civil servants had been guilty of maladministration but said it made no difference. Norfolk would still have refused to help Maurice and Audrey.

Disheartened, weary but still unbowed, the Balchins went back once more to the High Court. This time the judge who heard their application, Mr Justice Moses, was even blunter that Mr Justice Sedley and Mr Justice Dyson. He said that both government and council officials involved in the case had been ignorant and bungling. In an echo of Michael Lord in the House of Commons six years earlier, Mr Justice Moses said: 'I hope they don't sleep easily in their beds when they think about this case. What a disgrace.'

In August 2001, he gave the Balchins leave to seek a judicial review of the Ombudsman's ruling. The case was expected to be heard the following January.

Meantime, in the New Year's honours list of 2002 Michael Buckley, the Ombudsman, was like his predecessor William Reid, given a knighthood. It was the final twist of the screw.

This is the man who failed to help the Balchins even when the High Court gave him every opportunity to do so. Not only that but he has kept the Balchins waiting month after month to know their fate without any explanation or apology. It is all of a piece with everything else the family has had to endure.

Take the source of the family's ills – Norfolk County Council. Norfolk's elected councillors cravenly accepted that the cost-saving imperative of their officials was more important than a fair deal for individual local residents. Yet they wasted huge amounts of public money on a scheme that was eventually junked. One reason it happened was that both councillors and officials knew that nobody was going to make them accountable in any meaningful way.

Once local outrage over a case like the Balchins' might have shown itself at the ballot box. Now voters are so disillusioned that up to two-thirds of them do not bother to turn out in local elections and those who do tend to make their minds up on national lines. The result is that to all intents and purposes local councillors and their officials are not answerable for what they do.

The public can appeal to Whitehall or to the Ombudsman but as the Balchins discovered it would be foolish to place much faith in either. Provided they adhere to the letter of the law, they too cannot be called to account in any true sense for the injustices they perpetrate – not by the public, not by Parliament and not, it seems, by the High Court.

The flaws in the System suggest it is time to take a fresh look at how we make officials and elected politicians accountable. Perhaps it would help to concentrate the minds of those in authority if we could find ways of making them accept a measure of personal responsibility for treating individuals fairly – with penalties for those who fail to do so. Maybe, too, we need to give statutory backing to broad-brush definitions of 'fairness' and 'maladministration'. One possibility might be that outlined by Whitehall and the Tory Government in the 1990s when they said that failure to mitigate the unfairness of the letter of the law should count as maladministration. Had the authorities acted on that definition the Balchins might have had justice years ago.

The Balchins' story indicates an urgent need for a properly co-ordinated system of redress where there is no room for powerful people to slough off responsibility onto someone else. One of the most arresting aspects of the Balchins' tale is the way their fate has been bounced around between Government Ministers, civil servants, the Ombudsman and the High Court. Maurice, who is on legal aid, reckons the ongoing 'debate' between the Ombudsman and the High Court with the Balchins' case going back and forth between the two, has so far cost the taxpayer at least £2 million in legal fees. This is a tale where all of us are cheated.

What has happened to Maurice and Audrey suggests that the Ombudsman system itself needs to be revisited. There are now proposals for integrating the different Ombudsmen so that people like the Balchins who have been hit by local government and central government can be given redress against all those who have treated them so shabbily. But there is also a case for giving all Ombudsmen real teeth so they can *order* those in authority to reverse decisions and to pay compensation where appropriate.

Perhaps we should explore, as well, ways of giving the public a greater role in deciding cases once the Ombudsman's office has investigated a case. Ordinary people might take a more robust attitude to ending injustices than Ombudsmen who, no matter how well intentioned, are themselves members of the Establishment. The Balchins' case involves the conduct of civil servants. Both Sir William Reid and Sir Michael Buckley are former civil servants. The injection of some outside views might help to command greater public confidence in the system.

Whitehall itself and local councils might win greater credence among ordinary people if they stopped hiding behind the fiction – and it is often a fiction – that all decisions are taken by elected Ministers or elected councillors. Sometimes elected politicians do little more than rubberstamp the decision of officials. It was the bureaucrats who seemed to take the lead in doing down the Balchins at Norfolk County Council. The experience of Maurice and Audrey provides a powerful case for finding better ways to make the growing ranks of officialdom less secretive and more accountable for the way they treat people like the Balchins.

Bureaucracies provide a perfect climate for the cheating classes to flourish. Those who suffer at their hands need more than a vague hope of large-scale constitutional change that may never happen. They need more workaday, practical reform. And they need it soon.

Maurice Balchin is now sixty-seven. As he himself says: 'We're innocent people yet we've had a fifteen-year sentence. We've lost the best working years of our lives.'

In July 2002, Maurice went back to the High Court yet again. He listened as the court heard about the 'collective amnesia' of the Transport civil servants, about the Ombudsman's refusal to let the Balchins see all the documents relevant to the case and about how Norfolk Council had drawn up guidelines for buying blighted property once it understood that it had the powers to do so. Once again, the Court found in the Balchin's favour but that merely means that their case will now go back to the Ombudsman yet again. They still do not know if they will receive compensation. Even if they do, nothing can give the Balchins back their lost years of fighting, of living hand to mouth, of waiting and wondering when the cheating classes might give them justice.

2

THE BIKER'S TALE

Concern about the inadequacies of Britain's struggling health service has been made worse by a growing public awareness of incompetence and cover-up in the medical profession. Unlike civil servants or bankers or lawyers, doctors can destroy people's lives literally as well as metaphorically.

A series of well-publicised horror stories about medical blunders has badly dented the reputation of health professionals over the last few years. And claims of medical negligence have been rising steadily – as has the cost. According to the National Audit Office, the bill facing the Health Service for outstanding medical negligence claims has almost doubled in the last four years to an astronomical £4.4 billion. In the period 2000 to 2001, the likely bill rose by £500 million as the number of claims shot up to 4,115 from 2,411 the previous year. Despite efforts to reform the secretive, 'doctor knows best' culture of the medical profession with its unwillingness to admit mistakes, the figures suggest that change is slow in coming.

Frank Cunningham certainly believes there is a long road to go before the victims of medical negligence can be assured of a fair deal. He takes a certain grim satisfaction in the spiralling cost of compensation claims against the Health Service because it is putting pressure on the authorities to alter their ways. Not that Frank had ever expected the medical profession to let him down. He and his family had always had complete faith in their doctors . . .

Bikes dominated Frank's life. He was a motor mechanic by trade and a biker by inclination. He loved bikes. He loved the speed, the power, the glamour of them. He spent much of his spare time and nearly all his spare money on his bike. Why not? He was eighteen and he had no other responsibilities. He did not think of himself as a reckless rider but like any other biker of his age he rode for the thrill of it. He had a Suzuki scrambler motorbike for Motorcross riding. He knew there were risks but that was part of the excitement. Besides, he reckoned that he never took unnecessary chances.

He was practising when the accident happened. He was riding, with his mates, on some waste ground near his home in Cheetham Hill outside Manchester. Most of his friends had bikes too. That evening they were larking about, testing their machines, revelling in the exhilaration of the rides.

The terrain was difficult: uneven with sudden drops and hidden gullies. There had been a downpour earlier in the day and now it was slippery too. Frank had been going as fast as he dared but with a touch more caution than usual. Then, as he picked up speed after manoeuvring round some scrub, he felt his machine start to skid. He kept going and braked – a little too sharply – as he tried to correct the slide. But even as he struggled to regain control he could feel the bike toppling over. As if in slow motion, he felt himself thudding on to the rough grass. The bike landed on top of him.

His friends came rushing over. His leg hurt like hell. It was trapped under the bike from knee to ankle. The pain did not go away even when the others lifted the machine off him. Someone called an ambulance.

When it arrived the ambulance was unable to negotiate the bumpy ground. The paramedics had to carry Frank over to it on a stretcher. Although his leg was crushed he seemed to have sustained no life-threatening injuries and he was conscious. Perhaps he had been lucky.

The doctors who examined him at North Manchester General were young. They X-rayed his leg but at first they could not find any fracture. They went off to consult a more senior doctor who took a look at the radiograph – X-ray of the bone – and confirmed that there had been a break. He did not check on Frank himself.

The junior doctors put the leg in plaster and sent Frank home. It would take time to mend, they said, but there was nothing to worry about.

That night Frank was in agony. His leg seemed numb yet at the same time he felt a cold, consuming pain below his knee. The next morning the leg was no better and when he examined his foot protruding from the plaster it seemed strangely white.

He wondered if the doctors had made the plaster too tight. It felt as if they had. The pain was not easing. He decided to go back to the hospital. His mum went with him.

This time they saw one of the senior doctors. Frank explained that he could neither move his toes nor raise his leg – and the pain was severe. Mrs Cunningham added that Frank had been in agony all night. She asked why his toes were so cold.

'Surely that can't be right, doctor' she said anxiously. 'You feel his foot – it's like ice.'

But the doctor did not bother to feel Frank's toes or to check if he could raise his leg. He seemed unmoved by the Cunninghams' concerns.

'It's October,' he said. 'I'm not surprised your toes are cold with the weather like it is today. What I want you to do is come back in a week's time and we'll have another look at the leg then.'

There was no mistaking the tone. He was dismissing them. They had been with him for a couple of minutes – at most.

The doctor seemed harassed. The waiting room outside was full and he clearly had many more patients to see. All the same Frank felt reassured.

'If there was a serious problem he'd have spotted it,' he told his mother. 'I suppose it's bound to take time – after all it only happened yesterday. I'll probably be fine in a couple of days.'

Five days later the pain had become intolerable. The exposed part of Frank's foot looked like dead flesh. A week was not yet up but Frank could stand it no longer. He and his mother returned to North Manchester General. This time they saw a different doctor. This time there was no question of sending them home.

The look on the doctor's face told them almost immediately that something was wrong. He touched Frank's cold toes. The hospital would have to carry out checks on Frank's circulation. At once. The doctor would like one of his colleagues to give a second opinion but it was probable that Frank would have to stay in the hospital that night. They might need to operate on his leg . . .

Neither on that day nor at any other time did the staff at North Manchester General admit that maybe they should have acted sooner, that maybe there were tests which should have been run when Frank had first come in with a broken leg.

What the doctors realised when Frank went back to the hospital for the third time was that he had a blood clot in his knee.

The clot was travelling down his leg. Had it gone up his body it could have cut off the flow of blood to his heart and killed him. As it was the clot was cutting off the blood supply to his lower leg, which meant the tissue would be damaged. Already the muscles were starting to die.

Experienced doctors know that there is always a risk of a blood clot forming when a bone is broken. If limbs are twisted or under pressure – as Frank's leg had been when his bike fell on top of him – the veins can become constricted and a clot forms. Hospital staff should make a routine check of a patient's circulation to see if there is a clot. If they find one they can usually prevent irrevocable damage – provided action is taken within twenty-four hours. In Frank's case it was nearly a week before anything was done.

Even if checking for a clot associated with fracture was not standard procedure at North Manchester General, the suspicions of the doctor on duty should have been aroused when Frank came back the day after his accident complaining of pain and a loss of feeling in his foot. Instead he was sent home after the most cursory examination with no effort made to run circulation tests. That failure was to leave Frank with a gruesome reminder of his biking accident that will be with him for the rest of his life . . .

Surgeons operated on Frank within hours of admitting him. The aim was to cut away some of the damaged tissue that had been starved of blood. It was the only way that they might be able to save his leg.

That first operation was not successful. The doctors warned Frank that he would have to be operated on again.

In the end he had to endure a whole series of operations – ten in all spread over a six-month period. Frank knew that the hospital staff were now focused on his case and were doing their best, but they said he had an infection in the bone. And it appeared to him that the doctors' faces grew longer each time they came to see him.

Frank noticed that he never seemed to see the same doctor twice. Whenever he tried to cross-question one of them as to what had gone wrong, he met blank looks. The story was always the same. They all said that they were new to his case, that they had no idea what had happened originally.

And then one morning a consultant came to see Frank. He was sorry but he was the bearer of bad tidings. As Frank knew, they had tried again and again to solve the problem by operating but without success. Now there was only one course open to them.

Frank would have to lose his leg.

They amputated his left leg just below the knee. The operation went as well as could be expected. Physically Frank soon started to recover.

Mentally he was in poor shape. He was not yet twenty and the prospect of life as an amputee made him profoundly depressed. It was a depression from which he was not to recover fully for over two years.

As he lay in the hospital thinking bleakly about his future, he found himself wondering more and more often about why the doctors had not spotted the problem sooner. If they had tested him when he was first brought in he might have kept his leg . . .

Later, as he slowly learned how to walk again, first with crutches and then with an artificial limb, he resolved to find out whether the doctors had been guilty of negligence. If they had and he could prove it, he would sue.

He might not be a medical man but logic and common sense told him that he had lost his leg as a result of human error and not just because of some accident of fate. As he said to his mum: 'These days nobody should go into hospital with a broken leg and come out without any leg at all. Not when you're eighteen and healthy. It's not right.'

The decision to pursue the hospital authorities was a brave one. It was 1985 when Frank had his accident and in those days public respect for the expertise and integrity of the medical profession was stronger than it is today.

In the mid-eighties few laymen were alive to the risks of medical incompetence or to the professional freemasonry that allowed mistakes to be covered up. There *were* successful suits against doctors for negligence but it was uphill work and usually complainants won only if they had an open and shut case.

At first Frank believed he had a watertight case. He now had some idea of what had gone wrong and he found an early ally in his GP, who was horrified at what had happened. He introduced Frank to his brother, who was a solicitor and who agreed to take on the case.

Together they consulted medical experts who agreed that the hospital should have realised far sooner that Frank might have a clot associated with fracture. The experts said the medical staff should have checked his circulation immediately. Had they done so the problem would have been apparent. The experts were also confident that the X-rays taken when Frank first arrived at the hospital would show that the break in his bone was very close to the site where the clot was discovered. This was typical in cases of clots associated with fracture. Frank's team believed he was in such a strong position that the Health Authority might even settle before the case came to court.

But it was not to be that simple. Not only did North Manchester Health Authority deny negligence, they made it clear that they would fight Frank all the way.

One of their first moves came when Frank's team asked for the X-rays of his leg. The Authority refused to hand them over. It seemed the vital X-rays were no longer available . . .

The legal system, as always, took time.

Apart from pressing the Health Authority for evidence, there were efforts to see if it would settle out of court. That would be the quickest and cheapest solution – though Frank's lawyers warned him that even if the Authority did settle it would be at the last minute. The hospital administrators would try to drag things out as long as possible in the hope that Frank would become discouraged and give up.

It became clear to Frank that the doctors and the Authority believed they were playing for high stakes. If they lost it would seriously undermine the reputation of the hospital and its staff. Victory for Frank would also mean that he could expect a substantial pay-out. The Health Authority seemed ready to do all in its power to avoid that.

In the end it was not until 1991, six years after Frank had fallen from his bike, that he and his lawyers finally found themselves in court.

Despite their high hopes, the Health Authority did not offer to settle in the days before the court case. Once the hearing got underway Frank realised why.

In court the North Manchester Health Authority launched a three-pronged attack. Its lawyers claimed that hospital staff *had* checked Frank's circulation when he first arrived and had found it normal. They claimed that they had checked his circulation again when he returned to hospital the day after the accident. They explained the failure to keep any record of these tests by saying it had not been thought necessary because nothing was wrong.

Frank thought this claim was outrageous. He could scarcely believe what he was hearing and he felt sure that the court would not believe it either. Yet the judge, Mr Justice Henry, seemed unmoved.

The Health Authority's lawyers did not question that the damage to Frank's leg had been caused by a blood clot on his knee. What was in dispute was the cause of the clot and whether it could have been discovered earlier. The Authority's lawyers claimed that it was not a clot associated with fracture, which could and should have been spotted quickly. They said it was the result of 'compartment pressure syndrome' where the arteries are compressed by the muscle and they insisted that as is usual in such cases, a clot had formed some time *after* Frank had been examined and treated by the hospital.

Frank's own experts agreed that compartment pressure syndrome could cause a clot to form several days after an accident but they said the syndrome was extremely rare – so rare that there might be only one case a year. Yet nation-wide there were several cases a *week* of clot associated with fracture – and the problem became apparent almost immediately as it had in Frank's case.

Then there were the X-rays. The Health Authority claimed that the original X-rays had been lost or destroyed because they were too bulky to store. All they could muster were some miniaturised X-rays of Frank's leg. Frank's team had had to work with these and not only were the X-rays miniaturised they were also cloudy – like an over-exposed film negative. All the same, Frank's experts argued that the X-rays showed the conditions had been exactly right for a clot associated with fracture: the break in the bone was just where the clot had formed. Probably the broken bone had nicked the artery.

The X-rays were not proof positive of Frank's claim. They merely provided supporting evidence and even then much depended on the medical interpretation. All the same, taking all Frank's evidence together, things seemed to be going well for his team until the second day of the hearing. It was then that the Health Authority's lawyers dropped what turned out to be a bombshell. They announced that the original, full-scale X-rays had just been found.

Frank's people promptly asked for an adjournment so that they could study this new evidence that had so miraculously come to light so late in the day. Mr Justice Henry allowed a short adjournment but he did not criticise the Authority's failure to find the X-rays earlier. He did not question the fact that the Authority had signed an affidavit saying they had been lost or destroyed. He did not say what an extraordinary coincidence it was that the originals had been found halfway through the hearing and that they had evidently been discovered in Frank's own hospital file – exactly where they should have been all along.

Laymen might imagine that the appearance of the original, large-scale X-rays was a lucky break for Frank because it would help his team to prove their case. Not so. Far from strengthening his case, the original X-rays helped to undermine it.

The X-rays were never going to be conclusive. All they could do was to indicate that the conditions had been right for a clot associated with fracture. The trouble was that the original X-rays looked quite different to the small, cloudy miniatures – so much so that the Health Authority's lawyers were able to question the very credibility of Frank's team. They poured scorn on his experts for basing part of their case on miniatures that were so difficult to interpret and so unlike the large originals. In vain did Frank's team argue that the originals pointed even more clearly to this being a clot associated with fracture.

The Authority's barristers made Frank's experts look like amateurs who should not be given any credence as they had been prepared to rely on such flimsy evidence as a set of fuzzy miniature X-rays. Frank's case started to sink into a morass of conflicting claims from various professionals.

After four solid days of battling it out, the court delivered its verdict.

Frank lost.

That should have been the end of the matter. North Manchester Health Authority seemed to have been vindicated. The doctors and the administrators could relax safe in the knowledge that it would be almost impossible for Frank to pursue them now.

They knew that Frank had had legal aid to sue them for negligence. Now that he had lost there was little chance of him being awarded further legal aid to take the case to appeal. And he clearly did not have enough money of his own to hire a legal team. What with the months in hospital, the loss of his leg and the years of depression he had been unemployed for a long time. Eventually he had started doing bar work and clerical work but that did not bring in enough cash to pay legal fees.

When Frank applied, he was indeed refused any more legal aid. He visited a number of solicitors asking them to take on his case, explaining how the verdict had not been a fair one. He told them about the wholly incredible discovery of the original X-rays at the last minute. All of them said the same thing: he had more chance of flying to the moon than of winning his case now.

It was realistic advice – except for one miscalculation.

Frank had recovered fully from his depression now. Apart from the loss of his leg, he was strong and fit. He was also imbued with a deep sense of injustice. He was not going to give in . . .

Frank decided to pursue the case himself in the Court of Appeal. He had learned a good deal about the law and about medicine in the six years since his accident. And he was prepared to put in the hours of study that would be needed for an amateur like him to bring a case in the Appeal Court. He knew it would be a struggle.

Almost from the outset Frank felt as if he were taking part in some kind of obstacle race. The legal profession does not make it easy for laymen who trespass on its territory.

Frank, who still has dealings with the courts, reckons that judges could do far more to help non-lawyers through the legal intricacies but some choose not to do so.

Frank, who is nothing if not tenacious, found that larger public libraries have copies of *Supreme Law Practice* which gives guidance on what is and is not acceptable in the conduct of a case. Slowly, with help from well wishers including a number of professionals, he started to construct his appeal case.

His grounds for appeal would be the hospital's failure to disclose all the available evidence – in this case the original X-rays – until the very last minute.

Frank believed that the original X-rays had never gone missing and that he had some powerful arguments to prove this.

For one thing he questioned the Health Authority's claim that the original X-rays had been lost or destroyed. If, as the Authority said, storage were a problem, why had four sets of miniatures been kept rather than one? And why then did three large sets of the original X-rays eventually emerge? Surely only one would have been retained if there were a shortage of space.

Why had affidavits been signed saying the originals had been destroyed when they had not? Why not just say they were missing?

Frank also wanted to know why there were records of various tests carried out on him when he first went to the hospital yet mysteriously there was no record of his blood circulation being checked. The Authority claimed no record had been kept because his circulation had been normal. Was it the hospital's usual practice to keep records only when there was an abnormality? How did staff know when someone's condition deteriorated? Was the Authority's explanation really credible?

More than two years after he had lost his original suit, Frank's case went to the Court of Appeal. North Manchester Hospital Trust had hired a Queen's Counsel and a team of lawyers to oppose him but Frank refused to let that intimidate him. He reckoned he could prove from court transcripts that the other side had not always told the truth.

For three days he argued his case. At the end he was sure he must have won, but the three judges in the Appeal Court decided to reserve their judgement.

It was not for another three months, early in 1994, that Frank had his verdict.

The Appeal Court found in his favour by two to one. It ruled that the Health Authority had failed to produce sufficient evidence in time for the first court case. A retrial was ordered.

Still North Manchester refused to acknowledge that they might be in the wrong. If a retrial had been ordered, so be it. They would continue to fight.

One of the most shocking aspects of medical negligence cases is the way hospitals, medical staff and health authorities sometimes drag things out to the bitter end even when it is clear they have been at fault.

Frank, a young man who lost his leg below the knee because of negligence, had to wait nine years merely for the chance of a second, fairer hearing. During all that time he had not received one penny to make up for the pain, worry and disablement that he had suffered.

He had to wait another three years for the retrial that had been ordered by the Court of Appeal. Still the North Manchester Hospital Trust denied negligence, which meant Frank was still without any compensation.

When the retrial finally began, the Health Authority again tried to claim that Frank had been suffering from the rare compartment pressure syndrome. Yet Frank argued that the medical evidence did not support the claim – the physical conditions necessary to cause compartment pressure syndrome had simply not been in place. As the trial dragged on, Frank started to feel that this time he was winning the argument – not least because he was able to point out inaccuracies in the other side's case.

Finally, on the sixth day of the appeal hearing, the judge, Mr Justice Buckley, indicated the Health Authority should seek an agreement.

They offered Frank £325,000.

Fearful that the court might award him less if he turned it down, Frank accepted. It is estimated that the Health Authority must have paid out a further £300,000 in legal fees.

Twelve years had elapsed since the autumn day when Frank's bike had skidded over the waste ground and come crashing down on his leg.

There is a sad little codicil to Frank Cunningham's tale. That final £325,000 settlement made to Frank by North Manchester Health Authority was not quite the end of the story.

After he won, Frank wanted the conduct of the doctors and administrators at North Manchester to be investigated. He believed that some of the hospital staff had actually tampered with the evidence and he complained to Manchester's Fraud Squad.

He gave the police his evidence for making such an accusation; it included transcripts of the first trial of his case. Frank believed the transcripts suggested that his opponents knew all along that the original X-rays had not been destroyed. The police were sympathetic and promised an investigation.

Months went by. Frank rang the police and asked what was happening. He was told that inquiries were in hand. More time passed. He asked again. This time the police told him that they had finished their investigations and completed a report.

They did not expect any further action to be taken nor would the report be published. The reason? Public interest immunity.

Public interest immunity gives the authorities – civil servants, Government Ministers, the police – the right to keep information secret because they believe it is in the public interest. It is a wonderful wheeze because nobody can challenge them.

There are some occasions when most people would accept the need for official secrecy – when the police are in the middle of hunting down a criminal for example. But this was not one of those understandable occasions.

Frank could scarcely believe it. He wrote to the Chief Constable. The response was exactly the same. No further action – and the findings of the Fraud Squad's investigation were to be kept secret. All in the name of public interest immunity.

It is hard indeed to see how it could be in the public interest to keep the results of the Fraud Squad's inquiries secret. If there had been malpractice amounting to fraud it should be uncovered and the relevant people prosecuted – not least as a warning to other professionals who might try to cheat the public. If there were no malpractice then the names of those who might come under suspicion should be cleared publicly and nobody should be allowed to cast aspersions on their good name.

In Frank's case it was in no one's interests to plead secrecy on the grounds of public interest immunity – or on any other grounds – unless there was a cover-up. If there is nothing to hide why hide it?

And Frank? Frank still takes a gloomy view of the medical establishment and of the legal world. He acknowledges that there has been some attempt at reform but he says that on the ground it is often hard to see any real improvement.

Today he himself is still embroiled in legal battles over medical negligence but on behalf of others not himself. He divides his time between working for a children's charity and fighting four or five cases on behalf of people who cannot afford teams of lawyers. Using what he learned during his own case as a base, he has acquired considerable legal expertise. He certainly is not an optimist.

Frank's tale is not the most shocking or heartrending example of a medical negligence case. Plenty of other victims have had to fight every step of the way for justice for themselves or their families. Some have suffered far worse damage than the loss of a leg – such as being left to care for a brain-damaged child. Yet the difficulties that Frank faced are all too typical of what happens to thousands of others who demand justice from the medical Establishment.

In Frank's case, as in so many others, there was the refusal of the Health Authority to admit even the possibility of a mistake. Then there was the endless obfuscation by the hospital culminating in the mysterious episode of the X-rays with all its connotations of underhand dealing. There were the endless delays, the tendency of the courts to sympathise with the health professionals, the frighteningly high legal costs and the amount of time that Frank had to spend making himself an expert on various aspects of medicine and law. And always there was the absence of any sure, speedy alternative for getting redress.

Not that Frank didn't try. At one point he went to the Health Ombudsman. The Health Ombudsman said he couldn't help because the case was already going through the courts. Frank went to the Law Society, the solicitors' trade union, to complain about the conduct of some of the lawyers involved in his case. The Law Society referred him to the Legal Services Ombudsman. The Legal Services Ombudsman said there was no case to answer. Doubtless they all acted quite properly by their own lights, but it meant Frank had no option but to spend twelve years battling through our arcane legal system.

Defenders of the health professionals would argue that things have moved on since Frank won his case. A number of medical scandals, most notably that in Bristol where nearly 300 children suffered death or injury because of bungled heart operations, has led to insistent demands for reform. Faced with the public's growing willingness to complain about incompetent doctors and to make medical negligence claims through the courts, the Establishment has started to address the whole issue. Cabinet Ministers, senior judges and leading members of the medical profession itself have focused on how to give redress to the victims of medical negligence more quickly.

They have discussed it. They have spoken out about it. Some of them have come forward with detailed proposals for change.

Welcome though these moves are, the fact remains that they have not yet managed to solve the problem.

Most people agree that what is needed to help people like Frank Cunningham and all the other victims of medical negligence is a cultural change in the Health Service – and perhaps in the legal system too. Everyone is searching for a new approach so that health authorities and medical staff are more prepared to own up to their failings instead of automatically trying to defend themselves even when they know they are at fault. Everyone agrees that, in return, patients and the public need to be more understanding about honest mistakes, about the kind of errors that are made when, for example, inexperienced, overworked doctors are not properly supervised because of a shortage of senior staff – which is what seems to have happened in Frank's case.

The great difficulty is how to bring about that cultural change when it is so clearly in the interests of some doctors and health administrators to save money and save face by denying negligence. Another obstacle to reform is that a series of side battles are going on between various interested parties. Some patients fear that the real aim of the Government is not to improve the System but to cut compensation payments. Ministers, in their turn, say the costs of medical negligence are being hugely inflated by the lawyers. Lawyers are saying the costs could be brought under control if only doctors would stop being negligent. Doctors worry about 'vexatious' complaints from patients who are out to make a fast buck.

So far, there has been only limited agreement as to what concrete steps should be taken. The Government has introduced a National Patient Safety Agency and a Clinical Assessment Authority as well as new forms of clinical governance which means senior staff must accept responsibility for standards and not just let the most junior person in the chain take the blame when there is a medical accident. The Government has also set up a Commission for Health Improvement designed to act as a watchdog for the public, to monitor standards and make recommendations to Ministers. It works alongside the Health Ombudsman's Office which investigates complaints and which has wider powers to investigate medical negligence than it used to – though it can only make recommendations, not order the sacking of doctors or the payment of compensation. The Government is also considering setting up another new body called the Council for the Regulation of Healthcare Professionals that could investigate complaints from the public as well.

Ironically, perhaps, there is a risk of overkill with Ministers anxious to be seen taking action yet achieving little. As Sir Michael Buckley, the current Ombudsman, whose office covers complaints on health as well as general maladministration, has said:

> The stage is becoming crowded. There is an obvious danger of confusion and of duplication not only for the professionals but for members of the public including those who want to complain. With different bodies operating to slightly different standards and vying with each other for cash, 'customers' and prestige, there is a risk of negligent and incompetent doctors being able to disappear into the crowd. A plethora of watchdog bodies will simply encourage the medical profession to throw up its hands in horror and refuse to co-operate.

Meanwhile serious consideration is being given to ways of stopping lawyers taking huge rake-offs from medical negligence cases. Incredible though it may seem, around a quarter of the annual bill for compensation goes not to the victims of negligence but to lawyers in fees. The National Audit Office even found that in cases involving compensation claims of under £25,000, *more* money goes to lawyers than to the victims. These figures are concentrating minds in Whitehall and various schemes for making negligence disputes less adversarial and so cutting legal costs have been put forward. These do not always operate in the interests of patients. There is now a rule that the value of a claim must be big enough to justify the legal costs. This is often weighted against the patient because costs may be outside their control if a hospital decided to defend an indefensible case, as with Frank Cunningham.

The Government is looking at the possibility of a fast-track system where there would be a blunders tariff of standard pay-outs for victims of medical negligence – and a cap on legal costs. Lord Phillips, the Master of the Rolls, and the most senior civil judge in England and Wales, has gone further and urged a no-fault compensation scheme, something that is being considered by Ministers for brain-damaged babies.

All such proposals have their drawbacks. Standard payouts would raise fears that some victims would receive less compensation than if they went through the courts. A no-fault scheme could itself be costly – and some victims *want* to establish fault by doctors so as to stop others suffering in the way they have. For some that is far more important than financial compensation.

To date there is little evidence that the suffering or the negligence is being reduced – quite the reverse. In 2001, the annual bill for medical negligence claims rose to £450 million from £400 million the year before. By the spring of 2002, the Government had had to allocate a further £150 million to medical negligence costs.

Some say the figures merely show that the public is more willing to sue incompetent doctors, not that the incidence of medical negligence has risen. That maybe true but it is cold comfort to victims, to people like Frank Cunningham. Others say it is the growth of the blame-and-compensation culture that has encouraged an increase in medical negligence claims. Undoubtedly the blame-and-compensation culture has much to answer for but even Lord Woolf, the Lord Chief Justice has said it should not be used as an excuse for the rise in medical negligence cases.

As Frank Cunningham fought his long battle through the courts, one of the things he felt particularly bitter about was the way some judges seemed to sympathise automatically with the doctors. In an implicit admission that this had been the case, in 2001 Lord Woolf called for the courts to take a less deferential approach to the medical profession. The Lord Chief Justice wanted to end an assumption by judges that 'doctor knows best' though he said this was now happening, partly because of a greater awareness of patient rights and partly because of the sheer scale of medical negligence litigation.

Lord Woolf described this as 'a disaster area' and said it showed that the Health Service was 'not giving sufficient priority to avoiding medical mishaps and treating patients justly when those mishaps occur'. He added that the medical profession's tendency to fight every negligence claim led to 'particularly bitter and often singularly unproductive litigation'. In some well-publicised negligence scandals, those involved had acted 'as though they were able to take any action they thought desirable irrespective of the views of others'.

Assurances that the courts will take a tougher line with incompetent doctors is good news for victims provided the promises are matched by reality. But what of those at the very heart of the injustices, what of the doctors themselves?

As usual with the professional classes, doctors are allowed to regulate themselves – in their case through the General Medical Council. The GMC has powers to name and shame dangerous doctors and to stop them practising. Yet all too often there has been criticism that the GMC has lamentably failed to do its duty. The doctors in the Bristol baby scandal were a case in point. There, three doctors were found guilty of serious professional misconduct: two who had retired were struck off while one still practising was not.

In November 2001, the GMC came up with a package of reforms designed to speed the procedure for dealing with complaints against doctors. More to the point, perhaps, it was agreed that there should be an increase in the degree of lay involvement. It was decided that 40 per cent of the council's members should come from outside the medical profession.

Sir Donald Irvine, outgoing President of the GMC, has himself said that there are 'deep seated flaws in the culture and regulation of the profession'. He accused some doctors of 'secrecy and complacency about poor practice'. Certainly one of the things revealed by the medical scandals of the last few years has been the willingness of some doctors to keep quiet about the incompetence of their colleagues. Sometimes GPs who realised that a particular surgeon was not up to the job simply referred their patients to another hospital.

As with Government Ministers and the senior judges, the changing approach of the doctors themselves must be welcome but huge questions remain. How long will it take to bring about the cultural changes required in the medical profession – and among some lawyers? Is it enough to have 40 per cent lay representation on the GMC? Should the public continue to accept self-regulation? If doctors are allowed to continue policing themselves, is there any guarantee that they will not continue to do it on an 'of the doctors, by the doctors, for the doctors' basis? Would the public be more reassured if ordinary men and women were given a greater voice? Should there be greater, local accountability, not just for doctors but for health administrators? Above all, how far are the fine words of top people being matched by action on the ground?

Nobody should be too optimistic. The Government has said it will bring in a White Paper on Medical Negligence but insiders say it is proceeding slowly with officials and Ministers recognising that there are no easy answers.

Meanwhile, claims for compensation are rising all the time and, horrifyingly, many victims of negligence will have to wait years before their cases are settled. The National Audit Office report of 2001 said the 23,000 compensation claims then outstanding would each take an average of five years to resolve. That means that right now there are thousands of people waiting and hoping and enduring in exactly the same way as Frank Cunningham did.

'The only way to bring about change is to hammer the Government, to humiliate them in the courts,' Frank says, 'That's what makes a difference.'

3

THE DEAD MAN'S TALE

Secrecy is one of the great weapons of the cheating classes. It makes their lives so much easier if they can keep others in the dark about the negligence, trickery or unfair dealing of which officialdom is capable.

They control the system and they have laws to keep their secrets secret. Despite assurances that a new era of openness is dawning, they are finding ways to safeguard a culture of secrecy that dates back to the thirteenth century. Today's repressive approach can be traced to the early years of the last century when Parliament pushed through an Official Secrets Act that made no allowance for a public interest defence.

That is why the authorities have found the secrecy laws so invaluable. Slowly but surely the kind of justifiable secrecy needed to safeguard the State in areas like defence has been extended until the cheating classes can use it to cover up all sorts of embarrassments – right down to the truth about an accident on public transport.

Most members of the public do not realise how pervasive the secrecy laws can be. They believe that they are invoked only against spies or arms dealers or terrorists. They are confident that in Britain at least there is no risk of officialdom using secrecy laws against ordinary families.

That was what Sissel and Godfrey Fowler believed – until they were overtaken by tragedy.

It was early one morning when the call came that was to shatter the Fowlers' lives. Despite the hour Godfrey Fowler had been at his desk for some time. He reached for the phone, wondering fleetingly who else might be up and about at a time when most people had barely started breakfast.

It was the duty surgeon from the accident and emergency unit.

Professor Fowler knew him well. He knew all the senior medical people in Oxford. He had started out as a GP there forty years ago. Now he was a Fellow of Balliol and Professor Emeritus of the University's Department of General Practice, a department that he had played a key part in building up.

It was a Monday morning on the last day of July. That summer of '95 had been a good one for Godfrey Fowler and Sissel, his Norwegian-born wife. Six weeks earlier their elder son, Jeremy, had been married. Now Adrian, their younger son, the best man at the wedding, had been shortlisted for a prestigious job at the Scottish Office. An ecologist with a PhD, he was down to the final four from 150 applicants. He was travelling North for an interview that morning.

All was well with the Fowlers. Until the phone on Godfrey's desk rang that morning.

The surgeon tried to sound composed.

'I'm afraid Adrian's had a bit of an accident.'

'An accident?' said Godfrey. 'What kind of accident? Where is he? In casualty?'

'No,' said the surgeon softly. 'He's in intensive care.'

He did not need to say more. Professor Fowler understood immediately. Adrian had been badly hurt.

It was clear from the outset that Adrian might not survive. The brain scan looked bad. The medical team decided to operate to relieve pressure on the brain and stop the bleeding. Afterwards Adrian lay hooked up to a machine, hovering between life and death.

Then, twenty-four hours after he had been brought into the hospital, the decision was taken to switch off the machine.

Nobody seemed to know exactly how Adrian's accident had happened. It had taken place at Oxford station where he was due to catch the 7.03 morning train to Manchester on the first leg of his journey to Scotland. That much was clear.

What was not clear was how a strong, fit young man of twenty-nine had come to be fatally injured in the routine business of boarding a train.

The Transport Police came to see the Fowlers almost immediately. They expressed their sympathy and said that there would be a full investigation.

Later one of their officers, Detective Sergeant Dick Evans, gave the Fowlers the results of his colleagues' preliminary inquiries. There was still uncertainty about exactly what had happened but eyewitness reports suggested that Adrian had darted across the station bridge, down the steps and had tried to catch the train just as it was about to leave. He had tried one door and then another. They were locked. A door window was down. He had jumped on to the running board and put his arm through the open window to see if he could unlock the door from the inside. It would not budge. By now the train was moving and he was carried some twenty yards along the platform clinging to the outside of the carriage.

Perhaps he had tried to leap off and misjudged the distance. Perhaps by then the train was going too fast. Perhaps he had overbalanced because of the bag he was carrying. He was seen to tumble backwards, almost somersaulting down. As he fell he hit his head.

Apparently the only witnesses had been station employees. Nobody on the train – the driver, the conductor or the passengers – had seen anything.

The train had had central locking, which was why Adrian had not been able to open any of the doors. What was puzzling was why the station staff who had witnessed the accident had not stopped the train as soon as they saw what was happening.

The day after his son's death, Godfrey went to Oxford station to see if he could glean any further information about what had happened. He watched the 7.03 from London – the same train that Adrian should have caught – pulling in to the station. He noticed that the platform curved round so that anyone at the front of the train – the driver, for example, or the conductor – would not be able to see what was happening at the rear.

Godfrey noted that none of the staff was taking much interest in the 7.03. There was no one at the back of the train supervising its departure.

He spoke to one of the platform staff and asked if he had been on duty on Monday, the day of the accident. Yes, the man said, he had been on duty that day. Why? Who wanted to know?

Godfrey explained who he was. Immediately the man disappeared into the office and came back with the assistant station manager.

No, the assistant manager could not tell Godfrey anything about the accident. Why not? Because there was going to be an internal inquiry.

An inquest opened in Oxford a few days after Adrian's death. The coroner gave permission for the funeral to go ahead and announced that he was adjourning proceedings. The inquest proper would be resumed at a later date.

Thames Trains was the operating company responsible for Oxford station. On 7 August, which happened to be the day of Adrian's funeral, Thames held its inquiry into the accident.

Afterwards Detective Sergeant Evans informed the Fowlers that the inquiry had taken place and told them there were likely to be changes in railway procedure as a result. He revealed that the driver of the train had not been interviewed because he was on holiday. The conductor had not been interviewed either, because he was 'not well enough'.

Detective Sergeant Evans said that he thought it would be possible for the Fowlers to see the internal inquiry report.

At the time the Fowlers did not attach too much importance to the sergeant's rather guarded references to the report. They were still overcome with grief. In as far as they thought about it at all, they assumed that they would see the report in due course.

But Thames did not send the Fowlers a copy of the report. The head of the group wrote a letter of condolence and his deputy, accompanied by the local area manager, came to see them. The two men expressed their deep regrets about the accident. They told the Fowlers a little more about what had happened and explained the normal railway procedures.

They said that on the morning of Adrian's accident the conductor had been at the front of the train in the coach next to the engine. There was no hard and fast rule about which end of the train the conductor should be – sometimes he was at the front and sometimes at the back.

Three platform staff had been on duty when Adrian had tried to board. Their responsibilities included ensuring that the doors were shut and indicating clearance to train conductors. They had instructions not to restrain passengers physically.

Adrian's train had been scheduled to arrive and depart at 7.03. In practice it had had a statutory two minutes at the platform.

The Thames managers told the Fowlers that, in light of what had happened to their son, 'procedures would be modified'. But they implied that there was little that Thames Trains' staff could have done to save Adrian.

They were non-committal about showing the Fowlers the full report on the accident.

Godfrey and Sissel sensed that parts of the story did not add up. Clearly Adrian should not have tried to jump on the train at the last minute but had that made his death inevitable? Could he have been saved if rail staff on the platform or on the train itself had done things differently? Were the Fowlers being given the whole truth about what had happened?

The platform had not been crowded. As Godfrey had seen for himself, few people got on or off the 7.03 at Oxford. Which raised the question of how the accident could have happened without the three platform staff seeing it. And if they had seen it, why had they not stopped the train?

Above all, why did Thames Trains not insist that the conductor should always be at the back of the 7.03 when it pulled in to Oxford so that he could see any latecomers trying to climb aboard?

The Fowlers wanted to know more. They comforted themselves with the thought that things would become clearer after they had seen the Thames Trains report and studied its findings in detail.

Three months passed. Still the Fowlers had not been given a copy of the report. Godfrey was becoming anxious. He wanted to see it before the inquest resumed. He called Detective Sergeant Evans at the Transport Police. The sergeant promised to contact Thames Trains.

A few days later Detective Sergeant Evans wrote Godfrey a strangely Delphic letter. The policeman said that he had given Thames Trains '[his] views in respect of releasing any recommendations made'. The sergeant did not reveal what his views were and seemed unwilling to admit that recommendations for improving safety standards had been made at all.

He suggested that the Fowlers write to the director of Thames Trains 'and request a sight of any such report'. The letter added that 'the Report is not available to the public but Mr Gardiner, the coroner for Oxford, has been supplied with a copy.'

Godfrey formally requested a copy of the report as Detective Sergeant Evans had suggested. The Director of Thames Trains refused. 'The Board's solicitor has advised us not to release any part of this document at this stage', he wrote, adding that the recommendations were 'clearly aimed at preventing a recurrence of this type of accident'.

But how could the Fowlers or the public be sure this was true if they could not see the report? And why was a report designed to improve safety standards being kept under wraps?

The Thames Trains director said he was 'sure' that the coroner would 'incorporate our findings into his deliberations and that all relevant facts will be brought into the open'.

Perhaps, thought the Fowlers, it was just a matter of timing and ensuring that the proprieties were observed.

Even so, Godfrey took the trouble to write to Nigel Gardiner, the coroner, a man he had occasionally had dealings with in his work as a doctor. He explained that he and Sissel remained 'very ignorant about what happened at Oxford station on the morning of July 31'. He said that they expected to hear about this at the inquest but felt it would 'soften the blow' if they had some prior knowledge. The coroner replied that he was not at liberty to give the report to the Fowlers at that time.

Godfrey and Sissel say both the coroner and Thames Trains gave the impression that the Fowlers would be able to see the report eventually. There was no suggestion that it would be kept secret.

Nor did such a possibility occur to them. After all it was their son who had died in what was clearly a public transport accident.

The Fowlers did not question that it had been an accident. It was not because they wanted to blame someone for Adrian's death that they were anxious to find out exactly what happened. Nor did they have any thought of suing Thames Trains. They fully accepted that Adrian had been at fault in trying to jump on to the train as it was leaving.

Yet like many others caught up in a tragedy of this kind, they were desperate to ensure that it did not happen again to someone else. Only if the full facts were known could they and other members of the public be reassured that all necessary safety measures were being taken.

If safety standards could be improved as a result of Adrian's accident, then the Fowlers might be able to take comfort from knowing that some good had come from his death.

What worried them was the possibility that something might be overlooked. They felt that if they could see the Thames Trains' report before the inquest they would be in a better position to ask pertinent questions. But when the inquest resumed some five months after Adrian's death, the Fowlers still had not seen the report.

The inquest was a nightmare. The room where the coroner sat was pokey with seats for only twelve people. To the Fowlers' surprise and dismay, Thames Trains brought a large contingent of staff and advisers, including several lawyers and a barrister from London. The Thames group took up nearly all the seats, leaving Sissel to perch on a chair at the back where she could not see properly. Nobody made any effort to look after the bereaved parents.

There was an inquest jury headed by a formidable middle-aged lady who was keen to ask questions, but the coroner did not encourage questions. He simply wanted to find out whether Adrian's death had been an accident as opposed to suicide or murder. The court set about establishing the facts.

Thames Trains confirmed that the conductor had been at the front of the train with the driver. The curved platform meant that neither man would have been able to see latecomers trying to board at the back. Yet latecomers rushing from the ticket office would have to board at the back because of the station layout.

The senior conductor admitted that if he had been at the back of the train instead of the front he would have seen Adrian and the accident could have been avoided.

It was a signalman just outside the station who had looked out of his signal box, realised something was wrong and stopped the train. It was also the signalman who found that one of the doors on the train had not been properly closed but was stuck on the latch – a crucial piece of evidence.

The train Adrian had tried to board was a 'slammer' with traditional doors that opened outwards as opposed to sliding ones. The locks on such doors are not usually controlled centrally but this particular train had just had central locking installed. The aim was to avoid accidents but Thames Trains had given the change little publicity. Had Adrian known that the 7.03 had central locking he might not have risked his life trying to jump aboard.

Godfrey was certain that his son had not known, so he had leapt up and started opening a door. He must have done it at the very moment that the unseeing guard at the other end of the train had pushed the button that would lock all the doors automatically.

Not all the rail staff who gave evidence showed sympathy for Adrian or his family. One of the guards clearly felt that latecomers had only themselves to blame.

'All these bloody people trying to get on at the last minute,' he complained. He was asked to repeat that statement. He did so – this time without the 'bloody'.

The inquest found that Adrian's death had been an accident. The coroner announced that he would be making certain recommendations. These, like the recommendations in the unseen

Thames Trains report, would be designed to prevent a similar accident happening again.

The report itself was not produced in evidence during the inquest. The coroner did not ask for it. Thames Trains did not volunteer it.

Godfrey and Sissel had found the inquest upsetting and unsatisfactory. They felt cheated. Had they known that Thames Trains would have a team of lawyers at the inquest they could have hired a barrister of their own. They were not prepared to let the matter rest and Godfrey now decided that publicity was the only way forward.

The *Oxford Times* ran a front page story about the Fowlers' campaign to see the report on their son's death and to find out exactly what its recommendations were.

The paper also published a letter from Godfrey in which he reported how Thames Trains had assured him that its recommendations were aimed at preventing a similar type of accident in the future. 'My very recent observations at Oxford station provide no such assurance,' stated Godfrey. 'As a frequent rail passenger I need to know – and so do other passengers – what the recommendations are and that they are implemented. We have a right to know. Do they have something to hide?'

Sissel and Godfrey now suspected that the authorities did indeed have something to hide. As well as going to the press, Godfrey asked his solicitor to write to the coroner requesting a copy of the Thames Trains' report.

The coroner again refused and for the first time the Fowlers realised that they might have been tricked out of ever seeing the report on Adrian's death.

In his letter to the Fowlers' solicitor the coroner said: 'The position is that under the Coroner's Rules, I can supply notes of evidence, etc. to properly interested parties but I have no authority to supply anything else. No report from British Rail was produced at the inquest and so I am afraid it is a matter entirely for the Railway Authorities as to what information they supply to Dr Fowler.'

The coroner added that he had now made the recommendations that he had promised at the inquest. These related to 'publicity in connection with the installation and use of doors with this kind of locking mechanism'.

In other words the public were at last going to be given adequate warning that the 'slammer' trains had central door locking. Always provided, of course, that the coroner's recommendations were implemented.

The Fowlers had been the victims of a Catch 22 scam. Initially they had not gone to lawyers or to the press to demand that the Thames Trains' report be produced in evidence at the inquest. But the fact that it had not been produced at the inquest meant that ever afterwards the Fowlers could legally be denied access to it.

Nobody, not the coroner, Thames Trains or the British Transport Police, had warned them that this might happen. Nobody had told them that documents relating to train accidents could be kept secret forever – unless they were produced as evidence in court or the rail authorities gave permission for them to be disclosed.

Perhaps the most disgraceful aspect of this case is that Thames Trains, the coroner and the Transport Police had all hinted to the Fowlers that at some point they would be able to see the report. Yet all along the company and the coroner knew that unless the report was produced at the inquest the rules would enable them to keep it secret.

By the time the inquest took place in December 1995 bosses at Thames Trains must have been planning deliberately to keep the report secret. They knew, as did the coroner, that the Fowlers wanted to see it. Yet they did not produce it and the coroner did not ask for it.

Many people would say that neither Thames Trains executives

nor the coroner were morally justified in acting as they did. But there is no doubt that they had the law on their side. Nigel Gardiner's conduct was governed by Coroners' Rules. Thames Trains was backed by the secrecy provisions in the Health and Safety at Work Act 1974. Neither set of rules ensured any real accountability.

The Fowlers wrote to MPs – Labour and Tory – demanding to see the Thames report. They wrote to the Rail Users' Consultative Committee. They took their complaint to the Secretary of State for Transport, to the national press and to the broadcast media.

Almost everyone sympathised with them. Almost everyone seemed anxious to help. But always the Fowlers drew a blank. No matter who made the request Thames Trains still refused to release the report.

Sir George Young, the then Tory Transport Secretary, assured the Fowlers that efforts to ensure train door safety would continue but stated that Thames' internal report on Adrian's accident had not been intended for publication.

To the Norwegian-born Sissel Britain's secrecy rules were incredible as well as outrageous. Countries like America and Norway have had tough Freedom of Information laws for years, and in Sissel's homeland, where there was such openness that it was possible to find out how much your neighbour paid in tax, it would be unthinkable for a railway company to withhold information about an accident.

There had been pressure on British governments to introduce a Freedom of Information Act since the 1970s. Few politicians were keen and the senior civil service was against the idea.

But the demand was such that in 1994 the Tories agreed to a half-hearted compromise. They would not give the public a legal right to know but they would introduce a Code of Practice on Access to Government Information. The Fowlers decided to test it.

*

In March 1996, almost eight months after Adrian's death, Godfrey wrote to Her Majesty's Railway Inspectorate citing the Code of Practice and demanding a copy of the report. He said that disclosure of the report would be in the public interest. The Inspectorate is part of the nationwide Health and Safety Executive (HSE). The Fowlers understood that the HSE had been given a copy of the Thames Trains report.

It took the HSE a month even to acknowledge Godfrey's letter. Then there was silence. He wrote again in June. This time he had a letter back saying that the HSE was seeking the consent of Thames Trains to disclose the report.

Finally, on 1 August, almost exactly a year after Adrian's death, the HSE wrote to say that Thames Trains had refused consent. This meant the report was automatically exempt from disclosure under the Code of Practice. For the Code contained some carefully crafted loopholes which ensured that if bodies like Thames Trains did not wish to disclose information then they did not have to disclose it.

It was Catch 22 all over again.

The Fowlers refused to give up. They appealed to the HSE's Open Government Complaints Panel.

Their appeal was rejected. This time they were at least given an explanation. They were told that the Thames Trains report included information given in confidence by people who had not agreed to its disclosure. Employees might refuse to give any information about accidents if they feared it would be divulged without their consent. The Complaints Panel felt it would be against the interests of employees and the public to jeopardise the future supply of evidence.

The idea that witnesses to an accident will refuse to co-operate unless they are promised secrecy is a nonsense – on that basis nobody would ever speak to the police lest they be asked to give evidence in open court. Criminal trials would become impossible.

Some people might not want to speak out lest they incriminate themselves but that should trigger an investigation by the authorities into possible wrongdoing – not a cover-up. Witnesses to accidents should have no choice but to give evidence or risk prosecution. There might occasionally be a case for withholding the identity of a particular witness but that is quite different to keeping his evidence secret.

So what was the truth about Adrian's accident? On the face of it there would seem to be only two possibilities: either the platform staff saw what was happening to Adrian but failed to act; or they had disappeared into their office before the train started moving and did not see him trying to jump aboard.

We know that it was the signalman down the line who actually stopped the train rather than the staff on the station platform. And on his previous visits to Oxford station Godfrey's impression was that the staff were chatting to each other too much.

Thames Trains managers were culpable of failing to ensure that the conductor was always at the rear of the train when it pulled in to Oxford so that he could see latecomers. And there is no doubt that the company failed to advertise properly the fact that slammer trains had been fitted with central locking. However much Adrian may have been the author of his own tragedy, it would seem that Thames and its staff deserved censure.

The Open Government Complaints Panel let them off the hook.

But the Fowlers refused to let go. They took their case to the Ombudsman. Members of the public have to go through an MP to the Ombudsman – part of Britain's system for keeping ordinary people in their place – though there are plans to change this. The Fowlers were helped by Andrew Smith, a Labour MP.

The Labour Opposition, in contrast to the Tories, had promised to introduce a Freedom of Information Act if they came to power. It was now late 1996. The Major Government had been rocked by a series of scandals and divisions. Tony Blair's Labour party was looking increasingly confident.

Sissel hoped Mr Blair would make it – she had been a Labour supporter for years. And the Fowlers believed that a Labour Government would finally put an end to the kind of official secrecy that had made Adrian's death even harder for them to bear. They would not have to wait too long now. The election could not be far away.

Twenty-four hours after Labour's victory had been assured, David Clark still felt a sense of elation. At a celebration dinner with some of his fellow, re-elected MPs they talked of how they had always expected to beat the Tories but never on this scale. They regaled each other with tales of election night dramas, of who was in, who was out – and who would be given which job in Tony Blair's new Government. David Clark had been Shadow Agricultural Minister in Opposition and he thought it likely that he would be given the same portfolio now they were in power. In the event he was given a surprise.

He was called into Number Ten, ushered across the elegant hall with its black and white tiles, down the long corridor that separated the two parts of the old house and into the Cabinet room.

Tony Blair smiled at him.

'David,' he said, 'I want you to be Chancellor of the Duchy.'

David was stunned in more ways than one. Chancellor of the Duchy of Lancaster was a medieval title that had somehow survived into modern Ministerial life and he was a little hazy about what it involved. All he knew was that the Chancellor of the Duchy was part of the Cabinet Office team. He wasted no time in accepting the post before asking a pressing question: 'What exactly does it entail?'

'I want you to oversee and bring in our Freedom of Information Bill and our new Food Standards Agency,' said the Prime Minister. He said it with an enthusiasm that suggested he attached real importance to both measures.

David was pleased. He personally was strongly in favour of Freedom of Information. He believed that any bit of armoury the citizen could get hold of to fend off the overweening power of the State was worth having.

And he had never been one of those who imagined that the State would fall apart if the people had a right to know. If, as Chancellor of the Duchy, he was to be the Minister charged with fulfilling two election pledges that had the personal backing of the Prime Minister then he could not wait to start.

He did not have to wait. As soon as he had left Tony Blair he was ushered through Number Ten to the next door Cabinet Office. The Cabinet Office fronts on to Whitehall but the back of it links through to the Downing Street complex where numbers Ten, Eleven and Twelve all interconnect.

He was greeted by Sir Robin Mountfield, his Permanent Secretary – top civil servant – who led him along to his new office at the back of the eighteenth-century building. He quickly decided that it must be just about the best room in Whitehall. Beautifully proportioned, with its Georgian panelling painted in tones of ivory, it overlooked the Number Ten rose garden.

Sir Robin presented him with a civil service folder covering the major policy areas that would immediately confront the new Minister. For David Clark, for Labour and for the public's right to know it was a new beginning.

Godfrey and Sissel Fowler hoped it would be a new beginning for them too. They were delighted by Labour's victory. They believed it would bring their own personal victory over the forces of secrecy, silence and bureaucratic evasion within sight.

The new Chancellor of the Duchy quickly discovered that his civil servants had made no preparation whatever for a Freedom of Information Bill. The folder that Sir Robin Mountfield had handed to him when he arrived had no background brief on such a Bill. It surprised him. Officials were meant to spend the election period poring over party manifestos so that they would be up to speed on *all* the policy plans of whichever party was elected.

Sir Robin explained that Whitehall had done no work on a Freedom of Information Bill because the previous, Tory government had specifically rejected the idea of a statutory right to know. If the new Minister did want to introduce a law on openness then officials could turn the existing Code of Practice on open government into a Bill.

It occurred to David Clark that the civil service seemed very comfortable with the existing Code. He could guess why. The Code was weak. Hardly anybody used it and Whitehall had ultimate control over what was and was not divulged. The system allowed for complainants to go up through the Whitehall hierarchy. Ultimately they could appeal to the Parliamentary Commissioner – the Ombudsman – but he had no power to compel Ministers and civil servants to reveal that which they wished to keep hidden.

The new Chancellor decided the time had come to take a tough line with Whitehall.

It was now eight months since the Fowlers had taken their fight to the Ombudsman.

Their formal complaint about the refusal of Thames Trains and the HSE to let them see the report on their son's death had been made in October 1996. By the time of Tony Blair's victory in May 1997 they still had had no word from the Ombudsman.

Adrian's tragedy had taught them the need for patience. The mills of officialdom might not grind small but they ground exceeding slow. As for the new Government, well – there too they would have to be philosophical. With the best will in the world New Labour's new Ministers would not be able to push through reform overnight. It would take time.

In Whitehall the new Chancellor of the Duchy was doing his best not just to speed through work on a Freedom of Information

Bill but to ensure that it would give the public a real right to know.

On the first Monday after the election he called in Sir Robin Mountfield and stressed that the Prime Minister personally was backing a Freedom of Information Act. Realistically, it would not be possible to draw one up and steer it through Parliament that year. On the other hand if the Bill was worth doing, it was worth doing properly. They had the time to produce a state-of-the-art Bill.

Sir Robin never batted an eyelid.

A nine-strong group of civil servants was set up, aided by James Cornford, who had been chairman of the Campaign for Freedom of Information, a nationwide lobby group fighting for the public's right to know. One reason he was on the team was to confront officials on their own terms should they try to dilute plans for open government.

Not that there was any sign of that among the civil servants working on the Bill. All showed real enthusiasm and commitment. David Clark himself saw freedom of information as his own great policy reform. With some of his officials, he embarked on a whirlwind tour to find out what worked in other countries. They visited Canada, Australia, New Zealand and America – all far in advance of Britain in terms of giving their citizens a right to know.

When the little group returned to secrecy-bound Whitehall they set to work on a White Paper. David Clark wanted it ready by the beginning of the autumn. And he was determined that the new rules should be balanced in favour of the citizen and not the bureaucrats. He wanted his Bill to give people a legally enforceable right of access to official information of whatever date held by any public authority. Complaints were to be heard by an independent commissioner with the power to order disclosure. No longer would decisions on secrecy be left to Ministers or civil servants. Or railway bureaucrats.

*

Tony Blair himself wrote a preface for the White Paper pro-
claiming: 'The traditional culture of secrecy will be broken down
only by giving people in the United Kingdom the legal right to
know.' It was hailed in some quarters as 'visionary' when it finally
came out at the end of 1997.

Meantime, the Ombudsman, quite unaffected by the change
of Government, at long last delivered his verdict on the Fowlers'
right to know about their son's death.

The Ombudsman, or rather the Deputy Ombudsman had
taken a year to reach a decision on the Fowlers' case. His findings
were legalistic and convoluted. They evaded the key questions of
safety and the public interest. But they were unequivocal.

The Fowlers had no right to see the Thames Trains' report on
Adrian's death. Their complaint was not upheld.

Quite why the Deputy Ombudsman should have taken a twelve-
month to decide the Fowlers' case is unclear. What is certain is
that in the wacky world of the cheating classes delay is both a
weapon and a commonplace. As time goes by the facts become
harder to establish, and often the strength of grievance felt by victims lessens – or so the cheating classes hope.

Eventually the authorities can start making comfortable
excuses about how procedures have been modified so there is no
need for the public to start agitating.

'I welcome the Director General's assurance that Her Majesty's
Railway Inspectorate have improved their procedures for tracking
correspondence,' said the Deputy Ombudsman – one small
example of how complacency is the crutch of the cheating classes.
He sympathised with the Fowlers but said that in making his
assessment he must 'have regard only to the requirements of the
Code'.

Why? Why should compassion, common sense and justice be
cast aside in favour of adherence not even to the letter of the law
but to a non-statutory Code? Surely a good judge – or

Ombudsman – will look for ways of interpreting the rules flexibly if that is what fairness demands. If that is not possible because the law is so tightly drawn then he will use his authority to call publicly for the rules to be revisited.

Instead the Deputy Ombudsman found a whole gaggle of technical reasons for allowing the HSE and Thames Trains to keep their secrets secret. He stressed that Thames Trains had given its report to the HSE voluntarily but with no consent for it to be released. Therefore they were exempt under the Code of Practice from disclosure.

He accepted HSE claims that there was nothing in the report that would help improve public safety. Therefore 'the public interest would not outweigh the reasons for respecting Thames Trains' wish to preserve confidentiality'. This bland assurance about Oxford station's safety was breathtaking.

Without seeing the report neither the Fowlers nor the general public could know what safety changes were needed or implemented. The Deputy Ombudsman finished by saying that as he had already found against the Fowlers on two counts, it was not necessary to consider public interest arguments referred to in the Code of Practice.

For David Clark and his 'visionary' proposals for a Freedom of Information Bill, things were looking good. There was opposition within the government machine to some of his plans but it was bitty. The hard part would be to get his proposals through the Cabinet committee that would now scrutinise them in detail before they were presented to the Commons.

Even there the Chancellor of the Duchy felt fairly confident for he had recruited another more powerful chancellor to his cause: Lord Irvine, the Lord Chancellor. The Lord Chancellor, who has responsibility for the judiciary and the courts, is always a key figure but few have been more influential than Derry Irvine. A successful barrister, he took Tony Blair and Cherie Booth into his chambers when they were on the first steps of the legal career ladder. Years later Tony Blair made Derry Irvine not just his Lord Chancellor but the chairman of some of New Labour's key Cabinet committees – including that on constitutional reform.

David Clark went to see him at his offices in the House of Lords. As the two men sat in the Lord Chancellor's large, high Victorian room overlooking the Thames, David Clark told Derry Irvine about his ideas for giving the public a real right to know and about Tony Blair's support. He did not find it hard to persuade the Lord Chancellor to back him. When it came to freedom of information, his lordship had a libertarian outlook. He would do his best to give the Clark Bill a fair wind in committee.

There was a Cabinet sub-committee devoted to scrutinising freedom of information. Sometimes it met in the Cabinet Room itself and sometimes in a Minister's room. Most government departments were represented but few members of the Cabinet attended in person. They sent their junior Ministers along – with one exception. Jack Straw, the Home Secretary, always came himself. And nearly always he and David Clark ended up arguing – long, loud and acrimoniously.

David had expected some argument on the detail of his Bill but he had not foreseen any challenge on the basic principles. He believed that he had reached a deal with those likely to obstruct the Bill. Right from the start he had agreed that certain sensitive areas should be outside the scope of the new law: the security services, military intelligence, social security, the prosecuting arm of Customs and Excise, which might involve covert investigations – all these were to be exempt from any right to know.

In return all other areas of the Bill would be liberal, with the balance of the new law in favour of the public's right to know and against the Establishment's right to secrecy. The authorities would *have* to release information unless they could show that disclosure would cause *substantial* harm. Complaints would be heard by an independent commissioner with power to *order* disclosure of information. It would be a revolutionary change for secretive officials who would have to find new ways of working – inside and outside Whitehall.

David Clark's vision of the public's right to know would catch the HSE and Thames Trains, for the Clark Bill covered the rail companies. For them there would be no hiding place.

Jack Straw fought the Bill every step of the way. A lawyer by training, he used legalese and obscure legalistic arguments. One day there was a huge row over the meaning of a particular legal term. The shouting ended only when Lord Irvine who, as Lord Chancellor, ranks as the most senior lawyer in the land, turned to the Home Secretary and said in icy tones: 'I am *telling* you that this is what the term means.'

Jack Straw had never been a liberal but David Clark now realised that the Home Secretary was being fired up by senior civil servants in his Department. His responsibilities included the police and the security services, both of whom were deeply unhappy about giving the public any right to know.

So too was the charming but determined Sir Richard Wilson, the top civil servant at the Home Office and, like Jack Straw, a lawyer by training. In 1998 Sir Richard became Cabinet Secretary, the most senior civil servant in the land.

It was not good news for those who supported freedom of information.

For David Clark it was an uphill struggle to push the Bill through Cabinet. He won the key battles but only because he had the backing of Derry Irvine.

The rest of the committee fought their own departmental corners in a way that was invariably obstructive. They would argue that they had too many files to be able to keep track of any particular one, that it would be impossible to cope under the new rules, that there would be all sorts of administrative difficulties.

As Cabinet Secretary Sir Richard Wilson came to see David Clark once a fortnight to discuss Cabinet Office work such as freedom of information. Sir Richard was as engaging as ever but David Clark believed that behind the scenes he was trying to sabotage the Bill. Every Wednesday morning the top civil servants from all government departments met in the Cabinet Office under Sir Richard's chairmanship. They thought that the Bill would make their lives more difficult, force them to change their ways, add to their workload and challenge their authority. It seemed they spent a good deal of time at those meetings discussing ways of stopping the Bill.

The Fowlers had had one thing to celebrate. They had become grandparents following the birth of their son Jeremy's first child.

Even in their joy over the birth of the baby they still refused to give up all hope of finding out exactly what had happened on the day that Adrian was killed. They talked of going to the European Court of Human Rights but they knew that it would be expensive and take years. And as Sissel said: 'After all the trauma that we have been through, should we really be faced with that? We just want to see the report and learn exactly what happened, what mistakes were made and then get on with our lives.'

Besides, New Labour would surely end the secrecy surrounding their son's death.

That spring, as David Clark's Bill battled its way through a hostile Cabinet sub-committee, the Fowlers' struggle received recognition in an award from the Campaign for Freedom of Information, an award presented by the Lord Chancellor himself.

The citation to the Fowlers outlined their story and said: 'Professor and Mrs Fowler's determined efforts to obtain this information and ensure no repetition of the accident could occur have highlighted fundamental weaknesses in the existing Code – which must not be repeated in the proposed Freedom of Information Act. Protecting a co-operative relationship between a regulator and regulated industry should never be given higher priority than a family's right to know why a tragedy of this kind has occurred and whether everything necessary to prevent a recurrence has been done.'

As Lord Irvine handed over the award, Sissel had the satisfaction of knowing that at least Adrian's tale had reached the ears of the most senior law officer in the country. Afterwards she told the press: 'I am Norwegian. It is inconceivable that this could happen in Norway. Britain is more secretive and protective of vested interests than just about any other European country.'

Thames Trains was asked for its reaction to the Fowlers' award. A spokesman said the group was 'just abiding by the regulations'.

David Clark was running out of time.

With Lord Irvine's help, he kept winning the crucial battles over the Bill right up to the summer of 1998. Instructions were ready for the parliamentary draftsmen, the specialists responsible for the final wording of a Bill before it goes to the Commons. The Bill was 90 per cent there.

But there were rumours about a Cabinet reshuffle and speculation about which Ministers might be out. David Clark could read the runes as well as anyone. For him the outlook was not good. In a government dedicated to the cult of youth there was talk of him being too old, reports that he had few political friends, that he was dispensable.

That summer, in Tony Blair's first, limited reshuffle, David Clark was sacked. He was philosophical about losing his post as Chancellor of the Duchy. What hurt was losing his Bill – losing it in every sense of the word.

The Freedom of Information Bill was to be taken away from the Cabinet Office. It was being given over to Jack Straw and the Home Office, arch enemies of the public's right to know.

The forces of secrecy in the British Establishment managed to cut off David Clark just in time. And it was not because he was

an ineffective Minister that they wanted him out. It was because
he had been too effective in framing a Bill that would have given
the public a real right to know.

Nor was it true that he had no political friends. It was because
he had such a powerful political ally as Derry Irvine that he won
as many battles as he did. Yet although Lord Irvine held great
sway with Tony Blair he was primarily a lawyer and not a politi-
cian. Backstairs plotting was not his forte. He lacked the political
nous to save David Clark.

And without David Clark to champion freedom of information the Lord Chancellor could do little to stop Jack Straw
neutering the Bill.

Not that Jack Straw had been alone in wanting rid of David
Clark and genuine freedom of information. Peter Mandelson,
one of the masterminds behind the Blair revolution and a man
who was – and is – close to the Prime Minister, did not favour
openness.

He was one of the people Tony Blair would have listened to on
the subject of a reshuffle. Another was Alastair Campbell, the
Number Ten Press Secretary and the Prime Minister's Chief
Adviser. Alastair had once been heard to say that freedom of
information would be brought in 'over my dead body'.

One other person would have an opportunity to contribute his
mite to the Prime Minister on the subject of Ministerial promo-
tions or sackings: Sir Richard Wilson, the Cabinet Secretary.

It did not take long for Jack Straw and his senior civil servants to
water down the Clark Bill to the point where it was almost
weaker than the Tories' old Code of Practice.

Instead of having to demonstrate that disclosure would cause
'substantial harm', officials would only have to show that it
would 'prejudice' the public or commercial interests. A new
Information Commissioner would have the right to demand disclosure but he or she could be overruled by Ministers.

There would be another blanket exemption for all inspection

and investigation authorities that had the power to prosecute. As the Bill went through Parliament, this blanket exemption was changed and made subject to a public interest test. But it was decided that inspection and investigation authorities would only have to disclose information if the public interest in disclosure were greater than the public interest in confidentiality. This new rule, though far better than the original blanket exemption, still leaves plenty of room for the authorities to argue the toss.

It is a Whitehall truism that 'knowledge is power' – but only if it can be kept secret from everyone else. That is why the right to secrecy is so jealously guarded by the Establishment. Secrecy allows those in authority to be a law unto themselves with no risk of having to answer to the public. Secrecy allows them to avoid awkward questions. Secrecy enables them to cover up mistakes. Secrecy boosts their self-importance. And, despite all their promises about openness, they are not prepared to give it up lightly.

Four years after Adrian's death a disillusioned Godfrey Fowler wrote to the *Sunday Times* about the Labour Government's much-vaunted plans to introduce more openness: 'The culture of secrecy will be even more firmly entrenched with the new legislation than in the previous Government's Code of Practice and the proposed amendments to the draft Freedom of Information Bill will do nothing to change that,' he wrote. 'So much for election promises.

'What sort of country is it where information about the death of a much-loved son is the prerogative of a private company? My wife's family in Norway used to think that England was a just and civilized place – but no more.'

Now (in summer 2002), Godfrey and Sissel Fowler are even more disenchanted – and with good reason. Whitehall has decided it cannot stomach even the smallest moves towards greater openness. Almost unbelievably, Tony Blair and his top civil servants have decided to block the Freedom of Information Act from coming into force until 2005.

The official reason for this new delay is that Government Departments need more time to train staff and organize their records. The reality, according to some reports, is that officials are working desperately to destroy potentially embarrassing files before they are forced to disclose them. For Whitehall, despite all the efforts to protect its secretive ways, slipped up.

Jack Straw's Bill finally made it onto the Statute book at the end of 2000 and there were plans to start phasing it in during the summer of 2002 – hardly fast going by anyone's standards. Although the Government was forced by its own backbenchers to make some concessions on the Bill, they were nearly all cosmetic. Jack Straw had promised, for example, that only Cabinet Ministers would be able to override the new Information Commissioner's demands for disclosures – a flimsy safeguard for the public.

What Whitehall had overlooked was that the Freedom of Information Act, puny though it was, would boost people's rights under Data Protection legislation to see files about themselves. Officials had imagined that such rights would be used by the general public wanting to see their health or social security records. To Whitehall's horror, powerful figures like Lord Ashcroft, the wealthy former treasurer of the Tory party, had started using Data Protection rules to find out what Ministers and civil servants had been saying about them. Officials feared that the Freedom of Information Act, together with changes in data protection legislation being imposed by Europe, would allow people to find out more facts and figures that the authorities wanted to hide.

The tragedy is that the consequent decision to put the Freedom of Information Act on hold until 2005 means that ordinary people like the Fowlers will be damaged by Whitehall's ongoing obsession with secrecy. For all its faults, the new Freedom of Information Act *might* have helped the Fowlers had it been in force back in 1995.

The new Act will cover the HSE and *might* be able to force

private companies like Thames Trains to disclose information they want to keep secret. Quite how effective these new provisions will be, nobody will know until the Act is up and running. If it is ever up and running. What has been delayed once can be delayed again if powerful people inside the Government machine so wish.

Meanwhile Britain's culture of secrecy will persist and that is what is damning. After all, if Thames Trains had wished, it could have given the Fowlers a copy of its report at the outset. If Thames Trains' executives, the Transport Police and the coroner had wished to deal openly and honestly with the Fowlers, they could have warned Godfrey and Sissel that unless the report was produced at the inquest they might never be able to see it.

The Fowlers' case shows that the whole question of openness in Britain must be revisited. What is needed is the kind of law that would give people a real right to know with very few exemptions and absolutely nowhere for the cheating classes to hide. Yet the whole freedom of information debacle and the Fowlers' own story suggests that even that might not be enough.

Time and again, Godfrey and Sissel found that the system seemed to be rigged against them with the authorities allowed to police themselves. When they appealed against the Thames Trains' decision, Thames Trains was judge and jury in its own case. When they appealed higher up the HSE had its 'own' Open Government Complaints Panel, which duly found in the HSE's favour. When they went higher still to the Ombudsman's Office, which just happened to be headed by a former Whitehall civil servant, that too found in favour of secrecy. Which raises the question of how the public can ever have confidence in a system where the policing of the authorities is run by the authorities, seemingly for the authorities.

Perhaps we should start thinking about ways of giving the public much greater control over what is disclosed. Instead of an Information Commissioner – who will probably be a former civil servant or lawyer or some other suitably 'on-message'

Establishment figure – maybe we could look to independent review panels that include members of the public who can act as champions of the public.

Labour's failure to deliver open government has shown that battles remain to be fought. For the moment at least the forces of secrecy in Britain have won. But the war is not over yet.

The Fowlers are still hoping for reform. Godfrey Fowler says that Oxford station is now a safer place than it used to be, though he reckons it took over a year before any significant changes were made. That at least is some practical tribute to the memory of Adrian. A far greater one would be an end to the culture of secrecy that strangles honesty and fair dealing for so many people in Britain.

4

THE ARISTOCRAT'S TALE

Nobody can accuse the cheating classes of being squeamish. They are certainly not squeamish about being economical with the truth or intimidating those who stand in their way. Nor are they squeamish about the effect their actions may have on ordinary people's lives. They are not even squeamish about rotting bodies, death and the stench of corruption. At least, not *very* squeamish. It is true that Prime Minister Tony Blair threw up all over the back of his car when he visited the killing fields of the North but that was a purely personal moment of weakness. The politicians and the bureaucrats continued to lay waste the countryside, pretending all the while that they were on top of the foot and mouth epidemic.

Ordinary people felt devastated. It was not so much the disease itself. In a way that was an occupational hazard; many farmers could remember the last outbreak of foot and mouth back in 1967. What brought so many to breaking point was the cruelty and incompetence of the authorities. There was no escaping that. It did not matter whether you were scraping a living from a few sheep up on the fells or whether you belonged to an aristocratic family with a large estate. Like Liz Lowther . . .

Liz is a Viscountess. You might not guess it at first meeting. She does not match most people's idea of a titled lady. Born in Penrith she speaks with the soft lilt of the North country rather than the drawl of Sloane Square. Small and slim, she has shiny blond hair and a long fringe.

Admittedly she is fairly new to being an aristocrat. She and Hugh, heir to the Earl of Lonsdale, have been together for ten years but both had failed marriages behind them when they met and they were wary of trying again. It was only three years ago when they were organising a joint birthday party for Hugh, who was fifty, and Liz's daughter Kerry, who was twenty-one, that they decided to make it a triple celebration by quietly marrying the day before the guests arrived.

Neither of them looks their age. Hugh's dark hair is greying but his face has a boyish look and Liz appears younger than her forty-six years. There is nothing of the grande dame about her. Tough cookie might be a better way to describe Lady Lowther, as officials from the Ministry of Agriculture (MAFF) were to discover. Toughness is perhaps appropriate for she had married into a family of fighters.

The Lowthers have been fighting for over a thousand years. They came over not with William the Conqueror but with the Vikings. Later they fought in the crusades and at Agincourt. In the seventeenth century they secured the Northern counties for William of Orange. In the nineteenth Hugh's great uncle, the sporting fifth earl, created boxing's greatest prize, the Lonsdale belt.

The battle fought by Liz and Hugh at the dawn of the twenty-first century has been altogether less glamorous.

The Lowthers were not at their farm in Cumbria when it all started. It was February 2001 and they were skiing in Andorra, the tiny mountainous principality that lies on the border between

France and Spain. Liz's son, Bobby, and Kerry were with them. They had been there a couple of days when they switched on Sky TV to hear the news.

It seemed there was a confirmed outbreak of foot and mouth disease in Britain. It had been traced to a farm in Heddon-on-the-Wall in Northumberland. Technically, that was on the other side of the country from the Lowthers but in practice it was frighteningly close, as Hugh was well aware. He could remember the 1967 outbreak. He had been working on a farm away from home; his father had instructed him either to stay there for the duration or to come back to the family estate at once. On no account must he travel around and risk spreading the disease.

He had opted to go home and his family had been lucky – their animals had escaped the disease. Yet the outbreak had taught Hugh how quickly and how easily it could spread. This time round it was already having an impact. The TV in the Lowthers' room showed gruesome, uncensored pictures of piglets being slaughtered in an effort to prevent the sickness spreading. They were not the kind of pictures that would normally be shown on British television.

When Hugh and Liz phoned home it was clear that Kate, the girl who was looking after the house and the dogs for them, did not realise how serious the situation was. They told her not to leave Towcett House unless it was absolutely necessary. If she had to go out she must wash down the car, particularly the wheels, before coming back on to the property. She was to arrange for feed for the horses to be left at the end of the lane where it could be collected without outsiders coming on to the farm.

They had seven horses at Towcett, including two miniature Shetland ponies. They also had sheep on their land, though the flock belonged to a lady in Yorkshire and was on a field rented by one of their neighbours who looked after the animals. They had no sheep and cattle of their own but their tenants and other local farmers had both so the Lowthers were as anxious as anyone to keep the disease at bay. If it spread everyone would suffer.

They called Chris Wood, a neighbouring farmer. He understood much better than Kate how much at risk they all were. They asked him to put down a disinfectant mat at the entrance to Towcett and told him that they would be home in a few days.

The locals in Andorra seemed unimpressed when Liz and Hugh spoke of their fears about foot and mouth. Apparently there were regular outbreaks of the disease in Andorra. The farmers dealt with it by vaccinating their animals, just as farmers did in Brazil and Argentina, in South Africa, in Syria, in Vietnam. Vaccinated meat was safe to eat. And foot and mouth never affected humans. It was painful for the animals of course but they usually recovered. No, said the locals, foot and mouth was not a problem. The Lowthers should stop worrying and enjoy their holiday.

Hugh and Liz thought it odd when they arrived home at Manchester airport and there were no disinfectant mats – but perhaps the disease was being held so well in check that such precautions were unnecessary. They had heard a rumour about a lady from Cumbria who had been refused permission to land in Australia on the grounds that there was foot and mouth in northern England.

Yet that was meant to have happened in December when there had been no evidence of foot and mouth in Britain at all, proof perhaps that it had just been a silly story. Maybe they were being over anxious.

They were not being over anxious. They arrived back at Towcett to find that the disease had already reached Tirrel, a mere six miles away to the east. Horrified, they started ringing their tenants, telling them that they were back, asking what was happening, promising to give any support they could.

What they learned from neighbours and tenants made grim listening. The killing had already started. Far from vaccinating animals against the disease, the Government's plan was to eradicate it by culling the flocks and herds where it appeared. Culling had been the normal method of dealing with foot and mouth in Britain for some years. Yet it seemed to the more experienced farmers that the Ministry of Agriculture was not taking some of the basic measures it should have done.

Chris Wood had been driving up to Penrith from Cheshire the day after the first outbreak was announced on 20 February: 'We passed six wagons full of sheep on the drive back,' he said. 'There were 400 or 500 lambs in each truck. We can't understand why the Ministry didn't stop all movement of animals on Day One. They didn't impose a ban here for *four days*. I must have seen three thousand sheep on the motorway in two hours and when you think of all the animals on all the roads in the country over four days there must have been hundreds of thousands moved. How many of them were carrying foot and mouth? No wonder it's spreading so fast.'

Some of the Lowthers' neighbours were puzzled that there seemed to have been no moves to call in the army and shut roads in areas where foot and mouth had appeared. Already the sheer scale of the thing was threatening to overwhelm some of the villages near Towcett. Yet what really brought it home to the Lowthers was when Hugh went to buy some much needed supplies – not for him and Liz but for the dogs.

It was on his way to the farm shop just outside Tirrel that Hugh saw the great pile of dead bodies. Hundreds of dead cows and dead sheep lying in a massive heap. The stench was terrible. He knew that the village had just had foot and mouth – FMD as they were all starting to call it – but he had never imagined anything like this . . . so many dead bodies . . .

Disinfectant mats were down and disinfectant sprays had been used on the corpses, though that did little to disguise the smell. As Hugh and Liz were to discover, some of the farmers were having to wait a long time before the carcasses of their slaughtered animals were taken away. Each day the farmers had to spray the decaying bodies with disinfectant. After a few days the bodies would start to fill with noxious gases and by the end of a week they would blow up to two or three times their normal size.

Even for those who did not have to go up close to the rotting carcasses, there was no escaping the gagging stench that pervaded the fields, that seeped into the very stones of walls and buildings.

Sickened, Hugh made a bulk purchase of dog food and headed home. He was glad he had come on his own. He did not want Liz to see that heap of death and decay.

When Hugh arrived back at Towcett, it seemed like an oasis of cleanness and normality. He was welcomed by the usual, rapturous reception from the dogs: eleven black labradors and two golden ones, and a couple of small, jaunty Patterdale terriers. They are friendly enough to visitors – though they would set on any intruder – greeting everyone with a cacophony of joyful barking until ordered to be quiet.

It is an ideal house for dogs – comfortable and roomy with a lived-in feel. With its double-fronted façade and pillared porch it looks to be early Victorian, though its origins are older. Inside there are occasional touches of grandeur – an oversized piece of furniture, a great gilt-framed hunting scene – pieces brought from Lowther Castle. The Castle is now an empty shell, though Hugh can remember being taken around its richly furnished rooms as a small boy, just before his father had it gutted, saying that the family could neither afford its upkeep as a home nor find any other use for it.

Liz and Hugh may not live in the grandeur enjoyed by his forbears but the Viscount Lowther Estate still covers 5,000 acres and includes some fourteen tenant farms. Yet like many country people the Lowthers and their tenants and neighbours tried to support each other throughout the crisis, regardless of wealth or background.

Tirrel village was effectively sealed off. Officially it was only for a few days while the MAFF teams came to remove the bodies of dead animals. But the school had to be closed because some of the carcasses were lying nearby and most of the villagers cut themselves off voluntarily. They were prepared to do anything that would stop the disease spreading.

Some villages were shut completely, others remained more accessible. Arrangements were made for supplies of food to be left on the outskirts of the closed villages so that nobody had to go shopping and risk carrying the virus with them.

As Liz said later it was like living in a war zone. Or in the time of the plague.

Then the burning began. The stinking piles of dead animals were set alight in the hope of cleansing the countryside but it almost seemed to make things worse. The pyres burned for weeks. The smell was as suffocating as it had ever been and now people started to fear that the burning itself was a danger. Farmers with land lying downwind of the great fires found shreds of skin and hair from the dead beasts deposited on their fields by the sickly smoke.

Soon they noticed that often those same farms suffered an outbreak of the disease itself. Strangely, or perhaps it was not so strange, farms right next door to the pyres but upwind of the smoke seemed to be untouched.

Although Hugh did not want Liz to see the burning first hand, she learned the details of the horror just the same. She was spending much of her time on the phone and as the disease spread, nearby farmers rang to ask advice, to exchange details on what was happening, to seek some kind of comfort.

In those first weeks of March Liz, like so many others, men as well as women, was often in tears. She started to lose weight as the stress began to tell.

News came that the disease was at Great Strickland. Then it was found on the Strongs' farm, one of the Lowthers' neighbours.

Brian Strong noticed the presence of FMD on the Friday morning and he contacted the Ministry of Agriculture. Their slaughter
team came on Sunday morning and over 1000 head of sheep and
cattle were killed. Brian Strong and his sons had to help pen up
the animals ready for the cull. At around 11.15 am Liz rang Iris
Strong. Liz knew from Brian what time the killing was likely to
start and she comforted Iris as best she could while the slaughter
was going on in the farm buildings.

'Poor souls,' said Liz to Hugh later. 'It's so sad.'

Worse was to come for the Strongs. Having done their work
the slaughterers left instructions for Brian to spray his dead animals with disinfectant. He was to do it every day until the
contractors arrived to dispose of the carcasses.

So Brian Strong did as he was bid. Every day he and his sons
went out to the sheds with the disinfectant. Every day the bodies
of the animals he had known and cared for became a little more
bloated, a little more fetid. There was no escaping the smell even
in the house. As day after day passed with no sign of a disposal
team some of the dead creatures swelled up to the size of el-
ephants. All of them started to ooze foul body liquids so that
the men found themselves slipping and slithering over them as
they tried to keep the piles disinfected.

The Strong family needed a license to go shopping or receive
visitors. It was as if they were being kept prisoner. The strange
thing was that MAFF teams were able to go on or off infected
farms as they pleased.

It was then that Liz had an idea. Her own suspicion that the
authorities were mishandling things was hardening into certainty
but it was not until the Strongs' animals had been rotting for over
a week that she and Hugh thought of giving them their video
camera. At least they would have evidence of what people had
had to endure when the time came to call a reckoning.

Increasingly Liz felt that there would have to *be* a reckoning
for what was happening. Almost without realising it she was
becoming an activist.

It was not to the following Sunday that the men came to remove the animals from the Strongs' farm. The animals were so badly decomposed that their bodies fell apart when the front-end loader tried to pick them up.

It was several weeks after the animals had been taken away before a squad came to clean up the Strongs' farm. The work was being done by contractors who were paid good rates and competition for the jobs was keen. That was part of the trouble. There were not enough contractors to meet demand and the ones there were sometimes wasted precious time arguing among themselves over who should do which jobs and at what price.

Liz found it all puzzling. And scary. She could understand local contractors competing for the work and pushing up prices, reprehensible though that might seem at a time like this. But why was there no plan? Why was the Ministry of Agriculture not putting in hand emergency measures to speed things up? Why were there no arrangements to ensure that people like the Strongs were not subjected to weeks of rotting bodies, which must be a health hazard for humans as well as for farms still free of FMD?

Black, biting flies settled on dead animals, feasted and then landed on healthy animals. Swarms of them were biting people as well as domestic pets. Cutting grass or doing the weeding became an ordeal not a pleasure. Seagulls and crows pecked at animals that lay in fields for a week or more, yet the farmers were told they could not shoot them.

The unanswered questions became more urgent. Why had the army not been called in immediately? Why was vaccination not being considered as an alternative to the killing?

And what of the stories in the press about how MAFF had ordered extra trucks and extra supplies of coal and wood months earlier – as long ago as the previous autumn? If the Ministry did have contingency plans, why were they not being put into operation? Or was it possible that the Ministry had some sinister agenda of its own?

One feature of the 2001 foot and mouth epidemic is how many down-to-earth country people came to suspect that there was a Government conspiracy to encourage the spread of the disease so as to put farmers out of business. As FMD took hold so did the rumours.

Some believed that the Government had started the outbreak deliberately so that it could cut overstocking and reduce farming subsidies. A popular variation on this theme was that it was all part of a European Union plot to decimate British meat production so that there would be less competition for farmers on the continent. Particularly as established continental farmers would soon have to compete against low-priced agricultural economies in Eastern Europe that were set to join the Union.

The 'evidence' cited to back up these accusations included the Government's slowness in banning the movement of animals, its failure to remove carcasses quickly – surely a factor in spreading the disease – and the extra fuel supplies that MAFF had ordered long before the first case of FMD. Some believed that the latter could only have been wanted for the pyres of dead animals that the Ministry was expecting.

Fairly early on, about the beginning of April, Liz asked one of the local MAFF men about the reports of wood and coal being stockpiled the previous year. He did not deny it but explained that the Ministry always had to 'have a plan' – a contingency plan against emergencies. Asked why MAFF had failed to put its plan into action at the end of February he had no proper answer.

Much later, in May 2002, Brigadier Alex Birtwhistle who took charge of the cull in Cumbria when the army was finally called in during the fourth week of March, told an inquiry in Kendal that when he arrived there had been no organisation or agency in charge that had a plan to deal with the crisis. He reckoned that there had been more than 100,000 animals lying waiting to be disposed of and said that some of the bodies had been there up to three weeks. Small wonder if some farming people at the time had started to question MAFF's motives.

The more hard-headed put it down to incompetence and a lowering of standards among MAFF staff. In 1967 MAFF had 417 vets in its state veterinary service but by 2001 the number had been cut to 220. Some of Liz's neighbours said that thirty years earlier there had been first class vets at MAFF but now the only ones who joined the Ministry were those who could not make it in private practice.

Meanwhile the testing of animals to see if they had FMD was inadequate to say the least. Blood samples were being sent all the way down to Pirbright in Surrey. It took at least twenty-four hours before the results came through and sometimes farmers had to wait five days before the disease was confirmed and their animals were slaughtered. Offers of an American-made machine that could test animals on the spot and give results within a few hours were turned down by MAFF.

Even those who had no time for the more far-fetched conspiracy theories believed that once the outbreak had started the Government saw it as an opportunity to rationalise the farming industry. They reckoned Whitehall was hoping that FMD would force some farmers, particularly small ones, to close down. Whatever the cost in compensation payments, that would be a one-off, it was argued. The eventual saving in ongoing subsidies, year after year, would be very substantial.

Some of the evidence against MAFF is anecdotal, some more scientific but the case against is powerful. On the other hand the Ministry would argue that it was short staffed and hard pressed so mistakes were inevitable. Country people admit also that some of the farmers themselves were at fault, that they acted foolishly or, worse, that they encouraged the disease so that they could claim compensation. And leaders of the National Farmers Union were among the strongest opponents of vaccination.

Yet whatever the truth two things are certain. One is that the Government has been desperately anxious to draw a veil over the whole sorry episode, refusing to hold a proper, open public inquiry.

The other is that as the disease gained ground back in the spring of 2001 the trust between country people and government began to break down. That trust between rulers and ruled, between ordinary people and the authorities was further eroded in the long months of misery that followed. The risk now is that it will not be properly restored for years, that the countryside has been alienated permanently from urban Britain and from our failing Westminster democracy.

Perhaps it was not just cows and sheep that were made sick by foot and mouth disease. Maybe the tragedy found out a sickness in society.

George and Margaret Cass were the first of the Lowthers' tenants to be culled. MAFF had decided that the disease had been spread by animals going through Longtown Mart. Any contact with the place was now regarded as dangerous. George Cass had been at Longtown Mart, one of the biggest markets in the north, in February when FMD had first started and so the Cass's farm was to be taken out. George had to round up his animals by himself as they did not send enough men to help.

MAFF killed everything on the Cass's farm – every single animal. They did not test them first to find out whether they had foot and mouth or whether they were perfectly healthy.

The night before the animals were killed the Cass's daughter, Mandy, stayed all night in the barn with her half-dozen pet sheep. Her father told her she wasn't supposed to be in the building but she insisted on spending the last night with them. She pleaded with the slaughtermen at least to test these few before killing them to see if they could be spared. She promised they were pets and would not be going into the food chain; they were 'Mandy's girls' as she called them. They took no notice and killed them just the same.

The Ministry also insisted on killing the lambs with a bolt

gun. Mandy and her mother had asked them to inject the lambs to make their death more humane. The slaughtermen claimed it would be more painful to inject but that was because they had no intention of following the normal veterinary practice of sedating animals before putting them down. Often the MAFF teams did not use pithing sticks to churn the brains of slaughtered animals and to make sure they were dead. They were meant to do this but they did not bother. Certainly the slaughterers took no notice of Mandy and her mother just as they took no notice of George Cass when he warned them not to put the dead lambs in the clamp, the walled area used for silage, because it was leaking. As a result, when the new lambs had been given a bolt, their heads exploded and their small, tender bodies would not stop bleeding. The leaking clamp was on a rise and their blood ran out through the breaks in the wall. It ran down the farm lane, down the village street, into the stream and from there into the river Leith until the water ran red.

Far to the South, beyond the red waters and green fields of Cumbria, the grey landscape of Whitehall was being shaken by panic. Tony Blair's New Labour government had long been planning a general election for May. The Prime Minister and his advisers were confident that they would be victorious once more and so earn themselves a place in the history books as the first ever Labour Government to win a second term. At least they had been confident until the outbreak of foot and mouth.

At first the Prime Minister had accepted assurances from MAFF that the outbreak was under control. As the number of reported outbreaks rose from 100 in early March to 200 by the middle of the month, Number Ten started to realise that the disease could threaten their careful plans. Almost every day the television news was dominated by carnage in the countryside.

Labour feared the epidemic might affect the outcome of the election itself. It was certainly putting a question mark over the timing of the poll, with influential Labour voices urging that the election be postponed until June by which time foot and mouth would surely – surely! – be on the wane.

Desperate to conquer the disease as quickly as possible, Downing Street ordered that the killing be stepped up. Every time a case of foot and mouth was discovered, all the farms within a three-mile radius of the infection were to be culled – even if their animals showed no sign of the disease.

When the policy was first announced it seemed it would apply to all animals. Within a few hours the Ministry of Agriculture had a change of heart: those in charge had realised – belatedly – that there were already huge difficulties in disposing of so many dead animals, so the contiguous cull would be limited to sheep.

The politicians and the civil servants knew little about the countryside. They had failed to take any notice of the report on what had happened back in 1967. They relied instead on so-called experts, academics who, as it turned out, also knew little about the realities of killing in the countryside.

The main committee advising the Prime Minister was an informal group dominated by professors from London University's Imperial College.

For the first time ever they intended to rely on computer modelling to predict the spread of the disease. As some of their critics said at the time it was 'culling by computer'.

Months later, at the very end of 2001, when Dr David Shannon, chief scientist at the Ministry of Agriculture, retired, he attacked the advisory committee saying it seemed to him that it had had 'enormous power with no direct responsibility.'

'It was driving what the government was doing,' he said, yet it had concentrated strictly on disease control, taking no account of environmental factors and the impact of ever greater piles of dead animals littering the countryside.

There were the usual Whitehall cock-ups to contend with as well – more mundane perhaps but still devastating. A key official was on a skiing holiday when the outbreak began and nobody realised that it was against European law to bury cows over five years old.

The law had been introduced in the wake of the scandal over mad cow disease and with the best of intentions. The aim was to stop mad cow disease spreading to humans. But by now in Cumbria and in Devon and in other parts of the country the stinking bodies of dead animals had been rotting for weeks and it was impossible to identify how old they had been when they were killed.

It was towards the end of March that Brigadier Alex Birtwhistle went on a farewell tour of his troops just a week before he was due to retire. He arrived in Carlisle some twenty-four hours before Tony Blair was due to arrive on a personal tour of Cumbria. The Prime Minister was scheduled to have a meeting in a Carlisle pub with farmers and other representatives of the local community on 22 March.

The Brigadier's view, gleaned from talking to those he met, was that things were so bad there was a real risk of civil unrest. When Tony Blair arrived, making a flying visit en route to an international meeting in Stockholm, the reception awaiting him as his cavalcade drew up outside the Auctioneers pub in Carlisle was deeply hostile.

'Coward!' shouted one of the waiting locals. 'You don't give a shite about the North.'

Blair flinched as he legged it from his Jaguar to the safety of the pub. The protestors were small in number, only about forty of them, but they were bitter. Some carried banners saying 'Save Our Jobs'. Others shouted, 'The only good Blair is a dead Blair.'

The crowd included farmers, people who relied on tourism for their livelihoods and who now found themselves out of work and a couple of children whose pet lambs had been put down that afternoon. Inside the pub were official representatives of the farming and tourist industries plus local councillors – and Brigadier Birtwhistle. He had invited himself to the Prime Minister's meeting and told Blair that he did not think the local arrangements for culling and disposing of the diseased animals were going to hold up.

Instead he put forward a plan of his own that he had drawn up off the top of his head just before the start of the meeting. He reckoned that if he were put in charge he could drastically reduce the time between diagnosing an animal, killing it and disposing of the carcass. In fact he reckoned he could get it down to twenty-four hours.

Blair, described by the Brigadier as looking strangely vulnerable, told him to get on with it. He could have all the back-up he needed. This was the first time the army had been properly used to help with the emergency. The report on the 1967 FMD outbreak had stressed the importance of calling in the army at an early stage but the Government had ignored that. By the second week of March the Tory Opposition was demanding that the army be brought in but to no avail. Finally, just before Tony Blair's trip to Cumbria, the soldiers were sent in to help – only to be met with widespread derision. Farmers complained that the troops were armed with pens and clipboards rather than bulldozers and earth-moving equipment. One spokesman for the National Farmers Union described the use of the army as a 'public relations stunt'.

But it was not like that for long and certainly not in Cumbria once the Brigadier had been given free rein to act by the Prime Minister.

In Cumbria one of the first things Brigadier Birtwhistle and his soldiers did was to create the giant burial pit at Great Orton, not far from Hugh and Liz. It was there that they took thousands of animal bodies for burning. In the weeks that followed the nation was to become all too familiar with haunting television pictures of slaughtered cows with their legs stretched stiffly upwards as they lay burning on their funeral pyres.

And for weeks afterwards rarely a day was to pass without one of Tony Blair's aides in Downing Street calling on the Brigadier to demand that he get on with disposing of the cows and so end the terrible TV pictures.

Dennis Burn was the first of the Lowthers' tenants actually to have FMD on his farm. He was downwind of Brian Strong's farm and Liz wondered if the smoke from the pyres that blew over his land could have spread it.

The Rebanks were the next of the Lowthers' tenants to be taken out. Tom Rebank gave up his sheep to save his Charolais cattle. Sixty years of breeding had gone into his Suffolk sheep and that would be lost for ever. The cull was supposed to be voluntary but the Ministry told him it was sheep that seemed to be spreading the disease and as his cattle were still in their sheds they could be spared and would be able to come out later. But all the sheep must go.

Tom said he would let his lowland sheep go but not the ones up on the fells, the ones hefted to the land, which meant they had learnt over generations which was their territory and would not stray from it. He insisted that he himself had not been near the hefted sheep.

But the men from MAFF were not interested. They insisted on killing all the sheep. Bloodlines built up over many years were lost in an afternoon.

Later that year, his Charolais cattle, magnificent beasts that grazed in the field on the outskirts of the village, caught FMD and were killed. It was too much. Tom and his family decided to terminate the tenancy of the farm.

Liz and Hugh discovered that MAFF officials were becoming more willing to use bullying tactics against any farmers who tried to resist the cull. The Ministry would arrive and tell a farmer that they were taking his neighbour out so they would kill his sheep at the same time. They would do it on the farm or the sheep could be taken to Great Orton and they would do it there.

If a farmer protested, no matter how reasonable the arguments or how courteously they were put, the MAFF officials told him they would kill his sheep anyway but if he was going to be difficult they would take his cattle as well. Apart from anything else, this threat meant that the farmer would not get his regular milk cheque. He and his family would have nothing to live on.

Other threats were made by MAFF. Farmers were warned that if they tried to keep out the slaughter teams they personally would be made to pay the costs of testing and culling their neighbours' animals if foot and mouth did spread to their area. They would have to pay the clean-up costs too and the bill would run into thousands.

It was at this point, with more and more stories of bullyboy tactics coming in, that Liz started wondering what could be done to help the farmers defend themselves. She and Hugh were realising that it was not just in Cumbria that things were going wrong. They were reading in the farming press about the incompetence of officialdom and the lack of a plan in other areas, such as Devon. Cumbria and Devon were the two areas worst hit by FMD.

Liz contacted farmers in other parts of the country to compare notes and to see what could be done. Slowly, as that terrible spring of death wore on, they set up local groups, naming them by region – Heart of Cumbria or Heart of Devon. Collectively this network of self-help groups – or perhaps some would say resistance groups – called themselves Heart of Britain and they asked Liz to be their patron.

Aided by the Countryside Alliance, the national group dedicated to supporting the country way of life, Liz and her fellow activists started giving practical advice to farmers about to be culled. They told farmers to demand the full names of all officials, to ask at what time they would be coming to start culling a farm and to tell them that they would be making an appeal against the cull to the courts. They should then give the MAFF men the name of their solicitors.

The Countryside Alliance set up a helpline and a scheme that enabled people to obtain legal advice at minimal cost. Liz became the scheme's group leader and it was she who gave the farmers guidance on what practical steps to take to defend their land and their animals against the bureaucrats. She posted advice on the internet telling them they must not let anyone intimidate them. If Ministry officials threatened them they must be told to put it in writing.

Yet it was hard for the farmers. Sometimes a slaughter team of fifty people, all of them strangers, would turn up at a farm gate demanding to be allowed in so that they could kill everything in sight.

'You didn't stand a chance unless you were prepared and unless you had back-up,' says Liz. 'We'd tell farmers to block all the entrances to the farm save one. We suggested that they use vehicles and barbed wire to seal off all the other gateways and keep their animals well back from the roadside or their neighbours' stock. Otherwise they might be taken out on the grounds of dangerous contact.

'One problem was that the MAFF slaughter teams would turn up and you didn't know where they'd been. Sometimes they had come from an infected farm and they weren't always careful about bio-security. Yet the farmers were unable to move and even to have visitors they had to get a licence from MAFF.'

Sometimes even the most spirited defence did not work. One farmer tried physically to stop the slaughtermen coming on his land but they came back with soldiers, who marched up the drive, ignoring his protests, and started organising the killing. Later the farmer rang the authorities to ask when martial law had been introduced to Cumbria, for surely nothing else could justify what they had done to him. No, he was told, martial law had not been used. The soldiers were just assisting others to do a necessary job.

Not that the soldiers were always much use when it came to killing dumb animals – much less to moving decomposing

bodies. Many spent the time throwing up. Much of the dirty
work had to be left to locals. After a while it became simple to tell
which locals were working for the contractors because they
shaved their heads. That way it was easier to keep clean, easier to
wash off any flecks of putrid liquid from the dead beasts.

Sometimes there were 'accidents'. By the time the contractors
came to take away the dead animals from the Strongs' farm many
of the carcasses were hugely bloated. One or two were so full of
gases that a fork lift truck had to be used to get them into the
wagon. Once the operator did not get it quite right.

The prongs of the truck punctured one of the bodies and the
animal's insides burst out and splattered over two of the men
who were helping. Both vomited.

Many people were sick. Throughout the region there were
reports of an increase in the number suffering from asthma and
from strange flu-like symptoms that left people feeling breathless
and debilitated.

Down in London Tony Blair was still dithering over the election
date. Labour had booked costly poster sites, extra people had
been hired to staff the party's Millbank headquarters and everything was in train for a May poll.

Many Labour politicians feared that if the election were
delayed something terrible and unforeseen would happen that
might baulk them of a second victory.

What swung Tony Blair the other way was private polling,
which suggested that the voters might react badly if he showed
himself insensitive to the needs of the countryside and went in
May. Despite repeatedly leaking to the press that the election
would be in May, at the end of March Downing Street
changed its mind and announced that the election would be
7 June.

Blair was right to delay the election. Yet many in the countryside
would say he did it because it was politically expedient rather

than because he or those close to him felt it was the right thing to do by those who were suffering in rural areas. It was the political imperative that was the deciding factor in what happened on the ground in places like Cumbria.

Later, in November 2001 when the disease really was under control, Agriculture Minister Elliot Morley told the House of Commons that the Government did 'not have powers for a firebreak cull'. In other words attempts to enforce a policy of contiguous culling, of destroying every creature within three kilometres of an infected farm, had been illegal. Technically the cull had been voluntary. In practice often it had been no such thing.

Back in the spring when the policy was introduced, nobody in Whitehall, neither Ministers nor civil servants, cared whether people's legal rights were being trampled or whether millions of healthy animals were being destroyed unnecessarily or whether all kinds of cruelties were being endured by men and beast. The important thing for the politicians was to look in control, thereby winning the election and staying in power.

Up near Towcett the ban on moving animals even from one field to another was bringing hardship. Farmers were unable to move flocks to new pastures and if it rained and the exhausted ground became muddy there was no grass for the sheep to eat. Sometimes they would try to eat stones even though their mouths became torn and bruised.

The farmers themselves were nervous about buying in food and taking it to their animals lest they be branded dangerous contacts by MAFF officials which would mean all their stock would be culled. 'Dangerous contact' was defined as animals nose to nose over a fence where some of them had FMD or farmers who had been in contact with infected animals or to places where the disease was suspected.

MAFF officials themselves often broke the rules. Vets went

from infected farms to clean ones without disinfecting themselves adequately. MAFF lorries were often dirty too. Those carrying infected carcasses were meant to be sealed but often it was not done properly. Contaminated waste would splatter down on to the roads right beside fields where cows were grazing. Small wonder the disease was still spreading.

Lambs were being born now in fields where there was no grass. Only mud. Local people tried to help by bringing hay. One of Liz's friends, Carol, found a ewe giving birth to twins. One of the lambs was very weak, almost not breathing, and the weather was dank and chill. In desperation Carol, a plump, bosomy lady, took off her sweater and wrapped it round the lamb. She sat there in the freezing field, wearing just her bra, cuddling the lamb, breathing into its mouth, willing it to live.

It was a waste of time. Not that the lamb died straightaway. Thanks to Carol it survived the mud and the cold. As the days went past it even began to flourish and it showed no sign of foot and mouth.

But the MAFF men killed it just the same. It was the policy, they said. The lambs were on an infected farm. They had to go.

Liz and Hugh began compiling 'evidence' of what was happening so that later there could be no doubt about some of the things that the authorities had done. Since loaning their video camera to the Strongs to film the pile of rotting carcasses on their farm, they had started filming more widely. Sometimes they loaned the video camera out and sometimes Hugh went himself and filmed what was happening.

There were regular sightings of living animals rising up out of a pile of corpses. Once Hugh saw three baby lambs standing on their mothers' bodies in a field. Sometimes after a cow had been killed its calf still struggled to be born. Sometimes the slaughtermen, lazy and cruel in equal mixture, used the calves to lure cows to their deaths.

One farmer told the Lowthers how his cows had all run away

when the killing team came. The calves, very young and slow, stayed put. So the slaughtermen shot them. They did not shoot them dead. They shot them in the legs so that they gave out pitiful little bellows of pain. Then the mothers came back to protect their calves and the slaughtermen, pleased with their ploy, pleased that they did not have to chase after their quarry, killed them all.

Once Liz saw six men with shotguns riding on a quad bike. The driver took it slowly up the bank because it could easily have turned over. 'They were chasing about twenty sheep into a corner to shoot them but the animals were panicking,' Liz recalls. 'They should have quietly penned them instead of taking pot shots. Sometimes they killed them, sometimes they missed or merely inflicted wounds on the creatures. The men did not seem to care.' It seemed to Liz that the men were enjoying the sport.

Officialdom did its best to cover up what was going on, particularly the cruelty and the indecent haste of it all. Those working for MAFF were made to sign the Official Secrets Act to discourage them from talking.

Once when Hugh was driving through the village he saw a living cow being loaded on to a wagon full of dead ones, it's eyes were wide with pain and fear. Hugh started filming but a MAFF official drove up and ordered him to stop. Yet Hugh was not on his own that day. He had with him Duncan, a close friend of the family, who was young, six foot four in his stockinged feet and massively built. He got out of Hugh's car and marched up to the official.

'I'm standing on a public highway,' he said. 'And I can do whatever I like on a public highway. So can he,' he said, gesturing towards Hugh.

The man took a step backwards and started muttering.

'What's that?' demanded Duncan. 'You say it's a horrible thing to film? I say it's a horrible thing to *do*.'

The man retreated to his car and drove off.

Later Liz and Hugh called the RSPCA and gave them copies of the videos. The RSPCA said they should be able to use them as a basis for prosecution in at least some of the cases. They might even be able to ensure that some of the slaughtermen were sacked.

Yet nothing came of it. Despite the efforts of people like Liz and Hugh, there was often insufficient evidence to go to court.

Chris Wood's animals were taken out. When it was all over and the carcasses had been removed, his farm was eerily still and silent. After a while he could not bear it any longer. He called Liz and asked if he could borrow some of her horses to put in his field. Just so he could see some living, breathing creatures when he looked out of his window.

All this time Towcett itself had been free of the attentions of MAFF. Then, one afternoon in May at about four o'clock MAFF phoned Liz to say that they would be coming next morning to cull the sheep at Towcett House. They had taken out all the farms around the Lowthers already.

Jeff Carruthers who was next door had been the last to go. Liz had heard the sound of the shots as they killed his animals and she had kept a close eye on their field to make sure the slaughtermen did not try to come on Lowther land.

'We'll be there first thing to take you out,' announced the woman from MAFF. 'We understand that Mr Elwood has had contact with your sheep so we'll be there at eight in the morning to kill them.'

'Oh no you won't,' replied Liz.

'Don't you take that attitude with me,' said the woman, who was calling from Carlisle, the Ministry's headquarters office in Cumbria.

Keeping her voice as matter of fact as she could, Liz told her that MAFF would not be killing the Towcett sheep next day because if they set foot on Lowther land they would be sued for trespass. The sheep were perfectly healthy. She explained that Steven Elwood, who rented land from the Lowthers, had had no contact with the sheep at Towcett. Back in February when foot and mouth first started they had told him to stay away and they arranged for the sheep to be tended.

Steven Elwood was paid by Rachel Hall, the owner of the sheep, to tend them, but as soon as FMD began Rachel had asked a relative of hers, who lived near Towcett and who had no connection with any other farms, to go over and feed the flock every other day. It was true that Steven Elwood and his father had come up to Towcett a few days earlier – without the Lowthers' prior knowledge or agreement – but Liz had watched from the house and the Elwoods had not had contact with the sheep.

Liz told the woman from MAFF that she would be setting out the full details in a written statement that would be going to the chief vet in Carlisle and to the Hall lawyer. She would also be contacting Mrs Hall. Finally, said Viscountess Lowther, she was quite willing for a *clean* vet to come to Towcett by appointment to see for himself that the sheep were healthy

As soon as MAFF had rung off Liz called Mrs Hall. The sheep were hefted Swaledales and Rachel Hall was indeed prepared to fight for them. Mrs Hall would call her lawyer immediately to make an appeal against any attempt by MAFF to kill the sheep.

Liz wrote to the chief vet. Hugh prepared to stand guard against any invasion by MAFF. The next morning he went out with a flask, a supply of cigarettes and a book, waiting to see if MAFF would turn up with a killing team.

He waited all day. But they did not come. Nor did they come the next day or the day after that.

'We had to test the sheep – at one point we were testing every two days,' recalls Liz. 'But MAFF didn't take us out. They knew that we were likely to cause trouble so they backed off.'

*

The election campaign was in full swing and it seemed to the
Lowthers that every effort was being made to play down the
virulence of foot and mouth and to give the impression that it
was now fully under control. Yet that was not how it felt to most
of the farmers in Cumbria. Depressed by the seeming endless-
ness of it all, Liz wrote a letter to the farming press. The national
press and the TV seemed to have only limited interest in what
was happening in the countryside. There were still some pictures
of burning pyres on the television news but much of the coverage
was somehow sanitised. Liz reckoned that was how Downing
Street wanted it just before the election. She wanted to tell it like
it was.

> Nearly three months ago we were all looking forward to
> spring. Farmers were waiting for new lambs to be born,
> holiday cottages were spruced up ready for Easter, hotels
> were all ready for the season to start.
>
> What have we got to look forward to now that foot
> and mouth has cleaned us all out? Most of the animals
> in Cumbria have been killed or are living with a death
> sentence hanging over them. It does not seem to matter
> if they have the disease or not because MAFF will not
> tell you the blood test results anyway. The Government
> is trying to tell the world that foot and mouth is over
> in the UK and so they are not releasing the true figures.
> They are playing down the statistics because it makes a
> bad press.
>
> We still see smoke from pyres of animals burning in
> the distance. MAFF do their dirty work under cover of
> darkness and remove the dead bodies while village people
> try to sleep. Wagons come and go all night, carrying away
> thousands of animals.
>
> The next day the fields are empty and the villages
> silent. Never in my life have I seen so many grown
> men cry.

We are all living in a state of fear of MAFF turning up. We do not know who will be next either to catch the disease or be slaughtered because they are in the 3K zone.

People speak in hushed whispers for fear of Big Brother watching and listening. If we raise objections we are threatened by MAFF. We have been bullied and blackmailed into submission and now we are all angry.

The way the animals are being treated is barbaric in the urgency to kill them all and such a waste as thousands of them did not have the virus. The way the farmers have been treated in Cumbria is even worse.

None of the farmers we know have been paid any money yet for animals that were slaughtered over eight weeks ago. What are they supposed to live off – fresh air?

We suspect that by June 7th, election day, we will have hardly any animals left in Cumbria and the backlog of stinking, rotting dead animals will be either buried or burned. Mr Blair will congratulate himself on a job well done without a thought for the thousands of lives he had ruined.

Even Liz had become a little intimidated by MAFF. She did not want Ministry officials getting their own back by threatening her or the Lowther tenants. So she did not sign the letter 'Viscountess Lowther'. She just put: From a Farmer's Wife in Central Cumbria.

Tony Blair won his election and he won well with another overwhelming majority. Liz was not surprised.

Just before the election she had remarked that 'Mr Blair is not worried about getting votes from rural areas as he has all the city folks to vote him in again and some of them do not really care where the meat or milk comes from.'

She was only partly right. Fewer than six out of ten people

bothered to vote at all in the 2001 general election – the lowest turnout ever in modern times. That meant that only a quarter of the total electorate voted for New Labour. Alienation from politicians of all kinds had hit the cities as well as the countryside.

One of Tony Blair's first acts after he was returned to Downing Street was to abolish the Ministry of Agriculture, Fisheries and Food.

He replaced it with a new Department called DEFRA – the Department for the Environment, Food and Rural Affairs. The move looked good after all the criticism directed against MAFF. Many also thought it had real practical advantages, arguing that MAFF officials had shown themselves to be second rate, that all too often they were in the pockets of big, rich farmers and that they had failed the public both over mad cow disease and the foot and mouth epidemic.

Yet it takes a long time, often three or four years, before a new Whitehall Department starts to operate effectively. To begin with all is chaos with officials from different ministries jockeying for position, adjusting to culture clashes, arguing over differential pay scales and wondering often where they are going to sit, as well as trying to hammer out new mission statements with a bunch of new political masters.

To embark on all this in the middle of the worst ever foot and mouth epidemic was not felicitous. It added to difficulties on the ground rather than easing them. And there was no let-up in officialdom's oppressive treatment of the countryside. Evidence eventually emerged that right after the election the new DEFRA was behaving in exactly the same way as the old MAFF.

For some weeks Liz and Hugh had been hearing about the threats that MAFF/DEFRA officials and their slaughter teams were making to farmers who tried to stop them killing healthy animals. Sometimes the officials said that neighbouring farmers would feel great resentment against those who refused to be culled if foot and mouth then came to that area. Sometimes the threats were more specific. Farmers were told that if they resisted a cull and went to court to lodge an appeal then they would face huge court costs – costs that could bankrupt them. The Ministry claimed that the judges had already made it clear that farmers would have to pay the costs of MAFF/DEFRA as well as their own.

Proof that these threats were based on a lie seemed to come in a document purportedly leaked from MAFF/DEFRA, which was posted on the Heart of Cumbria website. It was dated 8th June 2001 – the day after the election. It said:

> The purpose of this brief is to provide MAFF staff with information to enable them to seek to discourage farmers from resisting MAFF's slaughter policy by citing the favourable judgements of the High Court. The strong possibility that farmers will be liable for MAFF costs in future cases should also be a deterrent . . .Although the judge did not award MAFF costs in earlier cases, it is likely that the court will now award costs in future successful cases.

As Heart of Cumbria activists pointed out and as the document itself seemed to confirm, there was no reason whatever to think that the courts would award MAFF costs against the farmers. Was this just another trick that unscrupulous bureaucrats could use to bully farmers into submission?

There were other weapons that the authorities were prepared to use against farming people, secretive, shadowy weapons that did little real damage but which added to the atmosphere of fear.

Hugh was driving home one day when he noticed a dark green car behind him that seemed to be sticking to his tail.

He took a circuitous route through one village and then headed off down a back road. The green car never left him. He put on speed and pulled up behind some trees so that the car was forced to go past him. He noted its number and later rang the police.

They said they would check. A few days later they came back to him. The car was nothing to do with them, they said. It was a DEFRA vehicle.

Anger was never far from the surface with Liz. As the summer wore on she knew that the injustices and misery endured by so many people in Cumbria must be exposed.

One day she had a call from a woman she had helped in the early days of the outbreak, a woman who had almost given up hope when she had seen all her animals killed and had wondered if she should take her own life. Liz had comforted her, told her that she must not let herself be beaten, talked her round. Now she heard that same woman saying: 'You helped me – tell me what I can do to help you.'

Liz thought for a bit. She knew that the Environment Minister, Michael Meacher, had talked of the need for a public inquiry into foot and mouth but the idea had been firmly vetoed by Downing Street. Number Ten claimed a public inquiry would cost too much and take too long. The time and the cost were legitimate concerns but equally compelling perhaps was the Government's desire to cover up the incompetent handling of the foot and mouth epidemic.

'You can help me start a petition,' Liz told her friend. 'We'll petition for a public inquiry and we'll organise a march on Downing Street to deliver it.'

They printed off posters headed: 'Foot and Mouth: Answers are Needed'. A list of questions followed:

WHY did so many healthy animals have to die?
Why did MAFF have to blackmail the farmers?

WHY did MAFF workers have to sign the Official Secrets
Act?
WERE you shocked by the way the animals were killed?
HAS your business suffered?
We Deserve the Truth. Please SIGN the Foot and Mouth
Public Inquiry Petition Now.

And hundreds did. The Lowthers asked people to pass on copies
of the forms that accompanied the posters to their friends and to
businesses in their localities.

Liz contacted local papers and the farming press to help spread
the word. Some of the newspapers, regional and national, backed
her. People called her asking for copies of the petition. Signatures
started piling up at local shops and post offices.

The Lowthers told everyone to hold on to their forms so that
they could be delivered to Number Ten after the march on
London.

'If all those who have been affected join forces with the farmers and march on Downing Street we will have real people
power,' Liz said. 'We can *force* a public inquiry.'

October 24th was set as the date for the march. Liz contacted
the Metropolitan police. They were helpful. At least 10,000
marchers were expected.

Then came September 11th and the terrorist attacks on
America that numbed the Western world. Shock gave way to
panic over the threat of germ warfare and anthrax attacks.
America prepared for war in Afghanistan.

As Liz put it: 'The march was scuppered.'

They found other means to pursue their demands. A group of
local farmers, including Chris Wood, got together and decided
to go to the courts to challenge the Government's refusal to
have a public inquiry – a *proper* public inquiry. Downing
Street had already agreed to no fewer than three official
inquiries. One on the future of farming and food, one a scientific

inquiry and one which was meant to look at Lessons to be Learned.

Yet none of these was to be held in public and none would have power to compel Ministers and officials to appear and give account of themselves.

Liz tried to co-ordinate the court appeal and ensure that different groups round the country – and their lawyers – acted together. She and Hugh were not taking part themselves because they personally had not lost any animals.

The various lawyers had agreed to act on a no-win-no-fee basis. They were going for a judicial review in the High Court. The date set down was 18 February and it was expected to last four days. It would begin just short of a year from the date of the first case of FMD.

Liz and Hugh went down to London for a day to get a flavour of the court case. They were not happy with what they heard. Not that they heard that much. The acoustics were so terrible that they missed much of what was said. It seemed to them that the judges looked unsympathetic.

Richard Lissack QC told the court that the Government's Lessons to be Learned inquiry was tainted because its chairman was a former adviser to the Prime Minister, its secretariat was based in the Cabinet Office in Whitehall – sometimes described as the 'heart of government' – and information from Ministers and top officials was not to be made public in the same way as other evidence. Probably it would not be made public at all.

'This is an administration which embraces the concept of open government more than any before,' said Mr Lissack. 'Why now, on this extremely important issue, does their appetite for openness fail them so selectively?'

The epidemic had opened a 'deep fissure' in the relationship between the Government and members of the rural community. Many of them harboured feelings of mistrust and resentment towards the Government and what was needed was 'truth and reconciliation'.

The judges said they realised that people would want a decision as quickly as possible. They would try to reach a verdict as soon as possible. The verdict, when it came, was unfavourable. The judges ruled in favour of the Government.

The end of the foot and mouth epidemic has been in keeping with everything that went before. To the very end Whitehall has remained unaccountable, secretive and impervious to the misery and injustice caused by officialdom's failings.

There can be little doubt about the scale of the damage done or about the incompetence of MAFF. Estimates vary but by the end of the summer of 2001 it is reckoned that over 10 million animals had been killed and the tragedy is that only a fraction of them were proved to have had the disease. At least two thirds, probably more, were healthy. In the early days they were slaughtered with little thought being given to what should be done with their carcasses; and often no thought given to the suffering of the condemned beasts.

The Ministry refused to use vaccination on the grounds that it would damage British meat exports because of the rules imposed by the European Union. Yet all the time the cost of the foot and mouth epidemic was rising in terms of compensation to farmers and losses to the tourist industry – something the Government clearly had not considered. In the event, the total cost was far greater than the value of the annual meat exports which were worth some £0.5 million. Again estimates vary, but total compensation to farmers was put at £1.7 billion, the bill to the taxpayer in terms of lost revenues and other costs was put at £2.7 billion, losses to the tourist industry at some £4.25 billion and the cost of cleaning and disinfecting at £0.7 million. Even if some of these costs are scaled down the total was far greater than the value of annual meat exports.

As ever politics and presentation have been the drivers – not good government or the public interest. Ministers talk of 'moving on', which is govspeak for burying the whole episode as quickly as possible. They also cite the public inquiry into mad cow disease, which cost millions and took years, as a reason for not having another public inquiry now into foot and mouth.

Which only goes to show that making public inquiries short, sharp and cheap is a much needed and long overdue reform. A government that had any respect for the notion of public accountability would surely find a way to do it, beginning by setting a deadline and a maximum budget and insisting that those running the inquiry operate within those limits. Another key move might be to ban all lawyers. Observers say that lawyers representing those who appear before public inquiries can have the effect of dragging out proceedings and bumping up costs.

No doubt some of the accusations against MAFF/DEFRA are ill founded. And some specific incidents might be explained away or even justified in terms of the need for swift, emergency action. But the evidence against Ministers and MAFF/DEFRA officials is overwhelming and becoming steadily more damning as more information emerges.

But should country people not put the agony behind them, stop raking over the past and start looking to the future? Certainly they should and they *are* looking ahead. Some of the Swaledale sheep that escaped culling at Towcett have been tupped and are back on the fells again with their lambs. Liz has decided to have no more farm animals at Towcett. Chris Wood is rebuilding and restocking his farm. There is hope again in the Eden valley.

Yet unless and until *all* the facts of the foot and mouth epidemic are brought out and 'owned' by those who perpetrated injustice, unless the people of Cumbria, Devon, Yorkshire and all the other country areas are told the whole truth there will have been no real lessons learned. The politicians and the bureaucrats will have cheated the public once more.

Which is exactly what has happened. When the report of the Government's so-called Lessons Learned inquiry, chaired by Iain Anderson, was published in July 2002 it failed to answer any of the key questions. It failed to discover *why* it took so long to bring in the army; it failed to identify *who* had ordered the closure of the countryside which resulted in such huge losses to tourism; it failed to identify *who* had decided on the contiguous cull that led to the deaths of so many millions of healthy animals; and it blandly accepted the Prime Minister's assurance that the Government had not been influenced by the timing of the general election. True, the report criticised MAFF/DEFRA but as *The Times* pointed out, Tony Blair was 'treated as completely off limits throughout'.

Because the inquiry was held behind closed doors, Ministers and civil servants were allowed to get away with pretending that they 'weren't present' when decisions were taken, that they were 'not sure' who *had* had made the decisions, that decisions 'just emerged'. It was risible. And it was exactly what Chris Wood, Liz Lowther and the other farmers had foretold when they tried to use the courts to force Ministers to hold an inquiry in public.

The lesson that has been learned by the cheating classes is that they can do it again. Although the Royal Society report on the epidemic called for vaccination to be used to combat any future outbreak of FMD, the Government is determined to push ahead with a new Animal Health Bill giving the authorities greater powers to enter farms and kill all the animals. They will no longer have to lay special emergency orders. And though farmers will be able to appeal to the courts, they will only be able to do so *after* the killing when it is too late.

This is the shocking thing. For the best part of a year an incompetent Government, driven by political interests, presided over the oppression of thousands of country people and over the killing of millions of healthy animals. Much of what it did was illegal. Yet its primarily concern is not to stop such a tragedy ever happening again but to give itself powers to behave in the same despotic way next time. What we must find is a mechanism that will allow people such as the Cumbrian farmers to insist that governments are cross-examined publicly in the wake of a national disaster like the foot and mouth epidemic. Unless we do so, all of us will lose.

5

THE POLICEMAN'S TALE

It is the tinpot dictators who are the worst. Great autocrats may curb freedom of speech or ban political protest and still have entire populations living fairly contentedly beneath their yoke – provided living standards are not too low and there is a certain order and fairness to their lives. Communist Russia may have been undemocratic and repressive but today many Russians look back to it as a golden age of stability and security.

What drives people to desperation is the kind of abuse of power that affects every aspect of their daily lives. Take the State-run Child Support Agency. Despite some effort at reform, it still brings a flavour of Kafka to Tony Blair's Britain. It may have been conceived as a way of making parents take responsibility for their children but it has become a monument to oppression and Whitehall incompetence.

At the time it was set up there was widespread public support for the CSA. The idea was that it would force fathers who were divorced, separated or just plain feckless to pay for their children's upkeep even if they had started another family.

It would be good for the children, good for their mothers and good for the taxpayer who would not have to shell out so much money on benefits.

Keith Dray thought it was an excellent idea when he first heard of it. He believed it would ensure a fairer deal for him and his family. Instead he became one of its victims.

Detective Constable Keith Dray set himself up to be a CSA target the day he went to investigate a burglary in the flats on a council estate in Ramsgate. Not that he could have known it at the time for then the Child Support Agency was not even a twinkle in the Government's eye. But that was the day in the autumn of 1982 that DC Dray met Gill.

It was the old lady in the ground-floor flat who had reported the burglary. She had heard suspicious noises and she knew that the couple in the top flat was away. She would offer to go up and help the policeman to look round but there was no lift and she did not think she could manage to climb two flights of stairs. Perhaps the girl in the flat above could help . . .

So it was that DC Dray found himself knocking on Gill's door.

'I'm sorry to bother you,' he said showing her his identity card, 'but we think there may have been a burglary in the flat upstairs. The thing is I'm on my own and we're not meant to investigate a burglary without someone else there to act as a witness. Otherwise I could be accused of doing the stealing. Could you spare a few moments to help me out? It's quite safe – there's no sign of anyone around.'

Gill, round faced and bright eyed, smiled up at him.

'Of course,' she said.' The baby's asleep so I can leave him for a few minutes.'

There was no doubt the top flat had been burgled. The television was missing and there were signs that drawers had been ransacked. DC Dray said the police would do their best but it was not always easy to catch burglars in cases like these. Gill made sympathetic noises. She could see it must be difficult. She and the policeman walked slowly downstairs. Gill hesitated a moment then: would he have time for a coffee?

They talked about thieving. And about babies. Gill knew about both. Her husband had been a feckless man at the best of times and eventually she had caught him stealing money from their own electricity meter. That was when she had shopped him to the police. She had had to because she could not take any more. He had been convicted of theft and burglary. He had left her of course but she was not sorry to have divorced him. He had moved out of their flat the day the baby was born.

'So he walked out and left you with a new baby?' DC Dray sounded shocked.

'No,' said Gill. 'He left me with four babies. I've got three boys and a girl.

'And he's never been to see them – never even sent any of them birthday cards let alone given me any money for them. Admittedly we married very young. I met him when I was four-teen, fell pregnant and I was still only sixteen when we married. I didn't mind. I really wanted the baby. But I suppose it wasn't the best start. All the same you'd think a man would take a bit more interest in his own kids.'

DC Dray did think so. He liked children. He had a little boy himself. Mark was not quite a year old and his father could not imagine leaving him to fend for himself. He and his wife Sadie were not as close as they had been once – they had even discussed divorce. But they both agreed that even if they split up they would always do all they could for Mark.

He made ready to leave. He could see how hard it must be for Gill on her own. If there was anything he could do perhaps she would let him know. He would have to come back to see the people upstairs about the burglary. He could pop in and see her . . .

Looking back Keith reckons his first meeting with Gill was the catalyst for the final break-up of his marriage. He and Sadie had been living increasingly separate lives for months. It was not that they had started having spectacular bust-ups – far from it. The relationship was civil enough but the spark was gone.

On the face of it Sadie was the successful one while Gill's life was a mess. Sadie was a librarian, she was earning good money – as much as Keith – and she was ambitious.

She had even talked of taking a few years off work to go to university so she could try for an even better job. In contrast, Gill's arrival at the legal age of adulthood had coincided with the birth of her first baby. She had known nothing but motherhood and financial insecurity ever since.

Yet she had not regretted it. Even when she had found herself unwed and pregnant at fifteen she had wanted the baby. For all the difficulties of her life she was a woman at ease with herself. And Keith Dray was very much at ease with her.

Like every other aspect of their relationship, Keith's divorce from Sadie was conducted in a civilised manner. The two of them even conspired to thwart the greed of the legal profession. They roughed out the terms of the divorce together and then made appointments to see different solicitors on the same day. Afterwards they met to compare notes over coffee.

They found both solicitors had said that the divorce would need to be more complicated and drawn out than they had planned. But Keith and Sadie stuck to their guns and insisted on going ahead with the deal they had worked out between them. If that meant less work and less money for the solicitors, then so much the better.

Their financial agreement was straightforward. Sadie did not ask for money for herself because she earned as much as Keith. So all they had to consider was the welfare of Mark who was still under two.

Keith agreed to pay £80 a month towards his upkeep. Sadie agreed there would be no problems about him seeing his son. The divorce settlement was approved by the court.

*

The deal meant that money would be tight for Keith's new family. He and Gill planned to marry as soon as Keith's divorce came through and he had agreed to take on responsibility for her four children as well as supporting Mark. He did not have much choice really – Gill and her children came as a package. But Keith was happy to take them on.

He liked all of them. Kelly, the eldest, was five. She and her three brothers, Glen, Gareth and the youngest David, who was not yet two, quickly came to regard Keith as the father none of them could quite remember. They were a happy family.

Keith knew that it was going to be a long haul financially. As soon as they married Gill lost her entitlement to state benefits for herself, Kelly and the boys. Yet there was no hope of getting any money out of her ex-husband.

In 1984 Gill and Keith had a daughter of their own, Emma. Three years later another little girl, Lorna, was born. Their circumstances became even more straitened but they did not think about it too much. They had a house in a pleasant part of Ramsgate. Gill kept it immaculate even if the furniture grew a little shabby because they could not afford to replace it. They had each other. They had the children. They managed.

It was from Margaret Thatcher that Keith first heard about the Child Support Agency. He was watching the television news when Mrs Thatcher came on to say that her Government was going to make errant fathers pay for the upkeep of their children instead of letting the burden fall on taxpayers. Keith turned to Gill.

'D'you hear that?' he asked. 'That could be really good for us. At long last someone might force that ex-husband of yours to pay towards Kelly and the boys.'

The mills of government grind slow. Initially just about everyone was enthusiastic about the idea of a Child Support Agency. Politicians of all parties backed the idea at least in principle. But

Mrs Thatcher had been out of Number Ten for three years before the CSA finally became a reality in 1993.

By then some warning voices were being raised. Labour politicians were worried that there might be difficulties making the CSA work in a way that was fair to everyone – including the second families of men who had remarried and had more children. But most people assumed that a fair balance could be found even if there were some teething troubles at the outset. Many welcomed the CSA – including the Drays.

The first inkling of trouble came with an unexpected phone call from Sadie. Keith knew that she had given up her job as a librarian to do a psychology degree at Canterbury University and she had just started the course. She wanted to become a teacher eventually. The last time Keith had talked to her she had been full of enthusiasm.

Mark was twelve now and doing well at school. Life would be tough financially while Sadie was at university but it would be worth it in the long run. By the time Mark was in his mid-teens she hoped to be earning quite a bit more than she had in the library. Everything seemed to be looking good for them.

Except that when Keith took the call from Sadie that morning she was in tears. Indeed she was not just in tears but sobbing hysterically. It was unlike her. As long as he had known her she had always been calm and collected, almost too much so.

His first fear was that something must have happened to Mark but as Sadie tried to get a grip on herself it became clear that the boy was fine. Whatever the problem was it had to do with money.

'I'm sorry,' she kept saying. 'I'm so sorry. They said if I didn't do it they'd cut my money off. They said you'd have to pay.'

As a policeman Keith was used to dealing with people who were very upset. He knew that the only way was to take things slowly.

'I'm sure we can sort this out,' he said soothingly. 'Now stop torturing yourself and start at the beginning. Who said these things to you and what is it I've got to pay?'

'The CSA,' said Sadie. 'The Child Support Agency. It's a new thing. It's just been set up.'

'Yes, I've heard of it. Gill and I thought it might be able to help us. We were rather in favour of it. But what's it got to do with you and me?'

Sadie was calmer now. She blew her nose, took a gulp of air and started to explain.

'I promise you none of this is my fault. The CSA says that I must fill in the forms to make you pay for Mark's upkeep.'

'But I do pay,' said Keith. 'I've always paid. There's never been any question of me not paying.'

'I know, I know,' said Sadie. 'I told them that. But it didn't make any difference.'

'Did you tell them that our settlement had been agreed by the court?'

'Yes. But apparently that doesn't count any more. We have to start from scratch.'

'Why did you go to the CSA in the first place?'

'I didn't. I'm doing this course at Canterbury, as you know, and I haven't got a salary any more because I've given up my job, right? So I had to apply for benefits. You and I talked about it. Well, I got the benefits all right but then I heard from the CSA. They said I had to fill in the forms asking you for money for Mark. They said if I didn't co-operate they'd stop my benefits. All of them. I had no choice.'

'What did they say when you told them I was already paying £80 a month?'

'They said that perhaps you ought to be paying more. The only way to find out was if we both filled in their forms. They were horrible to me.'

She started to cry again. Keith tried to comfort her. He told her she was probably worrying unnecessarily. Once the CSA knew all the circumstances they would see that everything was fine and no changes were necessary. At any rate, she shouldn't blame herself.

It would work out in the end. After all, if the CSA were prepared to be this tough with him there must be a good chance they would force Gill's ex-husband to start paying something for Kelly and the boys. That would be good news for all of them.

It was unfortunate that the person Sadie had dealt with at the CSA had been so unpleasant but that was just bad luck. They would not all be like that. Keith himself had worked at the Department of Social Security for several years. Most of the staff he had known there had always been sympathetic to genuine cases.

Keith did not realise that the CSA was different to traditional Government Departments. It was one of the new executive agencies brought in by the Tories. Though ultimately responsible to Ministers, these agencies enjoyed considerable autonomy. The idea was that this would give staff more freedom to employ modern methods, streamline services and give taxpayers better value.

Some backbench MPs were unhappy when they found that civil servants rather than Ministers were dealing with their constituency complaints. But it was explained that if there were a major problem then Ministers would step in because in the long run they would still be accountable.

The Child Support Agency was one of the few where this mattered. It turned out that in this highly sensitive area of family relationships the lines of accountability to Ministers had been stretched so thin they seemed almost invisible. Those who felt unfairly treated by the CSA soon discovered that in practice its staff was accountable to nobody.

The CSA's staffing policy marked it out. Under pressure from government to keep costs down, a high proportion of its staff were young and inexperienced. All too often they lacked the ability to distinguish between deserving and undeserving cases.

But the greatest weakness of the CSA was that the Government saw it as a cash cow. Faced with an ever rising social security bill, the Tories decided that forcing fathers to pay would be one way of reducing escalating costs. From the very beginning the CSA's foremost task was to raise revenue for the Exchequer. The cash went to mothers and children not direct to the State but every penny raised was a penny saved by the Treasury. Fair dealing was not top priority with the CSA. Meeting Treasury targets was.

Small wonder that the CSA's young, pressurised staff homed in on fathers who looked like easy meat. Fathers like Keith Dray.

In the end Keith and Gill sat down at the table and filled in their CSA forms together. Gill applied for maintenance for Kelly, Glen, Gareth and David, naming her ex-husband as their father. Keith had to tell the CSA about his pay and circumstances so that they would be able to assess whether he was paying the right amount towards Mark's upkeep.

He posted off the forms next day. They waited.

Four weeks later Keith heard from the CSA. Their initial assessment was that his payments for Mark should increase from £80 to £400 a month – an extra £320 a month. Payment instructions would follow in due course.

At first Keith wondered if the CSA had made a mistake. He wrote to the agency querying the new sum and asking how it had been reached. The letter he received in reply gave him little comfort. There was no mistake. The assessment of how much he should now pay for his son had been based on the information received from him and his ex-wife. The sum had then been worked out according to a formula. The CSA could not give him further details because it had a duty of confidentiality to his ex-wife and could not reveal the figures she had provided.

Keith rang the CSA but he was given short shrift by a brusque young man who refused to give his name or any further details about the formula for deciding how much fathers should pay. It was the first of many such phone calls. Keith continued to argue that there must be errors in his assessment. The trouble was that he never seemed to speak to the same person twice and the CSA staff were working off a computer that was never properly updated. Each time he called he was given a different sum. Sometimes he wrote to them, though he quickly discovered that unless he sent letters by recorded delivery they were ignored. When they did reply officials usually sent him pro-forma letters. It struck him that most of them did not know how to write proper business letters.

Meanwhile, Gill had heard nothing from the CSA about the assessment of how much her ex-husband should start paying for his four children.

Months passed and still Gill heard nothing. She and Keith tried making inquiries. The letters she received from the CSA – often unsigned and undated – amounted to no more than vague assertions that matters were going ahead and that Mrs Dray would hear more in due course.

While Gill waited for her ex-husband to be assessed, Keith was waiting for the CSA to send him the promised instructions on how to pay the extra money for Mark. Months passed and still no instructions came. Meantime he continued to pay Sadie at the old rate of £80 a month.

Life continued much as normal except that there was a faint sense of menace hanging over the neat little house in Ramsgate. At the back of the Drays' minds was the nagging question of what and when they would hear from the CSA.

At work Keith started hearing about other police officers who were having trouble with the CSA. All said that it was hard to find out what the rules were, what the formula was. And there were one or two horror stories about people being threatened by

CSA staff. At home Keith and Gill started to snap at each other. She was now working as a classroom assistant in a nearby primary school, which brought in a little extra cash but she was desperately worried about money.

With six children plus Mark they had always been strapped for cash and if Keith had to start paying over three hundred pounds more each month she did not know how they were going to make ends meet. The children felt the atmosphere and reacted by becoming more fractious, particularly the two younger ones. Emma was now nine but Lorna was only six.

Meanwhile Keith's relations with Sadie had deteriorated. He did not doubt that she had never intended to make him pay more for Mark. But now that the CSA had ordered him to pay extra, it certainly would make life easier for her, particularly while she was at college with so little income.

She had begun to ask Keith when he was going to start paying. His reply was always the same. 'They told me they would send me payment instructions,' he said. 'As soon as they send those I'll start paying at the new rate.'

Eventually the CSA did send him a definitive assessment. He was to pay just under £320 a month on top of the £80 he was already paying. This figure included the arrears that he had run up, according to the CSA, but the agency did not make it clear how much of the total was arrears and how much was the new regular payment.

Whether they realised it or not, the CSA now had Keith over a barrel. It is a disciplinary offence for a policeman to fail to pay a lawful debt. The risk of debt-ridden policemen laying themselves open to bribery or blackmail are obvious. Keith had to comply. He did not give up without a fight. He rang the CSA and asked exactly how much his arrears were. They refused to say. They told him they had the power to make a Deduction of Earnings order against him. That would include both the regular amount for Mark plus the arrears. The DEO would be for £317 a month.

Keith rang them again. A woman answered. He again demanded a breakdown of the payment so that he would know how much was arrears and how much was the regular payment for Mark. He was angry and it showed. But it did him no good. The woman at the other end said she thought his arrears accounted for around £40 of the total.

'But how is that worked out? How much do I owe in arrears altogether?' demanded Keith.

'I can't give you any further details,' said the woman icily.

'Well, why is it that I owe arrears?' asked Keith. 'You can't be demanding arrears from the time Sadie and I were divorced – our settlement was agreed by the court. And you told me that you would send me details of how I was to pay the new amount. Well, I've never had those details. So how much do I owe?'

'As I said, I think your arrears account for about £40 a month of the total you have to pay,' said the woman reluctantly.

'Fine,' said Keith. 'At last we're making some progress. Now, for God's sake tell me how you work that out.'

'Don't you take that tone with me,' rasped the woman. 'If you want to be difficult I'll put your arrears up from £40 a month to £100 a month. Now just stop arguing and start paying or you'll know about it.'

And still Gill had not heard from the CSA how much money she could expect from her ex-husband.

The question of how much he might be forced to pay was becoming more and more pressing. If it had just been a matter of Mark – even at the new higher maintenance rate – plus their own two girls then Gill and Keith would not have been in too bad shape financially. But with Kelly and the three boys as well, life was becoming impossible. If only their father could be made to pay his fair share.

Gill started making inquiries through old acquaintances. She heard that her ex-husband was in work as a builder. She also found out that he had married again and had twin girls. She duly reported what she had gleaned to the CSA. But still they did nothing.

It was not until 1995 – two full years after she first filled in her form – that Gill finally heard from the CSA. They had investigated her first husband's means. They had assessed him as being liable to pay £188 a month for Kelly, Glen, Gareth and David.

Regretfully, the CSA understood that although her ex-husband had been in work he was currently unemployed and living on State benefits.

Although technically he should make some contribution towards his children's upkeep out of his benefits, it was not the CSA's practice to pursue such claims. The administrative costs involved in adjusting his benefit did not make the exercise worthwhile. Therefore her ex-husband would not be required to make any contribution at all towards the upkeep of his children.

In other words the entire burden would continue to fall on Keith.

Keith had made a serious error in his dealings with the CSA. Somewhere along the line he had given one of the CSA staff his home phone number.

He was working shifts and he normally arrived home at about half past three in the afternoon. Suddenly he found that his afternoons were taken up with phone calls from the CSA. The staff, who never gave their names or at least not their proper names, demanded information so that they could review Keith's case. That at least was their claim.

In practice it seemed to him that they were bullying him ruthlessly so as to squeeze yet more money out of him. He kept on explaining that he was already paying for four children who were not his own but they were not interested in that. They told him that their formula did not allow them to make any allowances for second families.

Their task was simply to ensure that wherever possible men paid as much as they could afford to the children of their first families.

Keith in turn kept pressing them as to how much he owed in arrears. To his horror he found that some of them seemed to think his arrears amounted to thousands of pounds – the kind of sum that would bankrupt the Drays. Keith believed the total arrears should be in the hundreds not thousands but it was hard to prove when the CSA still refused to tell him the exact basis for its calculations.

They were still talking of putting his arrears payments up from around £40 to around £100 a month. And it seemed that almost every afternoon there were more phone calls from the agency . . .

Keith knew he was far from being the only one who was suffering persecution at the hands of the CSA. There were dozens of men in the police force alone who were under pressure from the agency – so much so that the Police Federation's lawyers could not cope.

In the past the Federation's solicitors had always covered domestic matters brought to them by members. But they announced that they could no longer do so. The rush of cases involving the CSA was simply too great.

Meanwhile ACPO – the Association of Chief Police Officers – also took measures to protect their men from the depredations of the CSA. ACPO ingeniously announced that because there were so many disputes between policemen and the CSA it had become virtually impossible to find out how much individual officers lawfully owed. Therefore, in future money owed by police officers under CSA legislation would be no longer be regarded as a lawful debt and those who ran foul of CSA rulings would not be disciplined.

ACPO's decision was a sensible one but it offered only small crumbs of comfort to the men who were the CSA's victims. And all the time the number of stories about the agency's unfairness and incompetence circulating in the press and by word of mouth was growing.

There were reports of several fathers who had become so desperate they had committed suicide. But alongside these tragedies were tales of men – like Gill's ex-husband – who had somehow escaped the net. Keith was sorely tempted to give up his own job and go on the dole himself. That would mean that for all practical purposes the CSA could not touch him.

What held him back was his self-respect, a refusal to be beaten – and concern about his pension. He had paid into it for twenty years and he was not prepared to have it jeopardised by the CSA. He would just have to keep going and see if there was another way to make the CSA start acting more fairly.

One of the most disturbing aspects of the CSA saga is the powerlessness of anyone – even influential people – to call a halt to the agency's abuses. Chief Police Officers are not a negligible group – and they were backed by the Police Federation, trade union of the rank and file. Yet it was the police who were forced to change their disciplinary proceedings – even though the rule that officers must pay lawful debts is sensible – rather than the CSA being forced to reform itself.

Not that the CSA escaped all public censure in the early days. There was an outcry over its double-edged injustice, with some fathers being asked to pay more than they could afford while some mothers received nothing from cheating ex-husbands.

MPs urged the CSA to clean up its act so that they could reassure the public all was well. But this was political hot air. It made no difference on the ground. The young, sometimes uncaring staff were still there. The secrecy over the assessment formula and even over staff names was still there. The ban on taking account of second families was still there. And the pressure was still on for staff to obtain as much money as possible from fathers so as to meet the CSA's financial targets.

When it came to finding ways of rectifying the system, there were few avenues open to the likes of Keith Dray. If the Chief Police Officers had to accept the CSA's writ, what chance did he have?

In the days before his fall Jonathan Aitken, old Etonian MP for Thanet South, was one of the most glamorous of the Tory party's high flyers. He was immediately sympathetic to the Drays when they went to see him at his weekly surgery. They were not the first of his constituents to complain about the CSA.

At the time the contrast in the lifestyles of Jonathan Aitken and Keith Dray could not have been more stark. Jonathan, flawed but brilliant, was a rich man. He had a home in the constituency and another, grand Georgian house two streets away from the House of Commons.

He had held high office in the Government while his business dealings took him round the world. And as the world was one day to know he always stayed in the very best hotels. It was his foolish decision to lie over who paid his bill at the Ritz Hotel in Paris that ultimately brought about his downfall and ended with him serving a prison sentence.

But for all that, he was a man of charm and energy, besides being a father himself. He was concerned about the way the CSA was treating his constituents and he promised to take up the cudgels on the Drays' behalf. Here at last was someone who might be able to achieve a result.

He wrote to Ann Chant, the head of the CSA, condemning the 'mistakes, poor communication and wrong judgements' of the agency's Hastings office and saying that they had reached quite unacceptable levels. He believed that Keith Dray, who had still not been told how much he owed in arrears, had been the victim of maladministration by the Hastings office. As an MP he had the right to refer the case to the Ombudsman's Office and he threatened to do so.

Ann Chant wrote back. She apologised for the way the Drays

had been treated. She said the agency would not increase his monthly arrears payments from £40 to £100 until the dispute over the arrears total had been sorted out.

That there was a dispute there could be no doubt. Ann Chant said the agency estimated Keith Dray's overall arrears at £5,867.59p.

Keith and Gill could barely believe they were being asked for nearly £6,000 – money which they had no means of raising. But nor did they believe they actually owed that amount. Even using the CSA's tricky arithmetic the total arrears could not possibly be £6,000. Less than a year had elapsed between the CSA sending him his initial assessment and the final, supposedly definitive one. What is more, as he pointed out to them, throughout that period he had often paid more than £80 for his son. Ever since he and his first wife separated he had paid extra for outings, clothes or equipment and he had done so without quibbling. He had also been paying for another man's children. He resolved to keep battling it out with the agency's office in Hastings.

Eventually, he and the CSA agreed a figure of £700 for his arrears. He and Gill felt a huge sense of relief. They decided that there was no point in asking Jonathan Aitken to pursue their case with the Ombudsman.

Yet if the Drays had hoped for some respite from the CSA they were to be disappointed. The agency reviewed all cases regularly to see if payments needed to be 'adjusted'. The harassment of DC Dray continued.

The CSA's demands affected every aspect of Keith's life including his work. For a long time he had wanted to go on an attachment to Scotland Yard to study the latest methods of combating serious crime. The opportunity came one summer. At first he was delighted.

Then the implications hit him. He would receive extra pay during the four-month attachment. This meant it would end just before Christmas – the very time that the CSA was due to review his payments for Mark. Fellow police officers warned him that if the CSA reviewed his case just as he received a fatter-than-usual pay packet then they would demand more money from him. And it would be no good trying to persuade them that the Christmas salary cheque was a one-off. They would assume he had had a permanent pay rise.

Nor would there be any way of hiding the extra cash he received for doing the attachment. The CSA had more powers than the police themselves. Keith had to have a court order before he could see a suspect's bank account. The CSA did not have to go through such formalities. And they could turn up at Keith's workplace at any time and ask any of his colleagues about his circumstances. They did not need a warrant, they not need to justify themselves, they did not even need an appointment.

Reluctantly Keith decided he would have to turn down the attachment. Then his superintendent sent for him.

'Am I right in thinking that you are turning down this attachment purely because of the CSA?' he asked.

'Yes, sir,' replied Keith. 'They're due to review me at Christmas and they'll assume the extra cash for the attachment is a pay rise. They'll insist I pay more for my boy and I just can't afford it. I've worked it out. Quite frankly it would bankrupt me. Literally. They might put my payments down again later but by then it would be too late.'

'There must be a way round this,' the superintendent mused, rubbing his chin. 'Tell me, does it all hinge on the fact that the CSA review is due at the same time as you do the attachment?'

'Yes, sir.'

'So if I could get your attachment shifted and you did it after the CSA review you might be in the clear?'

'Yes,' said Keith, hope dawning in his face.

The superintendent smiled. 'I'll see what I can do,' he said.

He was as good as his word. Keith's attachment was delayed

until after the CSA's review. For once luck – and a good super-intendent – had been on his side.

At home things were not so good. Gill was becoming more and more stressed by the CSA's bullying tactics. Things had reached such a pitch that she was frightened to answer the phone in case it should be someone from the agency.

She was in such a state that she was finding it hard to cope with her job in the local primary school.

The doctor gave her some tablets. He said she was having a nervous breakdown.

Detective Constable Nash was one of Keith's friends in the organised crime section at Dover where they both worked. Like Keith, Jim Nash had divorced and married again. He had two little girls by his first wife. He had never tried to evade his responsibilities towards his daughters but he too felt he was being persecuted by the CSA. As with Keith, agency staff had rung him at home and threatened to insist on even higher payments if he failed to meet their earlier demands.

For Jim, the opportunity to go on a course designed to update policemen on the law provided a brief respite from his everyday worries. They were a good crowd on the course and they quickly fell into the habit of going to the pub at lunchtime.

It was the penultimate day of the course. By 3.30 in the after-noon DC Nash was feeling decidedly sleepy, what with his intellectual exertions in the morning and a convivial lunch there-after. He was listening to the instructor with only half an ear. And then he heard the words 'harassment of debtors'. He sat upright and started listening. Perhaps this was something that could help him.

It seemed the law on harassment of debtors laid down that while reasonable steps could be taken to recover a debt, it was an offence to threaten someone. Anyone who was so threatened could make a complaint to the police . . .

Jim lost no time in alerting Keith and some of the other officers who were being hounded by the CSA. He had checked with
the instructor on the course and it seemed that this little known
law might offer some protection against the agency.

The officers did not raise their hopes too high. All of them had
looked to the law for protection before but always in the past it
had failed them when it came to the CSA.

Yet the law on harassment of debtors turned out to be a
winner. Keith wrote to the CSA citing the legislation and threatening to use it against the agency unless the threats and the
evening phone calls to his home stopped forthwith.

The effect was dramatic and immediate. The calls ceased.

The spring of 1997 saw the end of eighteen years of Tory rule
and the advent of a New Labour government. Labour had long
been critical of the CSA and many of its victims – including
Keith – were hopeful that at long last real reforms might be put
in place.

Superficial changes were apparent almost immediately. One of
the things that tried Keith's patience to the limit was that he
never spoke to the same person at the CSA. Plus the agency was
falling behind with its annual reviews of cases, which meant
there was even less chance of Keith having his payments for
Mark reduced let alone being recompensed for money he might
have overpaid in the past. He was told that his review for 1998
could not be carried out until the CSA had done the reviews for
1997, 1996, 1995 and 1994.

Keith came up against this bureaucratic logjam every time he
tried to remonstrate with a different voice at the end of the line.

Then one day he had a phone call that took him by surprise.

'Hello,' said a female voice. 'Is that Keith Dray?'

'Yes,' said Keith.

'This is the CSA here. My name is Alice. I'm your case officer
and I'll be dealing with you on all CSA matters from now on.'

Keith did not allow his hopes to rise too high. Bitter experience had taught him how foolish that would be. But Alice sounded pleasant and reasonable. Maybe the new Government *was* going to make a difference.

In the event Alice was apologetic but she could not speed up his reviews.

The new Government had never intended to close the CSA. The idea that people should take responsibility for themselves and that fathers in particular should take responsibility for their children was very much in line with New Labour thinking. But Tony Blair's administration did initiate a wide-ranging consultation about what changes should be made to the CSA.

And changes were agreed. The whole system was to be streamlined and simplified. Absent parents – mainly fathers – were to pay 15 per cent of their income for a first child, 20 per cent for two children and 25 per cent for three or more. Second families were to be taken into consideration. Mothers on income support would be allowed to keep some of their children's maintenance money instead of the State clawing back every penny. The reforms were scheduled to start coming into force in October 2001.

Yet almost immediately there were signs that the planned changes were merely going to worsen the chaos and confusion endemic in the CSA. Parents – over a million of them have dealings with the CSA – soon realised that some of them would gain from being on the new system while others would be better off on the old one. Individuals started manoeuvring to delay their CSA assessments or to speed them up so they could be on the system that was best for them. There were predictions that complaints against the agency, up by a third in 2002, would soar once the new rules came in. The Law Society, which represents solicitors, warned that the new 'cruder' child support formula would help CSA bureaucrats but only at the expense of fairness to parents.

The sheer scale of the mess and muddle started to emerge in

the summer of 2001 when it was revealed that the CSA was owed more than £1 billion in child maintenance. Even more damning was the Government's admission that around two thirds of this money – some £700 million – was being written off as 'uncollectable'. Then came the news that the reforms were being postponed from the autumn of 2001 to April 2002.

Towards the end of March 2002, as changeover day came within sight, the Government suddenly announced that the changes were to be postponed yet again, this time indefinitely. The reason? Flaws in the CSA's new £300 million computer system.

To the Drays, watching on the sidelines, the gathering disaster at the CSA seemed to have a certain grim inevitability. They were only glad that they themselves were no longer caught in the agency's toils. The CSA covers children up to the age of eighteen. In 2000, Mark reached his nineteenth birthday and as he was intent on travelling round the world for a couple of years rather than going to university, Keith no longer had to contribute to his upkeep via the agency.

Not that the CSA gave up that easily. In 2001, it sent Keith a new maintenance demand for Mark. It took officials until 2002 to apologise – and then they followed up the apology with yet another demand for payment. He is wondering whether to sue them for harassment.

Although Keith Dray is now free of the agency, he knows of other policemen with young children who are still, as he puts it, 'being ground down by the CSA'. And now there are to be greater powers to punish parents who fall out of line. Those who do not pay will face tougher penalties including fines or imprisonment and, in what must rank as a truly bizarre and arbitrary punishment, the loss of their driving licences.

The tale of Keith Dray is not just about the ongoing incompetence of the Child Support Agency – horrific though that is. It is about a shift in our society away from the old spirit of public service to a new, harsher ethos where economic imperatives take precedence over fairness to families. It is about the growth of a bureaucracy that is largely unaccountable to the public it is meant to serve. It is about ordinary people – competent, upstanding, articulate people – who find they have no comeback against unscrupulous officials who treat them in a manifestly unjust way.

The idea of making absent parents pay for their children came from the USA and right from the start the Americans warned the British that the financial savings to the Government should be regarded as a bonus – not a goal. Instead, the CSA was set up with the aim of making money for the Treasury. The object, first under the Tories and now under Labour, has been to reduce the social security bill for the taxpayer. That may be a laudable goal, but the balance between economic efficiency and common humanity seems to be seriously out of kilter.

Admittedly, most of the politicians and civil servants who originally set up the CSA now acknowledge that serious mistakes were made and in the last few years the agency has made a significant effort to improve its dealings with parents. It has improved its compensation scheme and its handling of complaints. It is also true that the long-awaited new system for assessing payments may bring about real improvements when it is finally introduced. Yet the underlying issue remains.

It is financial pressure from the top that encourages bureaucrats like those at the CSA to cheat and cheat again on people like Keith Dray. As they did. They cheated when they failed to make allowance for the fact that he was raising another man's family. They cheated when they tried to bully him into paying more. They cheated when they refused to tell him how much he owed in back payments.

People like Keith Dray believe that what is needed at the CSA is a more flexible system that does not insist on making every family fit a rigid formula – even a new, simpler one. There must be room for individual circumstances to be properly considered and without a weather eye on meeting Treasury targets.

The tale of Keith Dray also demonstrates how hard it is for ordinary people to have their wrongs righted. Here was an articulate man with special knowledge of the law because of his job as a policeman who was prepared to use all the usual avenues. He went to his MP who did his best to help him and even secured an apology from the top, but Keith's fundamental problems with the CSA remained unsolved. Today the agency has at least started telling people about the existence of a government-funded Independent Case Examiner who can deal with parents' grievances – in the past, the CSA kept quiet about the ICE. It is notable that the number of complaints to the ICE is now soaring – so much so that the Government has been forced to increase its staff. Yet the ICE can only make recommendations and even then the Examiner cannot deal with fundamentals such as complaints about matters of law. No matter how competent, an Establishment body like the ICE provides another example of the authorities, in effect, policing themselves. Meanwhile the CSA itself is still receiving nearly 20,000 complaints a year.

Perhaps what is needed to help people like the Drays is a new breed of powerful, independent review body where ordinary men and women have a dominant voice. Their role could be to ensure that organisations like the Child Support Agency treat individuals fairly with the balance weighted in favour of ordinary people and not the authorities.

The review bodies could have powers to enforce their findings – not just to recommend change. They could be given authority to overturn CSA decisions, to award compensation and to order changes in the agency's working practices. They could also name and shame individual officials where appropriate, though penalties would only be appropriate where bureaucrats had deliberately and knowingly treated someone unfairly – as in Keith Dray's case – not where there had been an honest mistake.

Perhaps there is another role that could be fulfilled by a truly independent watchdog. At its inception the Child Support

Agency was backed by politicians of all parties. What went wrong was that the legislation setting it up was not properly thought through and was inadequately examined by the House of Commons. There have been promises of Parliamentary reform and some progress has been made but the scrutiny of new laws before they go on the Statute book is still frighteningly inadequate. An independent complaints body could refer flawed legislation back to the Commons to be revised. It could even be answerable directly to the Commons as is the National Audit Office. That way it would be at arms' length from Whitehall and from Government Ministers who might try to suborn it to their interests by rigging its remit or packing it with cronies.

Undoubtedly the Blair Government has tried to address the chronic problems of the CSA that it inherited from the Tories, but after five years in power this so-called reforming administration still has not surmounted the underlying failures in the system. Unless or until it does so, there will be more Keith Drays.

6

THE PRISONER'S TALE

The wording on the exhibition stand at the Royal Courts of Justice in London was unequivocal. 'The courts,' it said, 'no longer send people to prison for simply being unable to settle their debts, only for serious misconduct such as insider trading or other frauds.'

It should have been a reassuring statement. The exhibition was sited rather forlornly in one section of the great, echoing hall that all visitors have to cross to reach the courts themselves. Its aim was to sketch the history of English justice and to give casual readers some idea of the work carried out in the Royal Courts. The tenor was optimistic and the magnificent, high Victorian building that houses the courts cannot fail to impress. It should all have been most reassuring.

Except that the claim made in the exhibition is wrong. It is not true that debtors in Britain are no longer sent to prison. Every year several thousand people go to prison because they cannot pay their debts. Most of them are poor and vulnerable. Many are women, usually on income support and often with health problems, mental or physical. They are sent to prison for such 'crimes' as failing to pay their television licences or falling behind on their council tax payments. At the start of the twenty-first century some were still being sent to prison for failing to pay the old Tory poll tax. For many of them it is not that they won't pay, it is that they can't pay.

Not that local politicians or town hall bureaucrats always allow themselves to be swayed by such distinctions. Some do not hesitate to take a firm line against what they regard as sob stories. They believe that they have to be tough on behalf of the whole community and they can be zealous in the cause. They – and their lawyers – have no qualms about using large amounts of public money to pursue minor debtors through the courts in the hope that they will be thrown into jail as an example to others. They do not wish to be unduly harsh these local government men but when it comes to the excuses put forward by defaulters, they have heard them all before . . . sickness . . . poverty . . . old age . . .

Hetty was old. She had never been strong. Even when she was much younger she had spent periods in hospital suffering from depression. Technically she was not poor because she owned her own house but most people would describe her financial circumstances as distressing. Not so distressing, however, as to count as extenuating circumstances to local officials at Thanet Council or to Thanet's magistrates. They were concerned only with the fact that Hetty had not paid her dues to society in the form of council tax. And they were prepared to be relentless in pursuing her . . .

Hetty had been beautiful once. It was hard to see it now. She sat in her front room, crouched and frail, with white hair and loose folds of skin around her face. Piles of books and papers were strewn over the furniture. Richard had had to move a stack of six-month-old newspapers before he could even sit down to hear her story. The place was not very clean. When he went to the kitchen to make a cup of tea he found the sink was filled with unwashed pans and crockery that looked as if they had been there for days.

As a lawyer, Richard did his best to keep Hetty to the points that would need to be raised in court but it was hard going. She found it difficult to concentrate and he could see that tears were never far. Several times she broke down. Often her mind wandered and she would start telling him about other times, other places. At one point she insisted on showing him her album . . .

The old photographs showed her as a shapely, buxom girl with hair falling in dark waves to her shoulders. In those days she had been a successful beauty queen, winning titles at holiday camps and seaside resorts. With her looks she had never had any difficulty finding a job – and she was always popular with young men.

It was a German she fell for in the end. He had been a prisoner of war in Britain and when they married they settled in a nice new house in North London.

Soon she was pregnant and she gave birth to a son. For a while everything seemed to be going her way. She was young, happily married with a lovely home and a new baby.

The idyll was brief. Although they had been married for only a short time, Hetty became suspicious that her husband was having an affair. It preyed on her mind. She could not stop thinking about what she felt was his betrayal. She became so depressed that she needed treatment. Inevitably, perhaps, her marriage broke up.

Her parents stepped in and looked after her little boy, though that only added to her unhappiness. 'They took my son off me,' she told Richard. 'They took him away from me.' Later, she found she was constantly denied access to the child. When he grew up, she lost touch altogether. She could barely remember when she had last seen him. Twenty years ago perhaps?

She had recovered from the misery of her marriage break-up and there had been other men in her life. In the 1960s, still attractive even though she was now in her forties, Hetty fell in love again, this time with a man several years her junior. The thing about John was that he looked after her. He decided that what Hetty needed was a fresh start. He took her down to Ramsgate in Kent and they bought a house there, the very terraced house with its large bay window where Richard and Hetty were now sitting.

For ten years she and John had been happy. Then, suddenly, he had died of a heart attack. He had been only forty-two years old. For the second time in her life Hetty was devastated. For the second time she needed help for severe depression and this time she started having physical problems too. The doctors said she needed a hysterectomy but the operation left her partially incontinent.

It was small consolation that John had done his best to provide for her financially, leaving a life insurance policy that had paid off the mortgage on the house. Still, it was something. She had held on to it – and if it were not for the house she would not have had Doug, who at least provided some company and security in her old age.

Richard knew about Doug. Doug was the lodger. He had been living in the house for years and paid £65 a week in rent – a vital top-up to Hetty's £86 a week pension. Doug's only stipulation was that she should pay for them to have Sky TV so he could watch the sport. Hetty paid £27 a month for the Sky subscription but the price she had had to pay in court had been far higher. Richard knew from studying the court papers that the Sky subscription had caused something close to outrage among the local magistrates and officials.

They reasoned that if she owned her own home and could afford frivolities like Sky then there was no reason why she could not pay her council tax arrears. They did not know that Hetty wanted the television mainly because she feared Doug would leave if she cancelled the Sky subscription. They did not seem to know what state her house was in or how fragile she was. Thanet officials saw Hetty as an awkward woman who was trying to dodge her liabilities and who must be made to pay.

Richard sighed. She was not going to be a good witness. As he himself said later, Hetty was 'off with the fairies' more often than not. But he was determined that this time the authorities would pay, not sad, confused Hetty.

It was time for the Wise brothers to act.

Richard and Ian Wise were an unlikely pair of lawyers. Tall and slim with soft, Midland accents and a gentle, rather intense manner, both were Labour radicals. Both were fired by a sense of indignation at the shabby, sometimes vicious treatment meted out to the vulnerable by the courts. Both had come late to the law and not by conventional routes. Ian had spent years working as a labourer in a tea factory before doing an Open University degree. Richard had studied economics and worked for the National Association of Citizens' Advice Bureaux. Ian was a barrister, based in London. Richard, based in their home town of Stoke, was the solicitor. At least he *acted* as a solicitor.

Technically speaking he had not done the final exams. He could only describe himself as a Public Law Supervisor – a 'loose character' in his own words. Technically he had to act under the supervision of a fully qualified solicitor but this had not stopped him being voted Human Rights Lawyer of the Year in 1999 by the Law Society.

The Wise brothers had made their name by challenging the casual way in which the courts jailed thousands of people each year for not paying debts such as council tax arrears or their TV licences. It was often women who were caught for not paying TV licences because they were at home when the detector vans came round. Magistrates sometimes imprisoned those unable to pay without bothering to make further inquiries and sometimes without making arrangements for the children.

Richard reckons that by 1995 around 22,000 people a year were being marched off to prison for debt. True, the days had long passed since people could be imprisoned for ordinary debts such as defaulting on hire purchase agreements. But those who owed money to the State in the form of income tax, VAT, council tax or court fines could still go to jail when financial orders were made against them. So too could those who had been ordered to pay by the State, such as parents who had fallen behind with their maintenance.

What the Wises had done was to contest in the higher courts this widespread, almost unthinking use of imprisonment by magistrates. They did so on the grounds that magistrates were not bothering to find out about people's means and nor were they considering other ways of getting people to pay. The Wises fought around a thousand cases taking them to judicial review by senior judges. They won all but three. The result was to force magistrates to start taking proper account of people's circumstances. Magistrates also had to start looking at alternatives to prison such as deducting money from people's wages. The numbers being jailed dropped dramatically, so that by 2001 there were only about 2,000 people a year going to prison for debt. Yet there were still far too many cases that fell through the net.

During their battles through the courts the Wises had built up ties with senior staff in some of the prisons – staff who were horrified at having to cope with defenceless people who were not criminals but who had been sent to jail for some minor debt. The prison officers would ring Richard to see if he could secure their release. Richard would call a barrister – sometimes Ian – who would get a bail order from a judge and often the unfortunate prisoner would be out that same day.

Some of them were not so lucky. That was how Richard had first come across Hetty.

Hetty had fallen behind with her council tax payments back in 1996. It was not altogether surprising. She had already had financial problems. Her house was in a poor state of repair. In the early 1990s a hole had appeared in the kitchen floor. She had borrowed £3,000 to have it repaired but the job had been poorly done. When the hole reappeared she found she had no comeback against the cowboys who had done the work and Thanet District Council had turned down her application for a home improvement grant. She had never managed to clear the first loan.

Years earlier she had raised £10,000 by remortgaging the house and she was still struggling to pay that off as well.

Then there were the bills for food, water, electricity, her TV licence. She had to buy incontinence pads . . . There was little left over. It was difficult to meet the demands for council tax as well. Almost without noticing she found that her arrears to the council were stacking up, until she owed back tax for two years – over £1,000. Thanet Council lost patience. Warrants were issued for her arrest.

Hetty appeared before the local magistrates' court and damned herself almost immediately by telling the court that she paid over £20 a month for Sky TV. She explained that she only had it for Doug but the Bench was unimpressed. Indeed they seemed to think it scandalous that a lonely old lady who led a spartan life with no holidays or other luxuries should spend money on a TV channel. They demanded to know how much she could afford to pay each week. Hetty offered £5 a week. The magistrates let her off the £461 that she owed for 1995 but they found her guilty of culpable neglect for failing to pay council tax for 1996 amounting to £679.08 including legal costs. In a bid to force her to pay up, they sentenced her to fourteen days in prison but agreed to suspend the jail term provided she gave them the £5 a week that she had promised.

Like many others in a similar position, Hetty had not thought through her offer properly and she had underestimated her weekly outgoings. Once she was safely back home she tried to put the whole business behind her and stopped worrying about her back payments. She worried instead about the hole in the kitchen floor and the broken fridge and her old debts to the bank and the building society.

Inevitably perhaps Hetty failed to keep her promise to pay back her debt to Thanet Council at the rate of £5 a week. She was ordered back before the magistrates, who demanded to know why.

Hetty did her best to explain. She told them about how the kitchen floor had fallen in, how there was the mortgage still to pay off and how Doug was not really helping . . . The magistrates were not satisfied. She had paid part of the debt so this time they sentenced Hetty to ten days in prison.

Sending someone as old and as ill as Hetty to prison diminishes all of us. Had she done something terrible, had she been found guilty of a serious, cold-blooded crime then a jail sentence might be justified – though even then there might be a question mark as to how far society would be served in sending her down. But Hetty had done nothing wrong. She could not cope financially but she was not dishonest. She was merely elderly, confused and poor.

They took Hetty and put her in a cell in Ramsgate police station. The officers who took her in charge were amazed that such an elderly woman should be jailed for the sake of a few hundred pounds. They knew she would not stay long with them – police cells are an expensive way to house prisoners and the local nick does not have the facilities to look after people for more than a day or so. That night Hetty would go to Holloway.

It would be quite a long journey and already the old lady was showing signs of acute distress. The police felt desperately sorry for her. The trouble was it was now late in the day and there seemed little hope of anyone getting her bail before morning. The officers in Ramsgate did their best. They rang one of the senior staff in charge of the bail unit at Holloway and asked her to see what she could do for Hetty. She rang Richard Wise.

The two had known each other for some time and had worked together before to help get women out on bail. It was ironic that prison officers who were meant to keep people inside should spend their time trying to keep some people out, trying to plug the holes in an uncaring system. In this case, it sounded to the officer as if the authorities, insensitive at the best of times, had excelled themselves.

'Richard?' she said when he picked up the phone. 'I've just had a call from Ramsgate police station saying they're sending up this elderly woman who is in a complete state. She's still on the prison bus. Can you help? How quickly can we get her out?'

Richard looked at his watch. He would need the notes of evidence from Thanet magistrates' court but he was sure he could arrange for a bail application to be lodged immediately. He was also confident that bail would be granted. The trouble was that no matter how quickly he moved, it would be too late to get Hetty home again that evening. She would have to spend one night at least in jail.

By the time Hetty arrived at Holloway she was already traumatised. She had never been anywhere near a prison before in her life, never been in trouble with the law . . . she who had been such a beauty, so proud of her husband, her baby, her home . . . that she should have come to this.

The prison staff did what they could for her. They treated her as gently as possible. The staff assured her that she would be out the next morning but she clearly found the prison frightening and claustrophobic. She would not be comforted.

That night they left her cell door open.

They sent her home the next day. As Richard had foreseen, bail had been granted on the grounds that there were plans to launch an appeal on Hetty's behalf. The next step was to have the magistrates' decision to send Hetty to prison quashed by a senior judge.

The law does not move swiftly and many months passed before there was a hearing. It was not until November 1999 that Hetty's case was finally considered by Mr Justice Jowitt. There was no sign of Thanet Council backing down but Mr Justice Jowitt quashed the decision. He sent the case back to Thanet magistrates for them to look at afresh. Richard reckoned that the hearing in the High Court cost over £4,000 – a bill that Thanet taxpayers would most probably have to pay.

Hetty, safely back at home and trying to put the whole experience behind her, did not know what this new court decision would mean for her or what she was meant to do next.

Richard talked to her over the phone. He explained that her case was being sent back to the magistrates who would want her to appear in court again. The first two times she had been in court she had had no legal advice and no one to explain all her circumstances to the court. She must make sure it was different this time. He said firmly that she ought to see a solicitor. He did not want to do the case himself because he was so far away in Stoke.

Hetty duly found a local solicitor who agreed to represent her. Yet somehow the case had moved on – and in a most unsatisfactory way. Thanet Council could have withdrawn at this stage and quietly written off Hetty's debt. That is what would have happened in any decent system. But it was not what happened to Hetty. There is no doubt they were within their rights. The law allowed them to take a tough line. Most of us would say they should have shown more compassion to a bewildered elderly woman in straitened circumstances. The authorities were determined to hold her to her original agreement that she would pay off her debt at £5 a week. And if she would not pay, then they were prepared to make an example of her. Again.

They were serious. Thanet had hired a senior barrister to

prosecute the case against Hetty. The legal charges would be £750 a day.

Even setting aside Thanet's unfeeling attitude towards an elderly woman, the conduct of its officials must be questioned on another head: value for money for local taxpayers.

Hetty had only owed £679.08 in council tax. Her debt was now down to £533. So why did Thanet's officials think it justifiable to hire lawyers who were going to cost more than Hetty owed, particularly as more than £4,000 had already been spent on the Jowitt hearing? Were the bureaucrats and their political masters playing fair by the public who would almost certainly have to pick up the tab?

Of course they did not want the cost to fall on Thanet's taxpayers. The hope of the bureaucrats was that Hetty herself would be made to pay the legal costs incurred by the council.

Thanet Council's legal fees raise another question: *why* should it cost £750 a day to persecute an elderly lady for non-payment of a few hundred pounds when there was little disagreement as to the facts of the case?

But perhaps it is too soon to ask that. Hetty's agony still had some way to go. So did the lawyers' creative billing.

Back in Thanet magistrates' court in March 2000 Hetty's new solicitor explained that her circumstances were rather different to what had been stated when she first appeared. Her outgoings were greater than she had realised and this was why she had found it so difficult to keep up the repayments. He assured the court that she remained anxious to pay off her debt and she was now offering to pay £20 a month by direct debit.

The magistrates seemed uninterested in Hetty's change of circumstances. They kept pressing to know why she had not paid the £5 a week she had originally promised. They said that if she was now offering £20 a month that just proved that she could and should have been keeping up the £5 a week payments which amounted to almost the same. They found the new offer unacceptable.

Yet £5 a week is not quite the same as £20 a calendar month. Calendar months are all a few days longer than four weeks – except for February in a leap year. This means that £5 a week works out at £21.17p per calendar month.

Richard reckoned that if Hetty had offered to stick to £5 a week instead of £20 a month she would probably have been all right. As it was the council and the magistrates held out for their extra £1.17p a month.

Yet could not even Hetty have afforded that extra £1.17p a month? Should she not have given in gracefully? Possibly. Most decent people would say that in such circumstances it should have been the authorities that backed down over the negligible sum of £1.17p rather than a frail old lady. But that is not what happened. For want of that negligible £1.17 pence a month, Thanet magistrates sent Hetty back to prison.

Hetty's second night in Holloway was not as bad as the first. As Richard Wise said later, she was more or less punch drunk by now. At least she knew what to expect this time and the staff were kind to her. The magistrates had sent her down for nine days this time. The first time round they had given her ten days but as she had spent one night in Holloway on that occasion, they gave her nine days now.

Not that she stayed for nine days. Richard had her out the next morning. And there was a small recompense for the two days she had now spent in prison. Not only does England still send people to prison for debt but we use time inside as a form of payment.

When Hetty went to jail for the second time her outstanding debt to Thanet stood at over £500. Had she served the full nine days' term the debt would have been wiped out. In her case each day inside was 'worth' over £50. She had already spent two nights in Holloway so she had wiped over £100 off the total owing. Her outstanding debt now was just over £400.

For Hetty that was still a very substantial sum. Richard was determined that she should not end up in prison yet again. He decided to go to the High Court for permission to apply for a judicial review of the magistrates' decision to jail Hetty yet again. This time he would go down to Kent himself and see her.

Which was how he came to be sitting in her front room in Ramsgate, listening to her story and trying to work out exactly how much she could realistically offer to the hard men of Thanet. A few days later he wrote a witness statement detailing their conversation. The statement, written to back up the application for a judicial review in the high court, was vivid.

'She told me on a number of occasions that she just did not know what to do,' wrote Richard. 'She felt that she could not see any way out of her financial problems and was totally depressed at having been sent to prison on two occasions in situations in which she felt that she could not have done anything more to have paid her council tax.'

Yet it seemed that Thanet District Council still wanted to send Hetty to prison. In other words they were still not prepared to let the matter drop.

The application for a judicial review duly went ahead and it was granted. Only at this point did Thanet Council finally agree to let Hetty pay back what she owed at the rate of £20 a month. But it was clear that officials still felt that somehow Hetty had cheated them of their due. And they had another grievance against her and her legal advisers: the outstanding costs of all the court hearings.

Hetty had never owed them more than £600. Now her outstanding debt was under £500. The total legal costs of trying to make her pay, of sending her to prison not once but twice and of pursuing her even into the High Court now stood at some £7,500.

The battle over costs went back to the High Court. This time it was Ian Wise, Richard's brother, who took up the cudgels on

Hetty's behalf. The council wanted her to have to pay the full costs of the case. The sum was roughly equivalent to Hetty's entire income for a year.

In the Royal Courts of Justice a little group of people gathered in one of the courtrooms before Mr Justice Gage to play out the final act of Hetty's tale. The barrister representing Thanet rehearsed the bald details of the case: how she had fallen behind with the repayments of her debt; how attempts to reach a settlement with her had failed; how she had been sent to prison; how the magistrates had decided that 'she had deliberately failed to pay' and that she 'couldn't be trusted'. 'The public is entitled to expect that she should pay her dues which the courts have decided that she should be able to pay,' intoned Thanet's barrister.

Mr Justice Gage listened for a while and then asked both sets of lawyers if they could tell him what the 'bottom line' was in this case. He had to ask several times before he received an answer. The bottom line, it seemed, was the matter of costs. Thanet's barrister maintained that it would have been appropriate for Hetty's legal advisers to accept that she should have a costs order made against her – in other words that she should pay.

The judge did not seem happy. He wondered aloud why it had not been possible to reach a settlement earlier given that the costs might have to be borne by public funds.

Ian Wise said he would indeed have expected a settlement to be reached far earlier – within a fortnight of Hetty being given bail – but the local authority had insisted on pursuing its costs. He added that Hetty was now paying her council tax by standing order – including the arrears. He also made it clear that there was an argument for setting out the details of the case in full all over again because they had an important bearing on the costs.

Mr Justice Gage said he could see that there were questions of principle here. 'But,' he said, 'the public would be shocked by the amount this case has cost when the actual debt was just over £400.'

He went on to suggest that one possible outcome to the case would be that Thanet should not 'on reflection' pursue their costs order.

'I am not condemning the council,' he said, ' but this is very close to being an empty exercise and a waste of public money.'

Leaving them to mull over the import of his remarks, the judge adjourned the court for a short break.

When everyone returned Thanet Council's barrister stood up and announced that they would not pursue the order for costs.

Hetty's case is shocking in many ways. It raises questions about the mores of a society that allows town hall bureaucrats to secure the imprisonment of a confused old lady for the sake of a debt worth only a few hundred pounds. Even if the debt had been far greater, common decency suggests that no one of that age should be jailed unless they have committed a most serious crime.

Nobody doubts that local councils have a right and duty to reclaim debts on behalf of the community, including sums owed by poorer people. It is unfair on those who pay up despite being hard pressed financially if others in similar circumstances are let off more lightly. And town halls are justified in pursuing some debtors so as to make an example of them. Yet surely councillors and officials have some moral duty to temper administrative rigour with compassion.

Thanet Council is unrepentant. Its debt recovery manager says that 'it is the local authority that has suffered' at the hands of Hetty, not the other way round. 'The Council takes the view that this is clearly the case of an elderly lady who chooses to be cantankerous in failing to meet her liability to pay council tax,' he says. 'She clearly has the money with which to pay.' Did it not cross the minds of officials that the thousands being spent were out of all proportion given the size of the debt and Hetty's impoverished circumstances?

The officials of course would have been conscious that it would be unlikely in the extreme that they would pay a penalty for such a dubious use of public funds. The fact that they were hoping to make Hetty hand over the equivalent of her entire annual income to cover the costs they had incurred only compounds their offence – and that of their lawyers.

For there should be questions too about the size of the bills put in by the council's lawyers. *Why* should it cost £7,500 to pursue one old lady through the courts for a minor debt? What expertise is required?

Town hall officials may have been the prime movers in this shabby little tale but the elected councillors who are meant to oversee the bureaucrats must also take responsibility. Did they know what was happening? Did they approve it? In the case of the magistrates too, there is an issue about the prudent use of public funds. Leaving aside the callousness of jailing someone of Hetty's age, there is the cost of keeping her first in a police cell – one of the most expensive forms of imprisonment – and then of transporting her to Holloway prison in London. Hetty was there for only two nights on separate occasions yet inducting a prisoner into a jail is one of the most time-consuming and expensive parts of housing short-stay prisoners.

Meanwhile the very same police and prison officers who were taking Hetty off to jail were simultaneously doing their best to have her released. Even Kafka couldn't make it up.

All credit should go to those who tried to help Hetty – though it is notable that in her case it was the footsoldiers of the criminal justice system, the police and the prison staff, who acted with humanity in contrast to those who were in charge.

The irony – and the hypocrisy – is that Hetty's error was to get into a muddle over money. Yet the men in the town hall and the magistrates court seem to have been guilty of greater financial imprudence than she ever was. The fundamental question of how to deal with debtors like Hetty who can't pay as opposed to those who won't pay is one that can no longer be ignored and needs to be addressed urgently. It is a major issue that requires a fresh approach at different levels. There will be no easy answers.

We need to explore ways of ensuring that councils – both elected members and officials – are more discriminating in their treatment of debtors and more sensitive to those who are vulnerable. Perhaps pressure could be put on councils to run better checks on the status of debtors – their age, health and relevant financial circumstances – before deciding to go to court and demand a jail sentence. Prison should only ever be the last resort and then only for those who are being deliberately recalcitrant. Councils need to be more imaginative about investigating other, less draconian options for collecting debts. Fairer, more effective alternatives to prison might include attachment of earnings orders or direct deductions from benefit payments.

Ian Wise reckons that instead of sending Hetty to jail, Thanet could have asked for a charge to be made on her house so that when it was eventually sold the council could reclaim what it was owed from the sale price. Admittedly, the council would have to wait for payment because the house might not be sold until after Hetty's death. Yet, putting a charge on the house would have been kinder to her and more financially sensible for the council – far more so than spending £7,500 on lawyers' fees.

One way forward might be for councils to improve their links with outside agencies such as Citizens Advice Bureaux. The CABs could suggest alternative payment plans in difficult cases and they could also alert councils to clients whose efforts to clear their debts deserve sympathetic treatment. This is already starting to happen in some more progressive authorities.

There are already provisions for surcharging councils that spend public money in a disproportionate or impractical way. Richard had thought of referring Thanet Council to the District Auditor on precisely these grounds. In the end he did not do so. As he himself said, 'I probably should have done so, but I just have too many other things to do.'

Understandable enough – but maybe we need to find more effective ways of alerting the District Auditor to cases like Hetty's where the costs of pursuing the debtor exceed the debt itself by a substantial margin. Maybe also we should consider making councillors and their officials liable to personal penalties not just when they mis-spend public money but when they treat individuals in a way that is manifestly unfair and that cannot be justified on the grounds of public interest.

Mr Justice Gage talked of 'proportionality' when hearing the arguments about costs in Hetty's case. The concept of proportionality, of not using a hammer to crack a nut, is one that has been emphasised increasingly by the senior judges over the last few years. There must be a case for insisting that councils should have particular regard to proportionality when deciding how to deal with debtors.

Some might say that Hetty's tale is proof that the System, however slow and creaky, works. In the end, a way was found for her to discharge her debt and she was not forced to pay Thanet's £7,500 costs. Even more to the point, the Wise brothers were able to use the existing arrangements for judicial review by the higher courts to bring about a dramatic and permanent reduction in the number of people imprisoned each year for debt.

Yet to imagine that we should not be unduly concerned about cases like Hetty's because there are now fewer of them is like saying that it is alright for children to work down coal mines provided the numbers are kept within reason. There should be no cases like Hetty's in the twenty-first century. We should not tolerate vulnerable people being treated this way any more than we tolerate child labour.

Nor should we have to rely on the work of committed individuals like Richard and Ian Wise to bring about some measure of reform. We should be looking to new structures and a new approach. As Ian Wise says, 'there has been a dramatic reduction in the number of people in prison for debt, but there is always the possibility that the trend will go back upwards. The real answer to the problem is to change the law and bring us into line with all west European democracies and abolish imprisonment for debt.'

Richard is even cynical about what he and his brother have achieved. 'There is no doubt that the magistrates have changed and they are much less likely to send people down for debt,' he says. 'But that usually means that debts are written off so councils are becoming reluctant to use the courts. Instead they are hoping for out-of court settlements which can put people in debt for years. The councils don't care where the money comes from and people are encouraged to borrow to pay off what they already owe so they end up more deeply in debt. There is also a greater use of bailiffs. I sometimes think that things are worse now that they were before.'

Richard is dismayed at the increased use of bailiffs – the bailiff system is one that has been widely condemned. A CAB report said 'intimidation, harassment and excessive fees' were often the hallmarks of bailiffs who regularly 'lie and cheat their way into people's homes' and 'use threats of violence and prison to pressurise people into paying lump sums they can't afford'.

The Labour Government has said it wants reform of this system and even published its thoughts on bailiffs in a Green Paper at the end of 2001. Sadly, firm plans for change seem to have been put on hold indefinitely on the grounds that there is not enough legislative time to push changes through Parliament. The Lord Chancellor's Department is thinking of putting out guidelines as an interim measure but these will not have the force of law and will be a poor substitute for a Bailiffs Act. It is ironic that the Blairites can find time in 2002 for a Bill to ban foxhunting but not one that might help to end injustice for ordinary people who fall into debt. For the moment there is little hope for the likes of Hetty. Hetty's tale is an example of how the cheating classes are willing and able to squeeze the poor till the pips squeak. It may also demonstrate how financial imperatives in local government as elsewhere can supersede the old public service ethic that might once have insured a better balance between economics and compassion. It is a trend that impoverishes all of us.

7

THE HANDYMAN'S TALE

The great professions – lawyers, doctors and bankers – have a reputation as people of expertise and integrity. They may be expensive to hire, they may take their time and of course there is always the chance of a rotten apple in any barrel but most members of the public still believe they will be safe in the hands of the professionals. Ordinary people feel doubly secure if the firms they deal with are well-known names.

And what if the unthinkable should happen, if the service from a top-notch firm is incompetent or dishonest? There's the rub. For the reality is that in Britain today those who find themselves up against the established professions often have little chance of redress. Ask Tom Walker.

Tom is a plump, rubicund individual with hobbit-like qualities of good sense and good humour. He used to be a flourishing businessman. His company, Decanor, was one of the most successful DIY businesses in the area and Tom was proud of it. He boasted that he had the best selection of wallpaper and paints for miles around. And they brought in a good living. It never occurred to him that he might one day lose his cherished company amid a welter of incompetence and secretive dealing by so called professionals. Yet that is what happened with Decanor. Not that Decanor is the company's real name. Nor is Tom Walker the true name of this particular businessman. The real Tom Walker is still trying to get redress for what he has suffered. He is battling his way through the courts in pursuit of the professional men who he believes caused him to lose his business, his home and even, for a while, his health. It is because that legal battle is still being fought that we cannot give his real name. The story that follows is Tom's story, based on fact, but the names of the characters, firms and places, the dates and the amounts, have *all* been changed to protect the identity of those involved.

This is a tale of our times. It is a tale that should be a warning to anyone who thinks that relying on professional advice is a surefire way of protecting themselves from unnecessary risk.

Certainly Tom was not a man who believed in taking unnecessary risks. He always sought professional advice on financial matters and he dealt with some of the very best firms. After all, an international accountancy group or a major bank would never give dud advice to a customer asking for help with a problem. Would they? Admittedly the Enron scandal in the US has changed public perceptions about finance professionals. Enron's auditors, Arthur Anderson, stand accused of trying to camouflage the group's liabilities. When the truth started to emerge, the shock waves were felt worldwide as the giant group went belly up. But even today people do not expect that kind of debacle to happen in their own town, among professional people that they know. And the Enron disaster was ten years into the future when Tom's tale began.

The problem was Jack Wilkinson. As he drove home that night out of town and down the long, steeply forested hill leading into his home village, Tom felt a mixture of anger and puzzlement. Jack Wilkinson was his finance director and the two of them had been together for years. Jack, who always looked the part of the accountant, was greying now but he and Tom had been friends since they were young. Jack had played a part in building up Decanor almost from the time Tom had set up the company in the early 1980s.

When Tom had wanted to expand, it was Jack, the accountant, who had drawn up financial plans to put before the bank; it was Jack who had done the company books, who had taken a shareholding in the new business and who had eventually moved over from the accountancy firm where he worked to be the full time finance director. Until he came across that strange letter in the files, Tom had never had cause to question Jack.

As the pressure of homebound traffic forced him to slow down, Tom remembered how the two of them used to meet once or twice a week for a drink outside working hours.

Sometimes they would go to the Bull, Tom's local, sometimes they would go to the small market town up the road which was generously endowed with pubs. Over the years, as Decanor grew and prospered, moving to bigger premises and opening branches in nearby towns, there had rarely been any serious disagreements between the two men. Until Tom found the letter.

It happened one morning when Jack was away. Tom was in the office sorting through some papers when he noticed the letter. Dated a few months before in early 1990, it was written to Jack from Decanor's accountants. What was startling was that it talked of Tom having a loan from the company. Tom read it through again. There was no doubt what the letter was saying, yet he was certain that he had no such loan. As Jack well knew — and so did the accountants for that matter — Decanor was doing well. So why should Jack imagine that Tom would want to take out a loan from his own business? Any payments made to him should have been regarded as salary or director's fees or dividends. Not a loan. And who was supposed to have authorised this loan account?

Tom touched the brakes as he approached the lane where he

would turn off for home. It was good that he knew the road so well for he could not help going over and over the events of the last few months in his mind. He had never had any proper answers to his questions. He had asked the accountants about the letter and about this loan he was supposed to have from his own company. They had advised him to discuss it with Jack. Tom had tackled Jack. Jack had claimed it was just an accounting procedure and there was nothing to worry about.

Yet the more Tom had thought about it the uneasier he had become. It was not as if the loan account was the only unexplained matter. There was the ongoing mystery of the company's stock losses that had been rising steadily to the point where they were wiping out a large chunk of the profits. Tom was not computer literate and it was Jack who recorded all stocks on the computer. He had seemed to be as concerned as anyone yet despite endless checking by Tom and his staff, there were always larger amounts of paint and wallpaper on the print out than in the stock rooms. Nobody could work out where the missing stock was going. Jack had announced that they were going to have to write off £40,000 in stock losses that year. Tom reckoned that altogether they must have lost some £150,000 in missing stock over ten years. He had written to Decanor's accountants again about the loan account and also about the stock write-offs. He had asked for a reply to be sent to his home address rather than the office. Still there were no satisfactory answers.

Then had come the bust up. It was triggered by a comparatively trivial, routine matter. Alan Green, Tom's marketing director, had just returned from a buying trip on the continent. A solidly built man with a pleasant, open face and dry sense of humour, he had dropped in on Tom and asked him to authorise his expenses for the trip. Tom duly signed them but to Alan's astonishment and indignation, Jack had refused to issue a cheque.

A meeting in Tom's office had degenerated into a shouting match and Jack had thrown down his keys and stormed out of the room. Tom sighed as he reached the entrance to his own drive and swung the wheel over. He simply did not feel comfortable working with Jack any more. He would discuss it with his partner Christine but his mind was made up. It no longer mattered that they'd been together for so long. Jack Wilkinson would have to go.

As he reached the end of the drive the lighted windows of his home looked even more inviting than usual.

Downstairs, in the large, farmhouse-style kitchen, Tom and Christine discussed what to do as they sat over dinner, watched closely by Monty and Winston, their ginger cats, and Tiggy, their mongrel dog.

Tiggy, fondly described by Tom as 'daft as a brush', could usually wheedle a titbit from his master. But tonight Tom was distracted. He told Christine that he had made up his mind to rid himself of Jack Wilkinson.

Christine, dark haired and dark eyed, nodded slowly. She felt that Tom would be doing the right thing but warned him to tread carefully.

'Don't worry,' said Tom. 'I'll ring the solicitors first thing in the morning and see what they say. I'd better talk to the accountants too.' He patted Christine's hand. 'I shan't do anything rash.'

Chadband's, Tom's solicitors, were quite clear what action Tom should take if he wanted shot of Jack Wilkinson. So were his accountants, Kenge & Tulkinghorn. The lawyers and accountants were unequivocal in their advice: the only way to cut all ties with Jack would be to buy him out.

Whatever Tom's concerns, whatever the reasons for the breakdown in his relationship with his old friend and partner, there was no evidence whatever that Jack had done anything improper. More to the point Jack Wilkinson owned 40 per cent of the company. Although Tom owned the majority 60 per cent stake, there was no way of severing Wilkinson's links with Decanor unless he would agree to sell his holding to Tom.

The lawyers and accountants were adamant about that. Such a deal would require considerable work if it were to be legally and financially watertight but the arrangements could be made if Tom so wished.

Tom did wish.

Agreeing a buy-out deal proved long, difficult and costly. Wilkinson's initial reaction was to hit the roof. He and Tom had another slanging match in the company's main office with Jack angrily walking out again. Tom was sure the customers in the showroom downstairs must have heard them shouting.

The row only made him more determined to proceed. Eventually Jack agreed to a deal – if the price was right and if the details were satisfactory.

Independent accountants were called in to value his 40 per cent stake in Decanor. They looked at the books, took account of the company's £5m worth of assets and its £3.5m annual turnover and decided that Wilkinson's shareholding was worth some £420,000.

The £420,000 figure seemed to be acceptable to everyone including, most importantly, Decanor's bank. John Gridley, the bank's corporate manager for the area, was one of the first people Tom went to see when he decided to buy out Jack. John had no objections in principle but he insisted that the bank must be closely involved to ensure there were no hiccups. He also wanted to bring in Blowers Jarndyce, the bank's lawyers and one of the biggest solicitors in the area.

Tom had no worries about the bank playing a major role. If anything the bank's presence would be an additional guarantee that things would be done properly. And it was understandable that the bank should want to be involved because it was giving Decanor a medium-term loan of £0.75m. Tom reckoned that for

John Gridley, a young, smooth-spoken man who was on his way up the career ladder at the bank, this was about the biggest deal he had ever done. Decanor was going to use some of the loan money to pay off Jack Wilkinson and to cover the costs of the lawyers and financial experts who were going to draw up the arrangements. The rest of the loan would go to pay off the mortgage on one of Decanor's properties.

Meanwhile Tom's solicitors and accountants had opened negotiations with the Inland Revenue. They explained to Tom that because the deal was being done through the company it would mean Decanor buying its own shares. Normally this was strictly illegal because it would enable companies to manipulate their own share prices. The only way it could be done was if the Inland Revenue gave special permission.

After what seemed to Tom like endless negotiations, the Inland Revenue eventually gave clearance for the deal. The lawyers were able to draw up heads-of-agreement in February 1991. And Jack, to Tom's great relief, finally left the company the same month.

Even then it took another eight months before everything could be finally sealed and settled.

Almost at the last minute there was a hitch. Jack's side had brought in Krooks Carstone, an accounting firm big enough to be almost a household name. They wanted to make some changes so that Jack would not have to pay so much tax on the deal. Tom said that he had no objections provided he and Decanor were not worse off in any way than they would have been before.

Jack Wilkinson was not at the final, crucial meeting when the deal was done. But given the rows they had had, Tom was not surprised when Jack failed to show.

It was a cold October day in 1991. Everyone, bar Wilkinson, gathered at the upstairs offices of Chadband's to finalise the deal. Alan Green, sitting with Tom at the big meeting table, asked where Jack was. Nobody took any notice. Everyone was too busy chatting, shuffling papers and making room for new arrivals.

'Where *is* Jack?' hissed Alan in Tom's ear.

'I don't know and I'm not bothered,' replied Tom. 'He's got his representatives here and the place is so thick with lawyers and accountants that I don't think we need worry.'

It was indeed an impressive turnout. John Gridley from the bank was at the head of the table. He was flanked by people from Blowers Jarndyce.

On one side of the table, representing Jack Wilkinson's interests, were two men from Krooks Carstone, the international accountancy firm called in by Jack's solicitors. In addition there were Tom's company accountants, Kenge & Tulkinghorn, who were represented by James Carboy, plus people from Chadband's, his solicitors. For good measure Tom had brought along his son Duncan, who worked at the company and who was sitting next to him.

On his other side Alan Green had started whispering in his ear again.

'Tom, who are those two men? I've never set eyes on them before.'

Tom looked over at them and shook his head.

'Don't know,' he said. 'Perhaps someone'll introduce us in a minute.'

'Could somebody introduce us to these two gentlemen,' said Alan, raising his voice and addressing the room. But the hubbub was still at its height. Again nobody answered him. He lowered his voice and turned back to Tom.

'Those two blokes could be a couple of window cleaners for all we know,' he said.

Tom looked at him for a moment and his pink cheeks creased into a grin.

'I don't think they'll be window cleaners, Alan,' he said. 'Window cleaners only charge a couple of pounds an hour. You have to be a very expensive lawyer or accountant to have been invited to this meeting.'

'D'you know yet what the full cost of setting up this deal is going to be?' asked Alan.

'I still haven't got the final figure but it's like I told you before. Between them these beggars are charging me over £80,000 to organise this buy-out. The only consolation is that at that price we shouldn't have any mistakes.'

Alan pulled a face. At which point one of the said beggars, a senior solicitor, called the meeting to order.

Tom was expecting to hand over a cheque for £420,000, the price agreed for Jack's shares. He presumed that the other side would give him Decanor share certificates in return. He had thought of burning the share certificates when he got home. It would mark the final severing of his relations with Jack Wilkinson.

In the event the meeting turned out rather differently. Instead of a cheque for the full sum of £420,000, a banker's draft for £354,278 was produced. John Gridley from the bank pushed it down to the table to the two men designated by Alan as window cleaners. The two strangers did not identify themselves. Nobody else saw fit to introduce them to Tom and Alan.

The meeting was told that a bond had been set up for the rest of the money – some £65,000.

No share certificates were handed over. Tom was disappointed but he did not question the arrangements. The experts must know what they were doing.

As he drove home he felt a sense of relief. He was rid of Wilkinson at last and now he could move forward. The short October day was ending as he reached home.

The hill that rises above the village stood out blackly against the fading sky. Beneath it the lights of the houses glowed warm and welcoming. The Bull was almost opposite Tom's house. He decided to look in for a quick pint by way of celebration. He was thankful that it was all done and dusted.

Almost a year passed before there was even an inkling of trouble. Even then it seemed as though it was a mix-up. Or a technicality. Or both.

It was the end of the summer and Tom and Christine were in Italy on holiday. Alan Green was holding the fort at Decanor.

One morning Kenge & Tulkinghorn, the company's accountants, sent over one of their people to go through the books. It was a regular event because at that time the company was paying the tax for all its employees on a monthly basis.

The man from Kenge & Tulkinghorn, a youngish guy, put his head round Alan's door and asked if he could have a cheque for the Inland Revenue.

'Sure,' said Alan. 'Come in – I'll do it now. How much do we owe? It's usually twelve or fifteen thousand, isn't it.'

"Fraid not, Mr Green. I need a cheque for £150,000 this time.'

Alan blinked at him. For a moment there was dead silence. Then the older man let out a disbelieving roar.

'You cannot be serious. You've made a mistake.'

The young man's face clouded. 'I'm sorry, Mr Green, but there's no mistake. It's £150,000 the Revenue wants. This isn't the income tax for your staff. It's Advanced Corporation Tax. You'll get it all back in a fortnight.'

'I will not get it back in a fortnight because I'm not paying it,' growled Alan. 'What's more, I think you'll have some explaining to do when Tom hears about this. He's back from Italy in a few days. He'll sort it out then.'

James Carboy, one of the senior people at Kenge & Tulkinghorn, took the trouble to come round to Decanor later that day. A tall, middle-aged man with a precise manner, assured Alan that there was nothing to worry about. He had been at the meeting to finalise the Jack Wilkinson buy-out the previous year and he said the tax demand was to do with that.

It was just an accountancy procedure – the company really would get the money back in two weeks' time.

Alan Green remained adamant. No way was he going to authorise a cheque for £150,000.

Tom and Christine arrived home at the end of August. They had had a great time. Now they were relaxed and fit. It was the last time they were to be so well and so content. The dark years were about to begin.

Alan drove over to see them as soon as he knew they were home. Urgently he asked about the tax bill. He found Tom as dumb-struck as he had been.

Tom rang the bank. He rang James Carboy at Kenge & Tulkinghorn. He arranged to see both of them the next day.

John Gridley from the bank came round to Decanor's offices at ten o'clock the next morning. He heard Tom out and tried to calm him down. Tom's face was becoming redder by the minute as he demanded to know what on earth was going on, why nobody had told him that there was a huge tax demand in the offing.

Tom also talked to James Carboy. He learned nothing new. Carboy confirmed that the demand for £150,000 was for Advanced Corporation Tax and that it related to the Jack Wilkinson deal. He assured Tom that he would get the money back. Like John Gridley, he told him not to worry.

The assurances of Messrs Gridley and Carboy had precisely the opposite effect on Tom to that intended. He and Alan became more worried and more suspicious. Nobody seemed able to give them an adequate explanation of what was happening. They decided to take a tough line. They would not pay a penny until the whole mess had been sorted out.

The next move came from Gridley. He told Tom the bank wanted to bring in a specialist accountant, a man called Edward Guppy. He would deal with the ACT.

Edward Guppy, a large, fair-haired Scot arrived with an assistant. The two took up residence in Decanor's offices and set to work. After only two weeks Edward reported to Tom that the whole matter was far more serious than any of them had thought.

He said that the Inland Revenue's original demand had been for £140,000 in Advance Corporation Tax. The trouble was that the figure was growing dramatically because of interest charges and penalties for non-payment.

The Revenue now wanted £180,000. If they did not get it they could send in the bailiffs.

The extraordinary thing was that it seemed the Revenue had sent in its first tax demand nearly a year earlier not long after the deal with Jack Wilkinson. Nobody had told Tom of that tax demand. Yet after a year's wait, it was hardly surprising if the taxman's patience was wearing thin. John Gridley and Edward Guppy advised Tom to set up a separate fund with money that could be earmarked for the Inland Revenue if it became necessary.

They decided that they needed to put in a total of £195,000.

There was only one drawback. Decanor was a successful company but not so profitable that it had £195,000 sloshing around in spare cash. What it did have was a £0.75m loan from the bank.

So how were Tom and Alan going to raise enough money to pay the taxman?

They did it by having a family whip round.

Tom's son and his wife remortgaged their house and put £35,000 into the pot. Tom's brother Ian chipped in with £15,000.

Alan Green's parents raised £15,000 from granny bonds – money for their retirement that they could ill afford but they lent it willingly.

It was a magnificent and loyal effort. What is more the Walker and Green families nearly pulled it off.

Then, without any real warning, the bank put Decanor's £0.75m loan on instant recall.

John Gridley at the bank tried to make the news as palatable as possible. He explained that it did not mean the bank was going to call in the loan immediately – just that it would be able to do so if it wished. In other words Decanor was completely at the bank's mercy. If Tom did not do exactly as he was told, the bank would foreclose on his company.

Nor was that all. From now on the loan was to be front loaded. This meant that instead of paying back both the interest and the capital over the period of the loan, Decanor would have to pay all the interest first. This would ensure that the bank got its profit. Decanor's trading record and its assets meant that the Bank was certain to receive its £0.75m capital in due course – no matter what happened to Tom Walker.

John Gridley told Tom that Decanor was looking like a 'rudderless ship'. Regretfully, he said, the bank had little choice but to take a tough line with the company.

By now a prudent man would surely have made direct contact with the people who seemed to be the cause of all his difficulties – the Inland Revenue. They were the people who had given clearance for the Jack Wilkinson deal and now it was they who were demanding a huge cheque for Advanced Corporation Tax. Today Tom Walker admits that he was naive not to call the Revenue himself and demand an explanation.

But that is with hindsight. At the time he put his trust in the assortment of bankers, accountants and lawyers who were advising him.

They were the experts. They would know best how to deal with the Taxman. He would do what they told him.

It took a great deal to shake Tom's faith in his so-called experts. He and Alan Green were encouraged to think that maybe Edward Guppy could sort things out. They believed that he was working for the bank. Tom and Alan say that only later did they discover that Decanor was paying for Guppy's services at the rate of £400 a day. The company was also meeting the costs of his assistant at £250 a day.

Tom says that when he queried these huge fees he was told that unless Guppy and his aide were kept on, the bank would have to liquidate Decanor.

Then came evidence of dubious dealing that even the trusting Tom Walker could not ignore.

In October 1992, following a meeting with the lawyers, the accountants and Edward Guppy, he was shown a letter from the Inland Revenue to Kenge & Tulkinghorn, his accountants. It was about the deal between Decanor and Jack Wilkinson agreed at the big meeting a year earlier. The deal had been illegal.

If the letter itself was devastating for Tom and Alan so too was the date at the top of it. The Inland Revenue had written to Kenge & Tulkinghorn eight months before, in February 1992.

'At the time,' said James Carboy of Kenge & Tulkinghorn, 'we decided that you had no need to know.'

Tom could hardly believe what he was hearing.

'Who is "we"?' he demanded furiously.

'All of us,' said James Carboy, 'including the bank.'

The deal that Tom had done with Jack Wilkinson and that had been approved at such expense by so many lawyers, accountants and bankers had been illegal from the outset.

Unbeknown to Tom and Alan the transaction done in that

crowded upper room back in October 1991 was not exactly in line with the deal agreed by the Inland Revenue. Yet failure to follow the precise terms and conditions laid down by the Revenue in such cases means the Taxman's approval is automatically withdrawn and the whole deal becomes invalid. What is more the Revenue is always tough on tax scams – which is what the new arrangement was.

What had happened was the result of Krooks Carstone's last minute advice to Jack Wilkinson. Krooks Carstone, the accountants brought in by Jack's lawyers, said that he would be able to save himself a substantial amount of tax if some changes were made to the agreed settlement. Why the bank, the bank's solicitors, Tom's accountants and Tom's solicitors all went along with the new arrangements is unclear. Maybe they were overawed by the Krooks Carstone name and its international reputation. At all events the net result was that the whole agreement became void in the eyes of the Taxman. And Decanor, Tom's company, became liable for ACT – Advanced Corporation Tax. Had everyone stuck to the original plan as approved by the Revenue, there would have been no liability for ACT.

All this would have been bad enough but there was another aspect that was even worse. The deal drawn up by Krooks Carstone also breached the Companies' Act – big time. It meant that Tom and Alan, innocent victims though they were, became liable to up to seven years in prison.

The key to it all was that Jack Wilkinson had already disposed of his Decanor shares before that final meeting where he was supposed to sell them back to Decanor. As part of Krooks Carstone's complicated tax avoidance scheme he had put the shares into a nominee company, a wholly owned offshore company specially set up by Krooks Carstone in the Isle of Man.

This meant he was selling Tom shares he no longer owned.

It also explained the two strangers at the meeting to finalise the deal. They were the representatives of the nominee company. At the meeting in the city they were the men who took the banker's draft for £352,000 after it had been handed over by John Gridley of the bank.

Tom had known from the start that Wilkinson was worried about having to pay tax on the money he would receive for selling his Decanor shares back to the company. Tom also knew that Wilkinson had called in Krooks Carstone to see if there was a way of minimising the tax bill. He was even aware that there had been talk of Wilkinson putting his money offshore but he had said at the time that he did not object as long as the arrangement was not detrimental to him or Decanor.

As long as his array of professional advisers assured him the deal was above board – as they did – he was happy. With firms of Krooks Carstone' standing looking after Wilkinson's interests, he was not even worried that his erstwhile finance director would embroil him and Decanor in anything dubious.

The Inland Revenue had realised early on that the Decanor deal was suspect.

The deal was agreed in October 1991. The Revenue's letter to Kenge & Tulkinghorn, spelling out exactly why the deal was an illegal tax scam, was written in early February 1992. To the Taxman, it seemed as if the whole deal had been designed simply to give Wilkinson a tax advantage. It was this detailed letter that James Carboy at Kenge & Tulkinghorn withheld from Tom for another eight months. Why was Tom kept in the dark for so long? Perhaps the answer is not hard to find.

Tom Walker had paid out a total of over £80,000 in fees to the so-called professionals who had advised him. If Kenge & Tulkinghorn, the bank, Krooks Carstone and all the other firms who had set up the original deal had admitted that they had made a huge error then Tom Walker would have demanded his money back – and might have sued as well.

The lawyers, accountants and bankers would have been exposed as being utterly incompetent.

The whole episode could have become a local scandal possibly with reputations damaged and business lost. How much better to play down the whole sorry mess.

What Tom's case shows is that a professional reputation or a well-known name is not always a guarantee of competence or of straight dealing. Nor is there any guarantee that professionals will come clean immediately if they discover they have make a mistake. That is the line that the lawyers and the bankers and the accountants like to give the rest of us. How often are we told that if we go to the professionals we will be guaranteed high standards of integrity and performance?

Tom, for example, continued to put his trust in the professionals even after he had seen the letter from the Inland Revenue showing that the Decanor deal was illegal. Yet seeing that letter in October 1992 was not the culmination of his troubles. If anything it was only the beginning.

By now Tom's illusions about Kenge & Tulkinghorn, Edward Guppy, John Gridley and all his other advisers were at last starting to be stripped away.

He decided to go to another firm of solicitors that he hoped would be truly independent and who were far enough away not to be mixed up in the Decanor deal. He found a firm on the other side of the country.

Alan Green went to see them. They heard Alan out and told him that in their opinion there was cause for concern at the very least. On the basis of what he had told them, it seemed on the face of it that Decanor 'had received negligent advice from one or other or possibly all of its advisers'. For an upfront fee of £3,000, the solicitors would investigate further.

They would also bring in a firm of independent auditors who could look at the books and find out what had really been happening.

When Tom told the bank of the plan for these new solicitors

to bring in independent auditors, John Gridley and Edward Guppy told him not to bother. They would stop him.

They would not sign the cheque for the upfront £3,000.

A few days later on a grey October morning Alan Green called into the main Decanor office. He found Edward Guppy there with Tom and his son, Duncan. The conversation was brief and brutal.

'John Gridley says you're an expensive luxury we can't afford,' said Guppy. 'You're out. Now sod off.'

Alan stormed out of the room closely followed by Guppy who ran and typed out a letter of resignation. He told Alan to sign it, warning him that if he refused he would leave with nothing.

Alan signed.

There was nothing Tom could do to save Alan. He knew that if he challenged Guppy and Gridley they would foreclose on the company. He was worried about his other staff losing their jobs.

Every morning he was physically sick.

The next eighteen months were a nightmare for Tom. Edward Guppy effectively took over the company. Many of the people Decanor dealt with seemed to think that Guppy was acting as a receiver or administrator for the bank. No matter how often or how forcefully Tom demanded to be told what was happening, he felt that he was always left in the dark.

He remained chairman of Decanor but he was a figurehead only and he knew it. He was not even sure whether Decanor had paid the Advanced Corporation Tax that the Taxman had demanded. When he asked about it, he was told that negotiations were in hand and that it was being sorted. He was also told to stop 'interfering' and to be more co-operative. John Gridley even said that he must learn to accept that the rest of them were doing what was good for him. It did not seem so to Tom.

Not that Tom did not try to help himself. He went to see his MP and explained that he was liable to be sent to prison for breaching the Companies' Act when all he had ever done was to follow the advice of professionals – accountants, lawyers and the bank. His MP wrote to the Department of Trade and Industry and received a letter from the head of the Companies House Executive Agency. The letter noted that although Tom had evidently contravened the Companies' Act, he claimed to have acted in good faith on the advice of solicitors and accountants. The letter went on to say that the boss of the Companies House Agency had no power to absolve Tom but did not plan to take any further action against him. If, however, there were to be a complaint from a member of the public, the situation would have to be reviewed.

Tom's family and friends promptly complained. An official duly came to see Tom and Christine to investigate. It was a bizarre episode, like something out of the *Yes Minister* TV series. The man sat at their dining room table looking through the papers they had provided but he was so short sighted that he had to hold all the documents within a few inches of his face. When he opened his important looking briefcase, it proved to contain nothing but a sandwich and a Twix bar yet he refused all their offers of refreshment. Tom and Christine were much amused – at least they would have been had it not been for the outcome.

The officer duly reported on their case. He said he could find no evidence of misfeasance.

Tom was told that the abortive deal with Jack Wilkinson was going to be resurrected and this time it was hoped that it would be done properly – the way it had first been planned before Krooks Carstone suggested alterations. This time it should win the approval of the Inland Revenue just as the original deal had done.

The share sale was duly re-enacted in April 1994. The idea was that the £354,278 that Decanor had paid for Wilkinson's shares should be returned to the company, whether by Jack or the nominee company Tom was never sure. As was now usual,

Edward Guppy took total charge of the meeting called to oversee the new deal.

It duly went through. After that the *coup de grâce* was not long in coming for Tom.

A few weeks after the deal was done, Tom went into the office to check some papers in the safe. Guppy confronted him.

He told him he must sell Decanor to his chief rival – Rouncewell's DIY.

'If you don't sell out the bank'll foreclose on you,' Guppy said. 'That'll mean that you personally will go bankrupt and you could go to prison. You must sell out.'

Tom stood there, looking at him. He knew he should not have been surprised but he found it hard to believe what he was hearing. Suddenly Guppy advanced across the room towards him and snatched the safe keys from Tom's hand.

Tom came alive again. He protested. He raged at Guppy. He swore that he would put a stop to it all.

A few minutes later the door opened and three men came in. Tom had never seen them before but Guppy seemed to be expecting them. He handed one of them the keys to the safe. The man thanked him and produced a tool kit. He started sizing up the keys. The other two locksmiths came over and sized up Tom.

'Perhaps you could show Mr Walker out,' said Guppy.

While the first man started changing the lock on the safe, his colleagues took Tom by the arm, one on each side, and started escorting him from the building.

Tom duly sold Decanor to Rouncewell's DIY, his chief competitor, although he feels the word 'sell' is something of a misnomer in this case.

'I gave it to them,' he says today.

He certainly believes that Decanor was hugely undervalued. The company owned two properties. The main one had been valued at £1 million two years earlier and the other one at £400,000.

Subsequently, there had been bigger offers. Significantly, the main site in town had retail planning permission which meant that potentially it was considerably more valuable – particularly as the area was booming.

What Tom wanted to do was sell one of the properties, pay off the bank loan with the money and still have some premises to carry on trading. But the bank would not agree. He was told he must sell to his rival for £300,000. It was what is known as a 'fire sale'.

Interestingly, perhaps, Rouncewell's DIY was a customer of the bank.

After he lost Decanor, Tom had a nervous breakdown. For weeks he was physically ill and mentally incapable of coping with any kind of problem. It was Christine who brought him back from the brink of total desperation.

Though still profoundly depressed, he was beginning to regain some control over himself. One evening as they sat in the dining room at home looking out through the long Georgian window over the lawn, Christine told him that he had to make a choice. He could give in and accept that the forces ranged against him were too powerful to resist. If he felt he had to do that Christine would understand. She would help him to put the whole thing behind him and try to build a new life.

Or he could fight back. He believed that he had been cheated of his due. What was more he had a file full of papers documenting what had happened to him.

Perhaps he could go upstairs, bring down the file and start sorting through those papers.

At least he would be able to see if he might have a legal case against Wilkinson, Gridley, Guppy, Carboy and the rest of them.

Reluctantly Tom fetched the files. That night he sat at the polished oak table and laboriously started to look through every letter, every report. He was surprised at how much written evidence there seemed to be.

He decided that he would take his battle to the courts. He would get his money back. He had nothing left so he would have to get legal aid. But one way or another he would have justice no matter how long it took . . .

Naive he may have been, but at each stage of his slow fall towards ruin Tom turned to people who could and should have given him the kind of expert, objective advice that would have protected him. Each one of them failed him.

The battery of lawyers, accountants and bankers who set up the deal between Tom's company and Jack Wilkinson included firms who would claim to be among the finest in the region if not in Britain. A couple of them had international standing. Yet they allowed the disaster to happen.

When Alan and Tom finally reached the point of being able to sue those who had let them down so badly, their lawyers were able to demand access to the other side's documents. One of the documents disclosed to them showed that Blowers Jarndyce, the bank's lawyers, had warned the bank *before the deal went through* that it might be illegal. If Blowers Jarndyce realised that the deal might be illegal – and they were at the meeting when it was finalised – why did they not warn Tom and Alan? Why did they not alert some of the other lawyers and accountants involved?

Perhaps the answer is that Blowers Jarndyce was working for the bank not for Tom Walker. The firm may therefore have felt it had no 'duty of care' to him. Moral obligations do not always seem to feature much in the conduct of professionals in Britain today.

But what of the bank? Why did the bank not stop the deal if it had been told that it could be illegal? The evidence suggests that the bank simply ignored Blowers Jarndyce's advice. During Tom's protracted legal battle over the Decanor case, the courts appointed forensic accountants to look into the evidence. Late in 2001, almost ten years since the meeting in that upstairs room where Tom's troubles began, one of the senior people at the forensic accountants wrote a report to the Legal Services Commission. Having sifted through the papers that the bank had been forced to release, he wrote in his report:

> There is correspondence in the bank's papers from
> Blowers Jarndyce stating that the revised deal broke
> sections 153 to 158 of the Companies' Act 1985. This
> letter is dated 11 October 1991. On 12 October 1991,
> John Gridley wrote back to Blowers Jarndyce and said that
> the deal was acceptable . . . The bank had been advised
> that the revised deal did not comply with the previously
> obtained clearances from Capital Taxes office of the
> Inland Revenue. John Gridley of the bank advised both
> Blowers Jarndyce and Decanor that the deal was
> acceptable.

Other papers disclosed by order of the courts reveal how quickly the Wilkinson deal had gone wrong. The documents show that the Inland Revenue had written to Tom's accountants, Kenge & Tulkinghorn, questioning the buy-out deal as early as November 1991 – less that three weeks after the fateful meeting where the settlement had been agreed.

The papers also show that Kenge & Tulkinghorn ignored the taxman's crucial letter of 15 February 1992 which said that the deal was evidently designed 'to obtain nothing other than a tax advantage' for Jack Wilkinson. The taxman finished that letter by asking if Kenge & Tulkinghorn 'would care to comment on my observations'. Evidently they did not care to comment. Four months later the taxman was forced to write again.

In a letter to Kenge & Tulkinghorn dated 30 May 1992 and headed Decanor Ltd, he inquires: 'I wonder whether you have now had an opportunity to consider the points which I raised in my letter of 15 February 1992 concerning the validity of the company purchase of its own shares. May I have your report.'

The letter goes on to list a series of questions to which the Inland Revenue wanted answers but again Kenge & Tulkinghorn were tardy in the extreme when it came to replying. The documentation shows that not until 8 September 1992, three months later, did the accounting firm send a terse note back to the Inland Revenue thanking them for their letter of 30 May and asking them to note that any further correspondence regarding Decanor should be addressed to Krooks Carstone.

It was only at this point that Kenge & Tulkinghorn bothered to give Tom some inkling of what was happening. Tom says that, even then, neither they nor the bank nor his solicitors made any attempt to explain or to apologise for giving him dud advice or to pay back the £80,000 plus that they had taken from him in fees. Nor, once they realised things had gone wrong, did they try to extricate him from the difficulties they had helped to create.

What makes the whole thing all the more puzzling and all the more galling for Tom is that Decanor had been doing so well. Gross profit margins were up. The decline in the housing market that was such a feature of the early 1990s actually helped boost business for Decanor rather than damaging it. As Tom says, people who cannot afford to move house opt instead to improve the homes they already have. And the DIY market offers retailers good returns. Tom also had some sizeable contracts to supply paints and wallpapers to big users including some retail chains. Even his stock losses had shrunk dramatically, down to a few hundred pounds instead of many thousands.

Yet few companies, however successful, could withstand a huge, unexpected tax demand plus loan repayments that were also substantially and unexpectedly increased. This is the position that Tom's company found itself in and all the evidence suggests that the bank had helped to put it there. So why did the bank not take a far more sympathetic view of Decanor's difficulties?

Today it is scarcely possible to open the business section of a newspaper without reading about some big industrialist endorsing the need for companies to show a greater sense of corporate social responsibility. In the case of major lenders, like the banks, that surely means they should do everything possible to help small- and medium-sized companies to stay in business – not pull the rug from under them at the earliest opportunity.

Do the banks not have a duty to safeguard their own interests and their own shareholders? Of course they do. But there is something very wrong when a bank is able to put a quick buck for its shareholders first and its responsibility to its customers and to the wider community nowhere. What is needed is a better balance between the two. If Tom's case is anything to go by, that balance is not always being struck.

Yet could Tom's case be a one-off? Might he have contributed more to his own difficulties than at first appears? Could any shortcomings at the bank not be the fault of a few individuals rather than a great institution? Maybe. All three of these possibilities could be true though it is not credible to imagine that a major bank leaves customer policy entirely in the hands of local managers. What happens at local level must reflect attitudes at the top.

What should concern all of us is the possibility that too many of our great financial institutions are now floating in an internationalist sea, where their priorities are international and where the interests of smaller businesses in local areas really do not count for very much.

There is one singular point about the way Tom was forced to sell Decanor to Rouncewell's DIY. One of the forensic accountants appointed by the courts believes that the retail planning permission that had been granted to Decanor's main site in town gave the properly a potential value far greater than the sale price to Rouncewell's DIY.

'With its retail planning permission, Decanors's main site could have been worth, potentially, in excess of £8 million,' he says.

*

After the forced sale of Decanor it took Tom some time to recover and to start rebuilding his life. His decision to pursue those who had, in his view, wronged him did not prove a straightforward option. For some eight years now he has been wrestling with the British justice system. It has not been easy. He has not come to the end of the road. And at times he has felt as if the legal system was operating in some other, more surreal world.

By the time he embarked on a court battle, Tom had little money of his own and he applied successfully for legal aid. But as the dispute continued through the courts he kept finding his legal aid had been withdrawn and he would have to re-apply. He is suing the bank, Kenge & Tulkinghorn and Edward Guppy. One of his tasks has been to persuade the courts to order the bank and others to disclose documents about the case. Some documents have been released but, at the time of writing, Tom and the forensic accountants still have not seen the all important Decanor bank statements for the early nineties that show what money went through the company and when.

He has been back to court, on his own without a lawyer because his legal aid has been stopped, to ask for the accounts to be disclosed. He was turned down. At the end of his hearing, which had lasted only an hour, the other side's solicitors asked for costs against Tom. He protested that he did not have the money – only to be told by the judge: 'If you have not got the money to pay you really should not be doing this'.

The judge ordered him to pay the other side's costs which were summarily assessed at over £500. 'Those have to be paid within fourteen days, Mr Walker,' said the judge. 'So you will have to find some money from somewhere.'

As the old adage says, British justice is like the Ritz – open to everyone. As with the Ritz, those who are not wealthy, those who have been ruined by the System, should realise that there is no place for them. The ironic thing is that the System has tried to help from time to time. Tom has had thousands of pounds worth of legal aid over the years. It is all paid for by the taxpayer and all largely wasted when the System pulls the plug on him, as it periodically does, before he has had a full and fair hearing.

The way legal aid operates within the justice system is by turns farcical and tragic. It seems to serve neither the taxpayer nor the men and women who look to the courts to give them a fair hearing. Tom is not the only one pursuing his former bank. Alan Green, his erstwhile marketing manager who was so abruptly sacked, is suing the bank and Edward Guppy for wrongful dismissal. In 2002, his case went to court for what was expected to be a five-day hearing. Alan says that half way through he was told by his own lawyers that the case was not going well, that his legal aid had been withdrawn and that if he wished to continue it would cost him up to £10,000 – money he does not have. He had no choice but to withdraw.

Tom had the same lawyers as Alan. On the basis of Alan's aborted, half-heard case, the lawyers wrote to the Legal Services Commission which is responsible for handing out legal aid, saying that Tom's legal aid should be stopped too. And Tom's legal aid was stopped.

Now it is perfectly reasonable for the Legal Services Commission to monitor legally-aided cases to ensure that the taxpayers' money is not being wasted. But what kind of justice system is it that allows a case to go to court and then stops it half way through before *both* sides have been heard? What kind of justice system is it that allows a case to fall not on the say-so of an impartial judge who has heard *both sides* but on the say-so of a hired lawyer who is second guessing the judge? What kind of justice system is it that allows all this to happen after an estimated £60,000 of taxpayers' money had already been spent on Alan's case? What kind of justice system is it that allows lawyers to charge £10,000 for two and a half days' work – work for which they must already have done the preparation?

The real irony is that when Alan checked he was told his legal aid had *not* been withdrawn in the middle of his court case. He tried to appeal but he was told that because he had voluntarily withdrawn from the case he had nothing – no court order – to appeal against. He would either have to start again from scratch or go back to the court on his own and ask permission for his case to be resurrected.

Alan and Tom are both keen to continue their legal battles. Both are fighting alone without the help of lawyers. Their problem is that if they lose they will be liable to pay the costs of the other side which does have lawyers. It's David and Goliath but with no guarantee of a fair fight.

How many other cases are there like Tom's up and down the country? How many people are there who have found our costly courts wholly inadequate to the task of speedily investigating claims of wrongdoing and granting redress where appropriate? How many people will nod sagely when they read that attempts to reform the justice system are being undermined by the great burden of legal costs?

Small wonder if people like Tom feel cheated, if they feel that a change of culture is needed among those who provide financial and legal services or if they believe that a far more radical shake-up of the courts is urgently needed.

Not that Tom Walker has given up. He is fighting on. It is now over ten years since he and his business first fell foul of professional advisers and that in itself is an indictment of the System. But Tom has not abandoned hope.

'We'll win,' he says. 'We'll win in the end.'

8

THE SICK MAN'S TALE

The financial world has always provided opportunities for the cheating classes to enrich themselves at the expense of others. Their conduct follows an age-old pattern. In biblical times there was the tale of a man whose very substantial debts were written off by the Chief Creditor and who reacted just as many corporate financiers would do today: he started hounding some poverty-stricken individual for the immediate repayment of a comparatively paltry sum that was owed to *him*.

Fast forward from first century Palestine to twenty-first century Britain and we find that little has changed. Corus, the former British Steel, makes a loss of £462 million and cuts its workforce by 6,000 yet Sir Brian Moffat, its chairman, has his basic pay more than doubled to £558,846.

Or take Abbey National. When chief executive Ian Harley was ousted in the summer of 2002 he was sent on his way with a payoff estimated at over £1 million.

Meanwhile, press reports say that our four biggest High Street banks 'are making more than £1 million an hour as they cash in on a boom in personal debt, credit card spending, loans and overdrafts'. When the Bank of England base rate is 4 per cent, they charge over 17 per cent on overdrafts and credit cards. Even as this is happening, bosses, like those at Barclays and Royal Bank of Scotland/Nat West, preside over massive job cuts yet are paid, respectively, £2.3 million and £1.5 million plus share options worth £3.5 million.

The strange thing is that many ordinary people persist in believing that great City institutions like the banks and building societies can be trusted to act fairly, not least to their smaller customers. Everyone recognises that they must safeguard their own interests of course but surely they can be relied upon to behave in a proper, decent manner. That was what Neil Palmer believed when he borrowed the money to buy a house for his growing family . . .

It was just a 1930s semi, similar to thousands of others all over the country, but Neil and Emma were delighted with the house in Broom Road. Of course it needed a great deal of work and it was not a patch on the modern flat that they had been renting but it was theirs. And had it been in better condition they would never have been able to afford it. They were pushing themselves to the limit financially as it was. But they were sure it was the right choice for them.

They liked the street it was in and the area – Hampton, near the great Tudor Palace at Hampton Court and not far from central London. More important, it was handy for Neil's large, close-knit family. He had been brought up not far away and his parents, sisters and brother all lived in the area. His mum helped look after Sam, their three-year-old son, when they were out at work. Also, the house had a garden where Sam could play and several of Neil and Emma's new neighbours had small children too.

The house had cost £68,000. That was more than they had meant to pay and with no savings they had had to take out a

100 per cent mortgage. A broker had arranged it for them through National Provincial, one of the big building societies. As a failsafe, National Provincial had insisted that they pay a one-off insurance premium of £1,000 to cover any shortfall in their mortgage repayments. Not that they were worried about falling behind because, as Neil liked to point out, they were earning good money.

He was a buyer for a firm that sold air-conditioning equipment while Emma had a part time job as a receptionist at a local business centre. She didn't enjoy it much – the people who used the centre always seemed to come to her with their complaints – but the hours were good and it enabled her to spend plenty of time with Sam.

If Neil needed an outlet for day-to-day frustrations, he and some friends had started a band at school called the Bitter Springs. The band only ever broke even but it had had some successes. They had made albums, they had been invited to perform in Europe and they had been on the radio. *NME* said Bitter Springs was 'one of the best kept secrets in Britain'. All the same it was fun. And Emma didn't mind too much about the time he spent rehearsing.

Neil and Emma had been together for five years. They had met in a pub at Christmastime. He had been twenty-four and Emma seventeen. He fell for her as soon as he saw her. Tiny and with long, fair hair, he thought she was the most beautiful woman he had ever seen.

Sam had been born in 1989 and they were thinking of having another baby. They had never actually got around to getting married but now that they were in the new house perhaps they might give it some thought. Maybe next year. Maybe 1993 would be a good year for them.

It was not. Eight months after they moved in to the house at Hampton the firm Emma was working for went into liquidation.

The family could ill afford to lose her salary. The monthly mortgage payments meant that their finances were already tight but they were confident that they would be able to manage. They were young and healthy. Emma would get another job, though it might be difficult to find one that would fit in so well with looking after Sam.

Had they but realised it, the downturn in the economy that was to be such a feature of the early 1990s had already begun. It was to wreak havoc with their lives.

Neil could not quite believe it when his boss called him in that Friday morning at work. It seemed that sales had not been going so well. The company was having to cut back. It was nobody's fault – certainly not Neil's. They were really sorry but they were going to have to make some people redundant. Sadly Neil was one of them.

The Palmers were devastated. For both of them to be out of work so soon after taking on the new house was frightening. They had moved in less than a year ago – and there was still so much work to be done. All they had managed so far was to redecorate some of the rooms and put in new heating. With no money coming in all their plans would have to go on hold.

Neil signed on the dole and started looking for another job but finding one as a buyer was not easy. In fact finding another job of any sort proved hard. He sent off dozens of applications but all too often he did not even get a reply let alone an interview. Emma was now pregnant again so it would be almost impossible for her to find work at present.

They soon found that Neil's dole money did not really provide enough to live on. He decided he would have to supplement it with some kind of temporary work and he tried doing shifts as a mini-cab driver. He worked mainly at night and his passengers were often drunk. He hated it.

Keeping up with the mortgage repayments was now impossible. Neil and Emma should never have been advised to take out a

100 per cent mortgage. Years later they heard that the broker who had arranged their mortgage had been sacked for cutting corners. Had he advised them better they might not have entered into the whole business so lightly. They admit now that they were partly to blame for their misfortune. Yet there is a question as to whether they and countless others should received better advice – particularly when a building society as big as the National Provincial was involved.

They might, for example, have expected better information about the £1,000 premium they had to pay to insure against any shortfall on their mortgage payments. They assumed that it would safeguard them if they fell behind. They were wrong. It was the National Provincial that was covered – not the Palmers. And the insurance covered only a tiny part of the loan, not all of it. If everything went pear-shaped Neil and Emma would still be in debt and with no safety net.

The rules on selling financial 'products' like pensions and mortgages have now been tightened up considerably. The rules on forcing borrowers to indemnify not themselves but the big financial institutions against default are unlikely to be changed. Most experts reckon it would cost too much to indemnify ordinary people. Yet it would cost little to insure that people understood clearly what their liabilities were.

As the months went by Neil and Emma fell further and further behind. At first they did not worry too much. They just assumed that they would be able to make up the payments once Neil found a job, which would surely happen soon.

Meanwhile they were having to borrow more money to make ends meet. They already had an overdraft at Lloyds bank and the sums they owed on their credit cards and to various catalogue companies were rising steadily.

Letters began to arrive from the National Provincial pointing out that they were in arrears with the mortgage and asking them to rectify this as soon as possible.

They would have done if they could. They still believed that
once Neil found a job they would be able to sort things out.
Meantime they did not reply to the letters. Neil became steadily
more concerned as the letters became more pressing but he did
not see what he could do.

In October 1993 their daughter Katie was born. Neil was over
the moon. All he wanted was to enjoy the new baby but harsher
realities intruded. The day after Katie was born he had a phone
call. It was the arrears manager from the National Provincial. She
wanted to come round to the house and talk to him. As soon as
possible.

As Neil said later the conversation 'was not pleasant'. She kept
asking him how he was going to repay what he owed. Social
Security was meeting the interest charges on the mortgage but
the capital had to be paid back too. If he was unable to pay then
the building society would have to start proceedings to repossess
the house.

What the Palmers did not know was that the sluggish economy was about to take its toll on the value of their home. A new
phenomenon was starting to make itself felt in the housing
market: negative equity. It sounded technical but it was very
simple. It meant that your house was worth less than you paid for
it. It should have been something that worried Neil Palmer but
as winter turned to spring in 1994 he had other worries.

He had found a lump in his scrotum. Emma said he should go to
the doctor as soon as possible. Apart from anything else he could
do with a check-up and it was best to be on the safe side.
Probably it would not be anything serious.

It was testicular cancer. The doctors tried to be reassuring. If
they operated immediately there would be a good chance of Neil
making a full recovery. Patients often recovered – particularly if
the disease was caught at an early stage.

Neil went into hospital. He was told later that the operation had gone well. The doctors reckoned they had managed to remove all the cancerous tissue. They thought he would be all right but they would have to see him again in three months' time.

Then at last the Palmers had a break. A letter came offering Neil a new job – a proper job as a buyer for a lighting company called Marlin. He had applied for it some weeks earlier but over the last year he had become so discouraged by his failure to find work that he did not allow his hopes to be raised. Besides he had been too taken up with his illness.

But now they might be able to start putting their finances back on an even keel. Neil was a realist. He knew that there was little chance of him and Emma keeping the house. The backlog of debt was now too great for that. They had started to accept that they would lose their home. It was almost a relief to be able to talk sensibly about being evicted.

Neil landed his new job with Marlin in March 1994. He had had his operation earlier in the year but he could not be sure he was better until after his check-up, which was due at the beginning of April.

Three weeks before his hospital appointment he found another lump. At least it might have been a lump. It felt different to normal but he was unwilling to admit it – even to himself. The hospital had told him to go back immediately if he noticed anything untoward. But perhaps he was panicking about nothing.

Perhaps if he waited just a little the strange tissue would disappear. After all he could not, must not, jeopardise the new job that he had wanted for so long.

He went to the hospital on the due date for his check-up. They admitted him immediately. The first operation had not, after all, rid his body of all the cancerous cells. He would have to have another operation. He would also have to have chemotherapy.

He had his second operation in April and the hospital warned him that he might have to have more. They were going to send him to the Royal Marsden at Sutton, one of the leading cancer hospitals, for chemotherapy. He would be in good hands. But there could be no question of him taking up his new job. He would not be fit enough. Marlin was very sympathetic when he explained. They would keep the post open for him as long as possible.

National Provincial would wait no longer. Over a year had passed since the Palmers had started to fall behind with their mortgage payments. The lenders' patience had run out. They were not prepared to grant the Palmers any more time to pay off their ever growing arrears. They had decided to repossess the family's house.

The Palmers were told that there would have to be a court hearing about the repossession. The National Provincial would present their case for repossessing the house. Neil and Emma would be asked if they agreed. The hearing would be at Surbiton court.

The morning of the hearing Neil went straight to the court from the Royal Marsden. He had just finished a course of chemotherapy.

The hospital had been brilliant and Neil was confident that his chances of getting better were good. But physically the chemo was taking its toll. He felt tired, he felt sick. Everything he ate tasted metallic. And when he arrived in court that morning he was completely hairless.

The judge and the court officials were sympathetic. They went out of their way to make Neil and Emma as comfortable as possible. At the end, when the other side had spelt out the details of the Palmers' situation and the reasons for repossession, the judge asked them if what the court had heard was correct. Neil and Emma agreed that it was.

The judge made the repossession order. He also told the lawyers for National Provincial that under no circumstances were they to put any additional pressure on the struggling family.

Neil and Emma felt very frightened. What would happen to them? What would happen to Sam and Katie? When would they be evicted? Where were they going to live?

After so many months of waiting and hoping and sometimes trying to pretend that this was not happening to them, the wheels of officialdom started turning more quickly. The Palmers were sent a formal notice of eviction. They were told they had between four and six weeks to get out of their house. After that the council would be responsible for re-housing them.

The council said it would not house them until the last minute, almost until they were on the street with Sam and Katie.

Neil still managed to spend some time with his band, Bitter Springs. They had decided to press another album. It came out just before Neil and Emma were evicted. The album was called Selective Memory.

The council found the Palmers a flat in Twickenham. They were only told where they were going a week before. The flat was privately owned, on the first floor and with two bedrooms. After their spacious house it seemed minuscule to the Palmers. The day they moved both of them felt utterly miserable. The flat felt even more cramped than they had feared, though the council promised that it would try to find them something better.

In the event they did not have to wait too long. Seven weeks after being evicted from their house the council's housing officer wrote to them saying that another flat had become available at Teddington. It, too, was on the first floor, which was hardly convenient for a family with two small children, but it *was* nicer, as both of them agreed when they went to see it. Yet as Neil said to Emma: 'It's not what I wanted for us.'

It was mid-summer when they moved to the Teddington flat. Neil was still having to go regularly to the hospital and he was still feeling weak and lethargic.

The doctors were pleased with his progress but he would have to have another operation to make sure there was no recurrence of the cancer in his lymph nodes. As yet there was no question of him being able to work.

He had kept in touch with Marlin, giving them updates on his illness. The managers he spoke to were always friendly. They were still keeping the job open for him. Yet neither he nor Emma had it in them to be optimistic.

At the end of the year Neil was given the all-clear. There are never any guarantees with cancer but as far as the doctors could tell he had conquered the disease. He rang Marlin. The job was still open.

By the start of 1995, things were looking up, though it did not always feel like it to the Palmers. Neil was well again and he had a regular income but being back to normal meant facing up to the fact that they had even bigger debts. With him being ill and both of them out of work for so long they had run up bills of some £5,000 – and that was without the bank loan.

For the next eighteen months they scarcely thought about anything except paying off their creditors: the bank, the catalogue companies, credit card companies and even the council for they were behind with the rent. Emma found a part-time job working on the assembly line at Marlin. It was what they called the mums' shift.

She only worked mornings and she could take off the school holidays. It was not big money but it helped.

Yet no matter how hard they worked it never seemed to be

enough. They started to cut down on food. Not that they went to bed hungry but often their dinner was beans on toast and nothing more. They began to have rows. Neil insisted that every last penny must go to pay off their debts. Emma said they should try to strike a balance, that they had to have some money to spend on the children and on making sure they had reasonable food. Usually Neil won. Yet still their debts hung over them like some impenetrable black cloud. They feared that if they went on like this they would end by splitting up.

It was Emma who suggested they should go to the Citizens' Advice Bureau. She had heard one of the girls at work talking about how it had helped a friend to sort out her money problems. One Saturday morning Neil and Emma trekked down to the CAB at Hampton. The woman they saw was sympathetic but told them bluntly that they were not handling their debts well.

They should work out how much they could afford and write to all their creditors asking if they would agree to accept a fixed sum each month. Staff at the bureau would help them write the letters. Neil and Emma did as she suggested and all the creditors accepted their proposals. They felt a little more in control.

As the months went by the pressure began to ease. It was a long, painful business. On bad days they felt they would never be free of their financial burden. But they started to make inroads into their debt. Now and again they allowed themselves to imagine that perhaps they would have a chance to re-establish themselves.

The months turned into years. There was no sign of Neil's cancer recurring. Feeling that he had regained his health gave Neil a new sense of optimism. He felt he was doing well at Marlin. He had been there four years now and he had a good relationship with his bosses. The company even offered him a £2,000 loan – on very favourable terms – to buy a car. He felt sufficiently confident about his and Emma's finances to take it on. The repayments would be automatically deducted from his salary.

By 1999 their financial position was stable. They had paid off so much of their debt that they were starting to put money aside each month. Their aim was to save enough for a deposit on a house. Not that they were putting every penny they saved towards the deposit. They had another plan in mind.

Emma and Neil had been together for twelve years. After going through so much and still managing to stick it out as a couple they had decided to get married. They had a romantic dream of going to Gretna Green for the ceremony and then having a holiday – with the children of course. It would be the first time Sam and Katie had ever been away, the first time they had all been on holiday together as a family.

They tentatively planned the wedding for July.

Emma was on her own when the letter arrived. Neil always left home earlier than she did, usually at 7.30 am, well before the post came.

In between giving Katie and Sam their breakfast Emma sipped her own tea and opened the long white envelope that had been on the mat that morning. It was from a firm of solicitors who wrote saying that they were agents of the Abbey National, which had merged with the National and Provincial. The letter said that the repossession and sale of the Broom Road house back in 1994 had resulted in a 'substantial loss' to the lenders. Although there had been a long delay since anyone had approached the Palmers, the Abbey National now wanted its money back. The sale of the house in Broom Road had raised £56,000 and the insurers had paid £1,200 to Abbey National. That was not enough to cover what was owed.

Taking into account the outstanding debt on their home loan, interest charges, arrears and various other items such as roof repairs and commission the Abbey National calculated that the Palmers owed £28,462.73p. The solicitors, acting on the Abbey National's behalf, would be grateful if the Palmers would contact them immediately.

Emma could not believe it at first. She and Neil had had no contact with the building society since the day they had been evicted from their house five years before. The judge at the repossession hearing had made it clear to the lender's lawyers that they were not to put pressure on the Palmers. And the National Provincial had not done so; they had not made any attempt to contact the Palmers from that day forward.

Neil and Emma had not thought for a moment that they still owed money on the house. Surely, surely they could not owe this huge sum. Not after all these years. Not just when they were starting to get back on their feet.

Emma looked again at the letter and the statement. There was the amount they owed, carefully broken down into its constituent parts. The sums were simple enough. The Palmers original loan of £68,000 had risen to £85,000 once interest and all the other charges were added. Take away the sale price of the house and the insurance money and the bottom line was they still owed £28,000.

Emma sat for a long time staring at the letter, still unbelieving. When she left the house she kept going over it in her mind, kept telling herself that it must be an error – and all the time knowing that it was not a mistake at all.

She managed to keep control until she had dropped off Katie and Sam with her friend Kim, who always took them to school. Without the children to distract her, the full horror of the letter swept over her. By the time she reached Marlin she could not stop herself shaking. She went immediately to find Neil. He was in a big, open plan office in another building and she had to walk right to the end of the room to find him. As she passed people looked up and stared at her curiously.

When Neil saw her his first thought was that something must have happened to one of the children. Then Emma handed him the letter. Like Emma, he could scarcely take it in at first. He read it through twice and then sat there as if stunned. Emma started to cry. For ten minutes or more they just looked at each other hopelessly. It was Emma who moved first saying she should go and start work.

Neil roused himself. 'No,' he said. 'We're going to go to the flat.' He went and found his boss, Linda, the manufacturing director, and told her what had happened. She was immediately sympathetic. Of course he must go home. He and Emma should take as long as they needed to sort everything out.

Miserably they made their way back to the flat.

'Neil, what are we going do?' whispered Emma.

Neil looked at her and took her hand.

'Well we'll have to check it out,' he said. 'I don't see how they can do this to us after all this time. But if it's right . . .' His voice tailed off.

The idea that a creditor could start demanding large sums of money years after the debt seemed settled and forgotten would strike most people as preposterous. Particularly when the creditor in question is a large, eminently respectable bank or building society. Yet in Britain today a mortgage company is legally entitled to demand its money back up to *twelve years* after the original debt occurred. What is scandalous is that creditors like the Abbey National have no legal duty to keep debtors fully and regularly informed of what they owe.

As they sat in their kitchen that morning Emma and Neil still could not quite take in the demand for £28,000. Later they agreed that it was like having a death in the family. There was the same numbing pain and sense of shock.

Eventually Neil galvanised himself and decided they must stop telling each other that it could not be true and find out for certain one way or the other. That afternoon they went to the Citizens' Advice Bureau at Twickenham.

The Palmers were putting their hopes in the words of the judge at the repossession hearing. They explained what he had said to the woman at the CAB. She asked them to wait while she checked. When she came back she had a grim look.

'I'm sorry to have to tell you that the judge's words were just his comments,' she said. 'They didn't have the force of law. He wasn't making a court order. And legally the Abbey National is quite within its rights to come back to you and demand the money after all this time. Legally there is little you can do. I'm so sorry . . .'

The Palmers' case is only one of many. Negative equity was once a rare phenomenon and when it did occur the building societies normally wrote off the debt. When it started happening on a large scale as in the early 1990s, they changed their tune. At the same time many of them were ceasing to be mutual societies, owned by their members and traditionally with a caring outlook. Instead they were becoming banks with a conventional profit motive.

The National Association of Citizens' Advice Bureaux (NACAB) estimated that in some areas up to a quarter of all the cases dealt with by their specialist money advisors involved mortgage shortfall debt. A study by the association found the debts ranged from £2,000 to nearly £70,000.

'To be unexpectedly confronted with a demand for payment of a debt dating back many years and running into tens of thousands of pounds can be overwhelming, destabilising relationships and household budgets and threatening to propel the family into long-term poverty,' the association's report said.

The evidence suggests that mortgage lenders have a deliberate policy of keeping debtors in the dark about the money they owe.

In The Long Shadow, its report on mortgage shortfall debt, NACAB says one reason why the impact of being pursued for mortgage shortfall debt can be so devastating is 'because of the unexpectedness of the demand years after repossession'.

The report says 'some lenders have argued that they do not wish to compound borrowers' problems by starting recovery action in the immediate aftermath of repossession'. Yet as NACAB points out, it is vital that borrowers be told the full extent of their mortgage shortfall debts as soon as possible so that they can make informed plans on how to deal with it as well as any other outstanding financial commitments.

Nor are people like the Palmers an isolated case. The NACAB study found that the first time borrowers heard from lenders pursuing mortgage shortfall debt ranged from three to ten years after repossession. A buoyant economy in most parts of the country means the number of cases has been falling but in areas like the North West there are places where negative equity is rearing its head again with some properties being given away for as little as £50. And NACAB reports that the tendency of lenders to go in for 'brinkmanship' has not changed.

It is easy to see why lenders do not want to be up front with debtors about the money they owe. For a start it gives them more chance to rack up interest charges. They also know that they will not be able to squeeze any money from people right after their homes have been repossessed. So they wait until people like the Palmers are getting back on their feet again, until they are financially stable and even starting to build up some small savings. Then the lenders swoop and demand their money back.

They know that most debtors will never be able to pay them in full but by playing cat and mouse with struggling families they can expect to wring something out of them. If they went in too soon, if they behaved honourably and warned people from the outset that they still owed money, then they might not receive a penny from families like the Palmers. For there is a way that people can avoid paying mortgage shortfall debt, or indeed any other debt, a way that is legal and above board.

Those who are penniless, those who have nothing further to lose can make themselves bankrupt. It is a drastic measure and, technically, bankrupts must make every effort to pay off their creditors. But if you are on a minimal income with no financial reserves whatever, then bankruptcy will not make you any worse off. And the beauty of it is that after a couple of years, you can expect to be discharged from bankruptcy with all your debts written off and the chance to start again with a completely clean sheet.

It might be an attractive option for those who have just had their homes repossessed and are then told there are still thousands of pounds outstanding on their mortgage. Which is why the mortgage companies often prefer not to tell them. Much better, from a lender's point of view, to wait until people are starting to re-establish themselves when they will have something to lose by becoming bankrupt.

Bankruptcy was suggested to the Palmers as a way out of their difficulties by the CAB. The advisers at the Twickenham bureau only hinted at it at first but it soon became clear to Neil that he must regard its a serious option.

It would mean abandoning any thought of saving for their future. Their hopes of becoming home owners again and taking out a new mortgage would be set back for years. On the other hand bankruptcy would put them beyond the demands of the Abbey National. As bankrupts they would still have to pay off their debts – technically – but only from the money left over after their basic living expenses had been met.

In the case of the Palmers, who still had other debts to pay out of a comparatively small income, that might leave nothing for the Abbey National. And once the three years of bankruptcy were over all outstanding debts would be written off. Neil was reluctant but he knew they would have to think about it. The other option was to do a deal with the Abbey National.

The Palmers quickly realised that Abbey National's lawyers were not going to hold out for the total £28,000 that was owing. And on the phone they seemed most distressed at the prospect of Neil going bankrupt. They assured him that it would not have to come that.

They said that the Abbey National 'may be prepared to offer a substantial discount on the total debt outstanding should you be in a position to raise a lump sum in full and final settlement'. Neil told them bluntly that he did not have even a few thousand pounds that he could give them to settle the debt.

The lawyers listened sympathetically. They were certain there must be a solution. Surely Mr Palmer could *borrow* some money. He must have family, there must be friends who could help him out . . .

The willingness of the Abbey National, to force a family back into debt is breathtaking. Encouraging the Palmers to take out a new loan in order to pay back an old one was almost certain to push them back into poverty at the very moment they were beginning to climb out of it.

Banks and building societies like the Abbey National would argue that they are profit-making organisations not charities. They would say they have a legal and perhaps a moral duty to their shareholders to maximise the returns they make and to pursue debtors. All of which is true. But as so often with the cheating classes the balance of rights and responsibilities is skewed against the citizen. The rights to that last pound of flesh lie with a rich and powerful institution while responsibility for paying huge debts that they never even knew they had lies with the Neil Palmers of the world.

Neil had made up his mind that he would have to go bankrupt but there was a catch. He could not afford it.

The Citizens' Advice Bureau informed him that it would cost

nearly £400 to file for bankruptcy – £120 in court fees plus a £250 deposit for the Government-run Insolvency Service.

The bureau also advised him that once he went bankrupt he would not be allowed to pick and choose which of his creditors he paid off. And there was one creditor he had to carry on paying: Marlin, his employer, which had lent him £2,000 to buy a car. He felt he could not renege on the deal. It was not just that his job might be on the line but that the company had treated him so well from the outset.

Probably they would be sympathetic if he went and explained the position to them but he did not wish to do that. He would finish paying off his loan from Marlin and then go bankrupt.

He wrote formally to the Abbey National's lawyers telling them that he planned to go bankrupt in due course. Again they tried to dissuade him, though this time weeks passed before they made contact.

Then one Friday afternoon in August, they called again. Neil was out and Emma answered the phone. This time the pleasant, persuasive manner was gone. If Neil did not do a deal then they would make sure he ended up in court and they would see to it that the whole family suffered . . .

Debt collection in Britain today has an ugly face. In practice it is largely unregulated. The harassment of people who have no money often goes unpunished and unremarked. It is not supposed to be like that of course. The Administration of Justice Act 1970 lays down penalties for harassment but only the most outrageous cases ever end up with a court prosecution.

Banks, building societies, insurers and solicitors all protest that they would not dream of piling pressure on anyone in *genuine* financial difficulty. But they say some debtors are out to defraud and then it is necessary to take a tough line. Staff at NACAB says that in practice the deserving and the undeserving are often treated the same. Sorting the defrauders from the 'genuine' hardship cases is troublesome so the big institutions rarely bother.

Suddenly the calls from Abbey National's lawyers became less frequent. Perhaps the firm had decided that if it exerted too much pressure on the Palmers then it might scare them into bankruptcy.

The family knew that they were living on borrowed time but the initial horror receded a little. They reckoned that if the burden of debt was going to start weighing them down all over again then they might as well live for the moment. They decided to get married and take off with the children to Scotland on their first ever family holiday.

It was not a big wedding – only eight of them – but it was a great day. After the registry office ceremony they all went out for lunch in a Gretna hotel. And Emma and Neil knew that they could contemplate a whole week away from their troubles. They were going to stay at Largs on the west coast. They had a little spending money and they would take the children swimming. Just for once they were all going to have a really good time.

Back home things seemed to get worse and better at the same time. There was still no word from Abbey National. Neil and Emma reckoned that this simply meant the firm was biding its time, waiting for the Palmers' finances to improve. And their finances were improving. Neil was given a pay rise. Their other debts were steadily going down and as the months went by Neil knew that it would not be long before he had finished paying off Marlin.

Perhaps that would be the time to take decisions about Abbey National and the mortgage shortfall.

Christmas came and went, the new millennium dawned and still the Palmers heard nothing from Abbey National. Soon it was over six months since its lawyers had contacted them. Neil had no wish to make the first move. He was finding himself in more and more of a quandary as to what to do. Marlin was thriving and he was doing well there. The firm had given him another pay rise and the prospect of going bankrupt was becoming less and less appealing.

His worry was that he was now earning too much to make it a worthwhile option. As a bankrupt he would be allowed enough for him, Emma and the children to live on but there might still be enough left over for the authorities to insist that he pay a regular sum to Abbey National on top of the other debt repayments they were making.

Now the initial shock of their demand had faded, Neil's strongest emotion was outrage at the way they had been treated by the Abbey National. He did not view them in the same way as his other creditors, to whom he felt an obligation. He was determined not to give them a penny more than was absolutely necessary.

The trouble was he did not know what terms he would get if he went bankrupt. There was no way of finding out in advance how much he would be allowed for living expenses and how much he might have to pay to his creditors, including the Abbey National. The other option was to stay solvent and find out how much – or how little – Abbey National would accept in full and final settlement. Yet he felt that if he even approached the firm they would take it as a signal that he now had some money and they would start pursuing him again.

He was caught on the horns of uncertainty . . .

The games that the cheating classes play with debtors should be outlawed. Many fall into financial difficulty either through no fault of their own or simply because they are bad money managers who are struggling along often on pitifully small incomes. The Labour Government has said it will carry out a review of debt enforcement. This is welcome but as so often with the Blair Government there has been much discussion and promises of initiatives in the pipeline but little action.

Common sense as well as compassion suggests that reform needs to focus on ways of distinguishing more effectively between those who won't and those who can't pay. It is in everyone's interest. Treating genuine hardship cases toughly not only causes misery but fails to yield worthwhile financial dividends for groups like the Abbey National.

Furthermore, people like the Palmers are put at a huge disadvantage when an institution like the Abbey National is able to rack up interest charges on a debt that they don't even know exists. The scandal is that the law lends legitimacy to this behaviour. Clearly changes are needed.

Requiring all lenders to keep borrowers informed from the outset about any outstanding debt would be a good first step. The present system of financial ambush when unsuspecting individuals are suddenly told that they owe thousands of pounds should have no place in today's Britain.

The big institutions have made some concessions on this front but it is minor league stuff. Banks and building societies have volunteered to observe a limit of six rather than twelve years for coming back to borrowers regarding an outstanding mortgage shortfall that must be repaid. Yet once they ask for repayment they can continue playing cat and mouse, leaving debtors alone for months or even years and then pouncing to demand their money. Each time they do the six-year clock starts ticking again.

As it happens, the shortening of the time limit would have made no difference to the Palmers. Neil and Emma received the Abbey National demand for £28,000 within six years of losing their home. They still had been kept in the dark for far too long.

Perhaps organisations that fail to be open and above aboard with those who owe them money should forfeit their right to reclaim the debt. NACAB has suggested also that the courts should have the power to cap interest charges as soon as a house is repossessed. This is the kind of measure that could have helped the Palmers.

So too would a requirement that all debts be settled or written off within the six-year limit. There is a strong case for saying that lenders should not be allowed to keep reopening negotiations over old debts – except in the case of deliberate fraud. Even then a time extension should be allowed only if granted by the courts.

Constant uncertainty was one of the worst aspects of the Palmers' case, as it is for so many debtors. Neil and Emma did not know what sort of settlement the Abbey National would accept and nor could they find out what the terms would be if they decided to go bankrupt. They were expected to make decisions on the basis of guesswork and horsetrading.

As NACAB says: 'It is essential that borrowers be provided with information on the full extent of their liability at the earliest possible opportunity. Otherwise the danger is that people will start rebuilding their lives based on the false premise that a line has been drawn under the trauma of repossession.'

This system of secrecy and of blind bargaining with debt collectors cannot be regarded as fair or efficient. Surely it would be better to have some well-publicised criteria for settling arrears. Where bankruptcy is an option, people should also have a right to know what the consequences are likely to be. Why shouldn't families like the Palmers be given some idea of how much they would be allowed to live on and how much they would be required to hand over to their creditors?

On a more general front there is a compelling case for having better scrutiny of the whole business of repossession, debt and debt collection. The courts already play a role here but it is clear that things can go badly wrong at a grass roots level which the courts cannot influence – particularly as some of the abuses are technically within the law.

Maybe there should be a new, independent watchdog to oversee personal debt and debt collection – a watchdog that gives ordinary people a major voice and which has powers to ensure fair treatment for debtors and creditors. It might be one way of forcing the cheating classes to be more accountable in an area that could affect any one of us no matter how financially comfortable we may seem.

Yet perhaps we need something else – something more fundamental than improved arrangements for dealing with debt. Perhaps we should think about an entirely different approach to those who provide financial services or key public services of any kind.

It may be time to insist that private sector organisations which offer public services should adopt a public service ethic instead of subordinating everything to profitability. Institutions that were required to recognise a wider duty beyond looking after shareholders – a duty to the public interest – might rethink their attitude to debtors or to other clients.

Banks, building societies, pension companies are all in the private sector and their *raison d'être* is to make money. Nothing wrong with that – profit is what puts bread into the mouths of everyone. But these institutions also provide a public service, whether it is loaning people money to buy homes or arranging financial security in old age. These services are essential to the wellbeing of individuals in the community. So could we use the law to ensure that these public service providers take account of the public interest as well as private profit? Could we give them a legally enforceable duty to do so?

The traditional distinction between the public and private sectors has become steadily more blurred over the last twenty years. It began in the 1980s when Margaret Thatcher's government started selling off state-owned companies such as the utilities. Most of them adapted to the private sector profit motive like ducks to water. To safeguard the public interest, regulators were appointed who were answerable to the State but who operated as independent arbiters. Their job was to ensure that the newly privatised groups struck a fair balance between the needs of customers and shareholders, between the public interest and private profit.

Measures have also been taken to strengthen the regulation of private sector financial institutions. But that is not quite the same as making them accept a public service obligation.

For example, it is in the public interest, both financially and as a matter of social policy, that families like the Palmers should not be tipped back into poverty. The likely result is that they will end up on the dole at public expense. Not only is this distressing for them but it is not a cheap option for the rest of us who have to pick up the tab as taxpayers.

Nor is it a fair option. The Palmers might be criticised for entering too lightly into taking out a 100 per cent mortgage. It is a criticism that they would accept. Yet the things that really went wrong for Neil and Emma were entirely beyond their control: both were made redundant; Neil developed cancer; and they took out their mortgage just as property prices were falling. It was not their fault that the bottom fell out of the market.

Yet big, rich institutions like the Abbey National are allowed to minimise their share of the pain while hard-pressed individuals like the Palmers are required to take the full impact of the market downturn. Such a system seems morally indefensible and financially bizarre. For there is no way that people like Neil and Emma can raise the sums demanded of them.

Once they have recovered from the initial shock they are likely to decide that their best bet is to go bankrupt. Such a drastic step cannot be good for them and nor is it in the interests of institutions like the Abbey National. A mortgage is in some sense a joint enterprise between lender and borrower. Normally both benefit. There is a case for saying that when things go wrong they should share the suffering and they should do so in proportion to their relative strength.

At present there is little sign of the big financial institutions accepting that they have a wider duty to the public weal.

Nor are there signs of the Government pushing them to do so. In the spring of 2002, Anthony Giddens, director of the London School of Economics and one of Tony Blair's leading intellectual allies, said Labour had 'not developed a policy framework relevant to corporate social responsibility, certainly not one with bite'.

Perhaps forcing financial institutions to temper the profit motive with public service principles would be one way forward. This would not mean asking them to behave like charities – simply requiring them to strike a better balance between money-making and social justice. It might serve notice on the cheating classes that they be allowed to cheat no more when dealing with families like the Palmers.

Neil and Emma still have not heard from Abbey National. They are beginning to hope that they will never do so now. They reckon mortgage lenders have had such bad publicity over mis-selling that most of them will think twice about continuing to pursue people like the Palmers for old debts. Yet they know they cannot be certain that the debt collectors will not strike again . . .

9

FUTURE PROSPECTS

So can we find a way to make the cheating classes serve our interests instead of their own? Can we devise mechanisms for ensuring that the bureaucrats and the bankers and the lawyers and all the rest give a fairer deal to people like the Balchins or Keith Dray or the Palmers or you and me? Is there some way of making the cheating classes more accountable? Can we soup up the engines of our democracy so that all citizens have a faster, smoother, safer ride?

The answer has to be yes. The question is how. In the 2001 general election a large chunk of the electorate turned its back on the political establishment and refused to vote. That jolted not just the politicians but other members of the cheating classes as well. As they are well aware, it is the political set up that underpins their position and here was proof positive that the public were no longer prepared to acquiesce in supporting the old order. For the first time in years they felt their cosy system being threatened by a disenchanted populace. In the spring of 2002 their fears were intensified when elections in France and

Holland suggested that a significant number of voters were disillusioned with the existing pattern of European democracy. Many were no longer prepared to buy into the political elite's views on such key issues as immigration and the need for big government from Brussels. A shudder ran through Europe's ruling class but in Britain, at least, their initial reaction was often to try to justify themselves rather than acknowledging that they must listen more to the public.

And what the public is telling them is that it is not just the political set up that is failing ordinary people but all the other areas where the cheating classes operate – notably the law, finance and the bureaucracy. Polling evidence shows that eight out of ten people now have less respect for *all* forms of traditional authority. The entire system is becoming inadequate even if politics will remain the main engine for change.

The puzzle is why the politicians do not earn themselves kudos with the public by driving through a programme of more stringent reform that would require providers of financial, legal or government services to offer a fairer deal to ordinary people. Undoubtedly the last few years have seen some laudable attempts by politicians of all parties to tackle the need for reform. Yet welcome though some of these measures are, they fall a long way short of what needs to be done to stop the rot in Britain today. There may be several reasons for this government reluctance.

One is the claim that reform – such as the ending of self-regulation – could lower standards instead of ensuring better services for the public. This point is argued strongly by some professional groups who say that the old system has stood the country in good stead for centuries and that it would be irresponsible to throw it out just because of a few difficult cases.

They stress that self-regulation, which had its origins in the mediaeval guilds, used to be seen as one of the cornerstones of public confidence in the professions. That may be true but however good the System *used* to be the evidence suggests that it is letting down the public now.

Opponents of change say there is also the difficult question of *how* to bring about reform. They point out that independent regulators, who are often a favoured option, can have weaknesses of their own. They may make bad judgements, fail to command public confidence or load down whole industries with red tape. Such concerns may be legitimate but they are arguments for finding better methods of reform not for giving up on reform altogether.

Cynics might say that there is another reason why governments are slow to introduce change. The very people who could drive through reform, the politicians, are prominent among the cheating classes themselves and they have a network of close ties with fellow members of the elite. Ministers work every day with Whitehall civil servants. They lunch with the press – journalists are another group allowed to police themselves. They dine with prominent businessmen and with leading figures in the City.

As for lawyers . . . a good number of Ministers, whether Labour or Tory, are lawyers themselves. Tony Blair is a lawyer. His best friend, Charles Falconer, is a lawyer. His wife, Cherie Booth, is a lawyer. This is not to suggest some grand conspiracy. But like the rest of us, politicians are susceptible to the views put forward by friends and colleagues, particularly if they have once worked in the same line of business themselves.

More significantly, Ministers know that while reform might bring political dividends from the voters it could also lead to reprisals. Ending self-regulation is a good example.

Ministers worry about taking on the doctors in case they retaliate by refusing to co-operate with Government plans for the NHS. They are scared of forcing independent regulation on newspapers in case the press attacks them. They are nervous about giving the public an effective method of scrutinising Whitehall decisions because that could lead straight back to the Government itself. And they do not want to upset business lest they lose the confidence of the City.

So they allow themselves to be seduced by the easy arguments for continuing with the status quo. They accept the Whitehall dictum that evolution is better than revolution – even if it does take forever. They let themselves be persuaded that improvements are coming through, albeit slowly, and that outsiders might not understand the complexities of professional issues.

It was no different under the Tories. In the 1980s Margaret Thatcher wanted to shake up the professions. Her Lord Chancellor, Lord McKay of Clashfern, even put forward proposals for a radical assault on the restrictive practices of the lawyers. But then, as now, the political will for change was lacking. The reform of the professions became Thatcher's unfinished agenda. A dozen years after her political demise, it remains unfinished still.

Yet when it comes to reform there is much that members of the public might do to help themselves. Maybe we need to look for a more direct democracy that can give ordinary people greater involvement in decision taking. As Robert Alexander said in his book *The Voice of the People*:

> The power to take part in major decisions which affect us
> is a basic freedom . . . Why should people not have a
> greater voice on specific issues? Why should they have to
> swallow (party) manifestos whole? Why should they not
> give their voice on important decisions which are taken
> between elections? The right to vote, priceless though it is,
> is only an occasional and fragile involvement in
> government.

Maybe the way to beat the cheating classes is to insist that more power be pushed down to ordinary people. After a quarter of a century of burgeoning bureaucracy and growing centralisation – in our cities as well as in Whitehall – it is time for the public to start setting out an agenda of its own.

Perhaps the first move should be to start a debate about the need for a fresh approach. Anecdotal evidence suggests that such a debate is long overdue. Tell people you are writing a book about those in influential positions who cheat on the rest of us and the response is nearly always a caustic comment as to how it will need to be a long book. Yet change will only come if ordinary people can find an agenda for reform that meets *their* needs.

There is little mileage to be had from proposing grandiose solutions like a new, written constitution. The political elite would not accept it unless they could subvert it to their own ends – as they have done with the endlessly delayed Freedom of Information Act, which gives more the pretence than the reality of openness. In any case ambitious constitutions do not always work the way we might like. The Americans have had one for over two hundred years, one that has served them well and that puts far more checks and balances on the powerful than we have in Britain. Yet for all that, America's Bill of Rights did not prevent decades of racist segregation or the Macarthyite witchhunts against those suspected of communist sympathies.

In present day Britain the Blair Government's decision to incorporate the European Convention on Human Rights into English law via the Human Rights Act was a praiseworthy move. Yet it has produced some bizarre results: suspected terrorists who threaten the community can seemingly use the Act to avoid extradition; other citizens can evidently use it to claim that their 'human rights' are being breached if they are disturbed by late-night aeroplanes – surely a devaluing of the human rights currency.

All too often the big solutions founder as they are twisted or watered down or bedevilled by detail. Often they do not even reach the starting blocks. Politicians – and others – waste inordinate amounts of time trying to come up with a Big Idea or a New Way. Their much-vaunted schemes often turn out to be no more than eye-catching propaganda initiatives designed to bolster a particular political brand. Even the more considered ones rarely live up to expectations.

So if we are to give ordinary people a better deal maybe we should junk the grand plans. Maybe we should go instead for less dramatic, more specific changes in our public and commercial life, not just in our political arrangements but in legal, financial and government services. These are all areas where citizens in a decent, democratic society should be able to rely on fair treatment but where they are so often denied it at present. The stories here highlight some of the areas crying out for reform.

The issue of access to justice needs to be revisited. The Biker's Tale and the Handyman's Tale underline some of the grave inadequacies here. Despite improvements under both Labour and Tory governments, justice still costs too much and is stacked heavily in favour of the rich.

As the Prisoner's Tale and the Sick Man's Tale illustrate, there is a pressing need to investigate the whole question of debt and of how to deal more fairly and more effectively with those who cannot pay as opposed to those who will not pay. In a country whose leaders boast of being modernisers, it is almost unbelievable that we are effectively still sending people to prison for debt – and often the most vulnerable people in the community at that. It is a system that serves neither debtors nor creditors.

Another area crying out for greater public scrutiny and control is our burgeoning bureaucracy. At both national and local level bureaucracies are becoming more intrusive and less accountable – witness the injustices of the Policeman's Tale, the Rich Man's Tale and the Dead Man's Tale.

Suggestions for various specific reforms have been put forward in each of the stories here. Some of the changes proposed are small, others more far reaching. Some are no more than a sketchy starting point for debate, others have more flesh on them.

The political community, however despised, remains the key to reform in other parts of the system. Yet it stands in need of reform itself. Both the party system and Parliament have long ceased to properly represent the interests of the public. Often they are merely vehicles for self-serving political professionals. As Professor Vernon Bogdanor says in his book, *Power and the People*, today political divisions on issues like Europe lie as much within the major parties as between them and all too often the party system stifles sensible debate. 'The result has been the growth of that most dangerous of all political cleavages: that between the political class and the people,' he argues. He adds that reform must be an attempt to 'fashion a new relationship between government and the governed'.

The question is how. On the democratic front there is a case for Britain borrowing from the Americans who have developed several ways of curbing overweening politicians and ensuring that more power remains with the people. In the US no President is allowed to serve more than two terms – eight years. Many American States and cities have limits on how long governors or mayors can serve. Even Mayor Rudi Giuliani of New York, who commanded such popularity after the heroic leadership he displayed in the aftermath of the September 11 attack, had to step down when his time was up.

Term limits are an antidote to control freak politicians and over mighty party bosses. They encourage fresh faces and fresh ideas. We should try them here. Instead of local councillors, MPs and Prime Ministers – especially Prime Ministers – being allowed to go on and on they could be restricted to a maximum of ten years in office. Nor would the expertise they had built up be wasted. They could move on to other jobs in public service or the private sector.

We might also follow America in making much greater use of referenda. In many US States any group of citizens can call a referendum provided they can persuade enough people to back them. In California, for example, referenda have been used to protect minority rights, ban smoking and limit local taxes.

Referenda are not unknown in Britain – the public was allowed to vote on devolution for Scotland and Wales and now the Blair Government plans to have a vote on whether we should join the Euro. Yet it is nearly always politicians not the public who call a referendum and the politicians do not regard the result as binding – unless it is the one they want. Perhaps it is time to change the culture. Why not let local voters call a referendum on a controversial planning case or on the pattern of school holidays or on whether London should have congestion charges?

Although referenda are usually only suitable for straightforward, single issues where a yes or no answer is required, they do give ordinary people a real chance to be in the driving seat – particularly if members of the public have the right to call for one. This is the kind of direct democracy that can make a real difference.

Referenda are not the only way to involve the public in decision making. We must pursue other, more effective ways of ensuring popular participation in decision making not least at the local level. We could look at directly elected supervisory boards for education and health.

Other candidates for direct elections are not hard to find. Estimates of how many people are appointed to sit on quangos vary but there is no doubt that the patronage state is very substantial. Robert Alexander says that in the year that Tony Blair came to power there were 'about 20,000 members of non-elected bodies administering institutions which are fundamental to the well being of people and communities'. Why should the majority of these individuals not be directly elected?

Some would say that the public has shown its distaste for elections by refusing to turn out and vote. That is true when it comes to electing politicians at local, national or European level. But the poll held by the Channel Four *Big Brother* programme attracted more votes than the last European elections – which suggests that people are not against voting per se. What many of them will not do is go to the polls to support remote, disconnected politicians.

One national body that could be subject to direct elections is the BBC. It is extraordinary that the people should have no say in choosing the chairman, governors and director general of the

BBC given that the corporation is funded through an earmarked tax – the TV licence fee – which virtually all of us pay.

Those who try to evade payment of this tax face severe penalties – in the past several hundred people every year have been sent to prison for failing to pay their TV licences. This is exactly the kind of abuse depicted in the Prisoner's Tale – and the kind that ordinary people would be most unlikely to tolerate if they could use their votes to influence policy. As the Americans said two hundred years ago when they were struggling to be free of British rule: no taxation without representation. Yet in practice top jobs at the BBC are handed out to government cronies.

Phone-in programmes on TV and radio and the internet could be used to let viewers and listeners question candidates for BBC office on what kind of programmes they would put on, how much money they would spend jetting round the world at the licence payers' expense, whether they believed in political correctness and how they would make themselves accountable to the public on a regular basis. Such technology could also be used to allow ordinary people to scrutinise a whole range of public opportunities.

When it comes to individual cases of abuse there are other measures that could curb the antics of the cheating classes. For example, the ending of self-regulation would be a step forward, albeit an obvious one. It would also provide further opportunity for giving the public a greater say. The present system whereby the cheating classes are allowed to police themselves may sometimes deliver satisfactory results for complainants but it has been seen to fail too often for ordinary people to have much faith in it.

A policing system geared more to the needs of citizens and less to the convenience of bureaucrats, lawyers, doctors and other professionals would surely command greater public confidence.

Yet preventing professionals from policing themselves would not of itself end exploitation by the cheating classes. So-called independent regulation often works on a crony basis, with friends of Ministers or former civil servants being given top jobs. So we should start exploring ways of giving the public a more direct say in deciding whether or not ordinary people are being given a fair deal.

One option might be to set up a series of powerful new watchdog bodies, citizens' tribunals, dominated by members of the public and with authority to hear grievances against those providing key services, to order that injustice be put right and to penalise those who knowingly and deliberately act unfairly.

There are various models that such bodies could follow. They could be based loosely on the citizens' juries now being developed in some towns to gauge people's views on controversial local issues. They take evidence and make recommendations. Admittedly these juries as currently constituted have some serious drawbacks: they are not accountable directly to the public and they are only consultative. This last is particularly important. The Audit Commission has found that 'a majority of local authorities do not consistently use consultation results to inform decisions'.

Yet citizens' juries do provide one way of involving ordinary people in the decision-making that affects their lives. Citizens' tribunals could be given greater authority and standing, with statutory powers to enforce their judgements – provided there were rights of appeal to the courts.

Various schemes could be tried for appointing members of citizens' tribunals. They could be chosen at random like juries in criminal trials or there could be a greater element of selection to ensure they represented different groups and interests in the community. Large panels of people from whom tribunal members would be drawn could be democratically elected in each area or region. Individuals might sit on a panel for a fixed term of several years, which would help to build up expertise. Special training could also be available, particularly for those chairing citizens' tribunals.

The system would have to be easily accessible to ordinary people and free to those on low incomes. It might be advantageous to ban costly, traditional lawyers and replace them with salaried advisers who could help people on both sides of an argument to put their cases clearly and succinctly.

But what criteria would these latter day tribunes of the people use to judge the lawyers, the bureaucrats, the bankers, the local councillors, the doctors or anyone else accused of cheating on the public? Giving the public itself a bigger role in judging those with influence or authority might help to even things up in the fair treatment stakes – but only to an extent.

One of the striking things about most of the stories told here is that the conduct of the cheating classes may be monstrous but it is nearly always legal. The Abbey National in the Sick Man's Tale and Thanet Council in the Prisoner's Tale were not doing any-thing unlawful. It would therefore be hard for any watchdog body, even an elected one, to do anything more than issue a slap on the wrist.

One of the defects of the present system is that when people seek redress from the courts or the Ombudsman they often find that they have no comeback because no law has been broken. Or they see their cases being bogged down in a legalistic morass with the other side using obscure points of law to justify shabby conduct.

Perhaps what we need are simpler, more straightforward cri-teria for judging whether members of the public have been fairly treated. Maybe what is wanted is a standard that rests not on legal niceties but on a broad-brush assessment of whether a bureaucrat or a planner or a lawyer has acted fairly and reason-ably. It is an assessment that ordinary people sitting on citizens' tribunals would be well qualified to make.

The concept of 'reasonableness' is already well established in English law. The last twenty-five years have seen the development of judicial review, which allows senior judges to overrule decisions by government and by other public bodies in certain circumstances. One of the criteria is if Ministers or others have acted wholly unreasonably – even if they have stayed technically within the law.

Judicial review, which was developed by the judges themselves to defend the public against the very type of behaviour exhibited by the cheating classes, has proved effective. There is a limit to what can be done by a small number of senior judges and the idea of reviewing administrative decisions could surely be more widely applied using general yardsticks of fairness and reasonableness in judging cases.

Maybe citizens' tribunals could fill the gap. There could also be guidelines on what constitutes fairness in terms of say, pricing. Whether the fees charged by the professionals in cases like those in the Prisoner's Tale would be considered reasonable could be a matter for a citizens' tribunal to decide. Open and speedy dealing could be another important factor in judging 'fairness'. The slow and secretive behaviour of the Abbey National in the Sick Man's Tale would surely breach any reasonable criterion of 'fair and open' conduct.

The stories here suggest that one crucial ingredient has gone from our public life. What we have lost is what used to be called the public service ethic – an approach, a culture that put a much higher value than we do today on treating individuals decently. It used to be found in government, both local and national, as well as in parts of the private sector such as the law and even in finance. Over the last two decades it has been steadily eroded.

In many ways the rolling back of the frontiers of the State that began in the 1980s was liberating. Barriers to prosperity disappeared and there was a new emphasis on performance, on competence and on value for money. Yet somewhere along the way the public service ethic died, driven out by a harsher competition ethic that put the emphasis on cutting costs and maximising profit.

Perhaps what we need now is to look at ways of bringing back that public service ethic, which would mean giving more weight to the fair treatment of ordinary people – particularly customers or clients.

It might be feasible to give all those who provide professional, financial or government services a legally enforceable duty to act in line with the public interest. Such a public interest or public service requirement could apply equally and without distinction to the public and private sectors. After all, why should there be different rules for the two sectors? As far as ordinary people are concerned there is often very little difference between a private sector banker offering a loan service and a public sector bureaucrat handling a planning approval. When things go wrong it is equally hard to hold either to account, as the Handyman's Tale and the Rich Man's Tale show.

To make a real difference a public interest requirement would have to be backed up by penalties. A doctrine of personal responsibility that would force individuals to accept liability for dealing unfairly with the public could be an essential ingredient of reform. The evidence suggests that fear is the key to dealing with the cheating classes. They cheat knowing that they will get away with it, that their victims will find it hard to get redress. If, on the other hand, they knew that they personally would pay a high price for knowingly treating the public unfairly then they might think twice. There could be penalties for wilful injustice, as opposed to honest mistakes, they could range from a reprimand to fines and dismissal or even imprisonment – with a right of appeal to the higher courts.

Give the public some means of insisting that their grievances are heard and judged quickly, cheaply and fairly and we might go a long way to ensuring a better deal for everyone.

But would such a system not trespass on the powers and privileges of the politicians whose support would be needed before it could be introduced? And are not many of those politicians paid-up members of the cheating classes? The answer to both questions is yes – but our political masters might yet be persuaded to accept some of the measures outlined here.

Why? First because such moves might prove popular with the public and politicians are desperate to win back the interest and confidence of disenchanted voters. They are discovering that warm words no longer cut ice with the electorate. Something more substantial is needed.

Secondly such reform would not impinge on politicians personally – at least not often. Most of the decisions they take are on strategic policy matters not on individual cases. Citizens' tribunals and the Public Service Requirement would cover *only* individual cases. Politicians, therefore, could rarely find themselves in the dock and their control of most areas of general policy would be largely unaffected.

Ironically our politicians find themselves grappling with what might be called the paradox of power. The ones at the top are intent on centralisation and on concentrating power in their own hands. They appear to be doing so with frightening success. Yet even as their control tightens they find that all too often power is slipping away from them. It is going to the European Union. It is going to the senior judges. Above all it is flowing away from Government Ministers to the markets, to the finance men and to great global companies.

The supranational forces that are sucking power away from domestic governments are not going to disappear. They need to be balanced by pushing control of local matters down to the local level. Giving ordinary citizens more power over the things that affect their own daily lives may be an essential way to make inevitable globalisation acceptable. Our politicians may find that in the end they have no choice but to go with the flow, bow to pressure from the people and hand more power back to the public.

In May 2002, Philip Gould, Tony Blair's pollster and strategy guru, wrote in the *Spectator* of the 'need to build a participatory democracy in which self-confident citizens are fully engaged in

the political process and in which politicians respect this engage-
ment and use it to fuel change'. Mr Gould does not get down to
specifics and New Labour has a history of talking about giving
more power to the people while doing the reverse. All the same,
Mr Gould's plea for a new kind of democracy is recognition that
the elite must act to stem the groundswell of discontent with the
present system.

As for the other members of the cheating classes – those lawyers,
bankers, planners, bureaucrats, local councillors, accountants
and Whitehall civil servants who mete out unfair treatment to
ordinary people – in the face of growing disquiet over their performance they might find it increasingly hard to argue that the
public should *not* have more say or that they themselves should
not be forced to accept new rules and a new public interest obligation.

They might point out that different people would have different views as to where the public interest lies, which is true
enough – but who better to judge than the public themselves?
They might say that the public could not be relied upon to get it
right every time, which is also true – but then nor do the judges,
impressive though the senior ones are.

One essential ingredient of reforms designed to curb the cheating classes is that the public and even more the media would have
to be far more forgiving about honest mistakes. They would also
have to be generous about officials or professional people who
found themselves having to decide between several equally
unpalatable options. No blame should attach to those who make
genuine errors even if their decisions were overturned.

Others will have ideas of their own about how to stop the rot
in our society, how to rein back the cheating classes and ensure a
fairer system for everyone. One thing is certain. There is much
that could be done by all of us.

Our democracy is failing but it is not yet dead. Our rights to
freedom of speech are being eroded but the political class has

not yet reached the point where they can silence us. The biggest bar to ordinary people speaking out and insisting on more recognition, more accountability and more power is apathy and . . . fear.

Not fear of retribution, fear of imprisonment or punishment by the State – although that is becoming more of a threat – but fear of ridicule. Too many men and women are concerned that if they enter the debate, if they make suggestions for reform they will be made to look foolish because their ideas will be shown up as flawed.

Do not be intimidated. That is just what the spin doctors, the rip-off merchants, the unrepresentative elite, the cheating classes in all their guises want. Take heart. Your ideas may be imperfect but they will be at least as good as theirs.

Think of the way they have failed to deliver on their promised reforms in health and transport. Think of their handling of the foot and mouth crisis – a textbook example of bad government. Think of the Law Society, the solicitors' trade union, which spent years failing to clear the backlog of complaints against its members. Think of the local councils who have been dragged through the courts on corruption charges. Think of the Financial Services Authority, the powerful regulator that failed to spot the scandalous inadequacies at Equitable Life.

The elite does not know better than we do. Its members do not have any God-given right to treat us meanly or greedily or unfairly. We have the right and the ability – every bit as much as they – to explore new ways of giving all citizens a better deal, to insist on reforms that will stop the rot, end the elite's abuse of power and force the cheating classes to bow to our just demands.

INDEX